THE ANGLICAN COMMUNION AT A CROSSROADS

The ANGLICAN COMMUNION at a CROSSROADS

The Crises of a Global Church

CHRISTOPHER CRAIG BRITTAIN *and* ANDREW MCKINNON

The Pennsylvania State University Press | University Park, Pennsylvania

Library of Congress Cataloging-in-Publication Data

Names: Brittain, Christopher Craig, author. |
   McKinnon, Andrew, author.
Title: The Anglican Communion at a crossroads : the
   crises of a global church / Christopher Craig Brittain
   and Andrew McKinnon.
Description: University Park, Pennsylvania : The
   Pennsylvania State University Press, [2018] | Includes
   bibliographical references and index.
Summary: "Analyzes the tensions within the contemporary Anglican Communion, addresses the theological
   arguments and social forces involved, and explores
   the dynamics of religious conflict in a global era"—
   Provided by publisher.
Identifiers: LCCN 2017056506| ISBN 9780271080895
   (cloth : alk. paper) | ISBN 9780271080901 (pbk. :
   alk. paper)
Subjects: LCSH: Anglican Communion. | Church
   controversies—Anglican Communion.
Classification: LCC BX5005.B75 2018 | DDC
   283.09/051—dc23
LC record available at https://lccn.loc.gov/2017056506

The Pennsylvania State University Press is a member of
the Association of University Presses.

It is the policy of The Pennsylvania State University Press
to use acid-free paper. Publications on uncoated stock
satisfy the minimum requirements of American National
Standard for Information Sciences—Permanence of
Paper for Printed Library Material, ANSI z39.48–1992.

CONTENTS

ACKNOWLEDGMENTS

A book that has taken the better part of ten years to research and write has incurred a good number of debts for its authors. We are particularly grateful for the generous contribution of time and thoughtful insight we received from all of those (here unnamed) church leaders from across the Anglican Communion who agreed to be interviewed. Though it would not be possible to write a book with which they all would completely agree, we hope that they will recognize the value of their contributions in these pages, and we hope that the book gives something back in return. We are thankful to have received initial research funding from the College of Arts and Social Sciences, University of Aberdeen; research for the Pittsburgh case study was generously supported by the Engaged Scholars Studying Congregations Network (funded by the Lilly Endowment).

Chris would like to thank Aberdeen colleagues who have provided valuable feedback and support of this project, particularly Tom Greggs, Paul Nimmo, John Swinton, Pete Ward, Don Wood, and Phil Ziegler. He is also indebted to the leadership team of the Engaged Scholars workshop: Nancy Ammerman, Larry Mamiya, Bill McKinney, Omar McRoberts, Jim Nieman, Steve Warner, and Jack Wertheimer. Special thanks to Steve Warner and Barbara Wheeler, who served as mentors during his fieldwork in Pittsburgh. Discussion partners in the "Ecclesiology and Ethnography" network and in the Society for the Study of Anglicanism consistently offered stimulating responses to work in progress. Chris is particularly grateful for the support offered by Katja Stößel and Patricia Craig.

Andrew would like to thank colleagues in sociology at Aberdeen, particularly John Brewer, Steve Bruce, Bernie Hayes, David Inglis, Gearoid Millar, John Nagle, Marta Trzebiatowska, and Rhoda Wilkie, and colleagues in the British Sociological Association's Sociology of Religion Study Group; Grace Davie, Gordon Lynch, David Martin, and Anna Strhan deserve special mention. Paul Gifford kindly offered his expertise on religion in Africa, providing helpful comments on a draft of chapter 3. As always, Andrew is grateful for the love and support of Les and Sandy McKinnon; Christy, Mariusz, Simon, and Lucy Stepien; and family in Toronto and Prague. Martina Klubal and Phoebe McKinnon grace him each day with joy (and playdough).

Early versions of various chapters were given a first run before a variety of audiences. Early versions of chapter 1 were presented at the British Sociological Association Annual Conference (Cardiff, 2009) and at the Sociology Department Seminar Series at the University of Aberdeen (2009); a first published version appeared as "Homosexuality and the Construction of 'Anglican Orthodoxy': The Symbolic Politics of the Anglican Communion," in *Sociology of Religion* 72, no. 3 (2011). A symposium convened by Abby Day titled "Contemporary Issues in the Worldwide Anglican Communion" at Canterbury Cathedral Lodge (2013) provided a forum for the first airing of the argument of chapter 2. That conference presentation was first published as "Anglicans in a Globalizing World: The Contradictions of Communion," in Abby Day, ed., *Contemporary Issues in the Worldwide Anglican Communion: Powers and Pieties* (Farnham, Surrey: Ashgate, 2016). We are grateful to Oxford University Press and to Routledge (which acquired Ashgate) for permission to publish the much revised versions that appear in this volume. An attempt at the argument of chapter 3 was presented to the Sociology Department seminar at the University of Aberdeen in 2015, and the claims in chapter 5 were given a first dress rehearsal at the annual meeting of the British Sociological Association's Sociology of Religion Study Group at the University of Chester in 2012. Some of the interview data and analysis found in chapter 4 are included in Christopher Brittain's *Plague on Both Their Houses: Liberal vs. Conservative Christians and the Divorce of the Episcopal Church USA* (London: Bloomsbury T&T Clark, 2015). We thank Bloomsbury T&T Clark for permission to include this much revised material. We are grateful for the opportunity to float our ideas in these fora, as well as for the various questions and challenges received in response. We would like to thank Kathryn Yahner for her support for this project and Suzanne Wolk for her skillful copyediting; this is a much better book for their contributions.

INTRODUCTION

Since the middle of the 1990s, the global fellowship of Anglican churches worldwide, known as the Anglican Communion, has been caught up in an increasingly intense conflict that has taken as its focus disagreement over the place of gays and lesbians in the church. Perhaps the most memorable scene to date took place on the lawn at the University of Kent in August 1998, where the decennial Lambeth Conference, which gathers bishops of the church from the four corners of the globe, was being held. As a group of fellow bishops nervously looked on, and an army of press passes scouted for a good hook and compelling visuals, Bishop Emmanuel Chukwuma of Enugu Diocese in Nigeria attempted to exorcise a "demon of homosexuality" from the Reverend Richard Kirker. Bishop Chukwuma declared loudly to a journalist that the book of Leviticus demands the death of anyone caught in a homosexual act. This prompted Kirker, general secretary of the Lesbian and Gay Christian Movement, who had been passing out leaflets, to ask the bishop, "Would you be prepared to stone us to death?" James Solheim, director of news and information for the Episcopal Church, recounts what followed:

> The bishop tried to lay his hands on Kirker, "In the name of Jesus, I deliver him out of homosexuality," he said as he attempted to grab the general secretary. "I pray for God to forgive you, for God to deliver you out of your sinful

act, out of your carnality," the bishop shouted as a crowd gathered. Kirker responded, "May God bless you, sir, and deliver you from your prejudice against homosexual people."

"You have no inheritance in the kingdom of God. You are going to hell. You have made yourself homosexual because of your carnality," the bishop said.

With sweat pouring from his face, the bishop screamed again and again for repentance while his wife stood nearby murmuring "Alleluia." The bishop said, "We have overcome carnality just as the light will overcome darkness. . . . God did not create you as a homosexual. That is our stand. That is why your church is dying in Europe—because it is condoning immorality. You are killing the church. This is the voice of God talking. Yes, I am violent against sin."

When Bishop David Russell of South Africa tried to intercede, pointing out that Archbishop Desmond Tutu "supports the inclusion of homosexuals in church," Chukwuma marched off muttering, "Desmond Tutu is spiritually dead."[1]

The press reported extensively on the scene, captured by BBC camera crews; the media played the clip repeatedly, in the UK and around the world. It was the very definition of a public relations train wreck.

It is all too easy to take this scene as a small-scale model of the recent conflicts in the global Anglican Communion as a whole, even if such a telling would oversimplify to the point of distortion. While different storytellers may be inclined to use different emphases and different vocabulary to describe the characters, Chukwuma and Kirker can easily be made to stand in as representatives of currents within the Communion at large. Kirker might be variously described as a gay man from the Global North, a Christian, a sinner, a liberal, a revisionist, a heretic, a prophetic voice, a sign of acquiescence to the spirit of the age, or an advocate of Jesus's radically inclusive love. Chukwuma could likewise be variously described as a church leader from the "majority" or "mainstream" of the Anglican tradition, a pseudo-Pentecostal, a bulwark of the faith, an opponent of neocolonialism, a bishop of the Global South, a defender of the Bible's authority, a remnant of orthodoxy, a homophobe, or a fundamentalist. While the nouns and adjectives employed vary, the sense of "two sides" contesting for the soul of the Anglican Communion abides, and such ways of framing the situation are repeated over and over again in one bad-publicity headline after another. In our view, these terms are much too simple, and they very often represent a rush to judgment. Academics and church leaders alike have often told us that one or more of these terms tell all that is required to explain why the conflict has emerged in recent years; there is little more to say.[2] We disagree.

The sources of contemporary tensions in the Anglican Communion, and what they mean for members of this global family of churches, are the subject of this book. In the polemical context of the global Communion's present conflict, there is a tendency among many commentators to point the finger at those they deem responsible for all that plagues the Anglican Communion.[3] In our research, we have made every attempt to stand back, as much as we can, from polemics and position taking. As researchers from two different disciplinary backgrounds—theology and sociology—we have taken as our starting point a principle once encouraged by the former archbishop of Canterbury, Rowan Williams. He suggested that "one of the first tasks we need to pursue in the current climate is simply to look at what Anglicans say and do."[4] In this study we have sought to understand the conflict through careful observation and attentive, open-ended qualitative interviews. Our only disagreement with the archbishop's statement has to do with his inclusion of the word "simply," for we have found the task of organizing, conducting, transcribing, and analyzing more than one hundred interviews with members of the Anglican Communion from most regions of the globe anything but a simple undertaking.

Our research has led us to conclude that the Communion's struggles are the result of a complex interweaving of many factors, including the forces of globalization, the rise of new communications technology, and the impact of decisions made in different periods of the Anglican tradition's history. We argue that despite the messy polemics, and the church leadership's unsuccessful repair attempts, the global church is not necessarily at an end. It is clear, however, that different groups of Anglicans conceive of the "end" of their Communion—in terms of its purpose, meaning, and future direction—in quite different ways. For some, the global church ought to be a "big tent" that embraces diversity in recognition of the plurality of a world created by a triune God. For others, the Communion should operate like a family—with intimate and familiar relationships that nurture close collaboration and mutual responsibility. Still other Anglicans begin with the assumption that member churches should in the first instance gather around common beliefs and practices rooted in holy scripture. That different Anglicans orient themselves to the Communion's current conflict from such distinct starting points goes a long way toward explaining why resolution and reconciliation have thus far remained elusive.

While disputes over the legitimacy of LGBTQ clergy, along with the acceptability of same-sex marriages in the church, are certainly a major element of the disagreement in contemporary global Anglicanism, this study will show that such matters are better understood as "presenting symptoms" of wider and more general tensions. This book attends to the many differences and disagreements among Anglicans; however, we also demonstrate that such diversity does not necessarily signal the inevitability of schism and fragmentation. We suggest that much depends on how one tells the story of the conflict, on how the present situation in the global church is framed.

Following a brief overview of the history of conflict over these "presenting symptoms," the remainder of this introduction turns to a brief summary of some basic details of Anglican ecclesiology and governance for those less familiar with the complicated internal workings of the Anglican Communion. We then summarize our approach to our field interviews.

Homosexuality and the Church: A Brief History of the Anglican Disagreements

The Lambeth Conference of 1998, where Kirker and Chukwuma encountered each other on a hot August day, resulted in many resolutions, most of which have been largely forgotten.[5] What has been remembered is Resolution 1.10. This has come, at least for some, to signify the "official teaching" of the Anglican Communion and the very mark of orthodox belief for Anglicans, even though such resolutions have no such formal status. In practice, those who so understand it typically remember that Resolution 1.10 identifies "homosexual practice as incompatible with scripture"; they are often less likely to recall the part of the motion that "calls on all our people to minister pastorally and sensitively to all irrespective of sexual orientation and to condemn irrational fear of homosexuals." An earlier version had gone further and condemned "homophobia," but an amendment proposed by Bishop Taita Taveta from the Province of Kenya changed this to the final wording of "irrational fear of homosexuals."[6] In practical terms, Lambeth 1.10 states that the bishops "cannot advise the legitimising or blessing of same sex unions nor ordaining those involved in same gender unions," which is far from an unequivocal condemnation but also indicates that the church's leaders disagreed among themselves on the question. The final clause of the resolution also "recognised the significance of" the Kuala Lumpur Statement on Sexuality,[7] a hard-line conservative document that took the church's position on the matter as settled and beyond discussion or legitimate disagreement; the conference did not formally "endorse" such a position. It was clear, however, that there were in reality a variety of views in the room that day. A preliminary indication of this was the tally of the vote itself, in which 526 voted in favor of the final motion, with seventy opposed and forty-five abstaining. About a hundred bishops at the conference seem not to have voted.

Those conservatives who had been organizing for several years to arrest what they identified as a liberal drift in the United States, Canada, and the UK declared it a victory.[8] Not all the bishops of the church felt that justice had been done, however, or that the conference had upheld a Christ-like perspective in such a resolution. There was nothing like unanimous agreement that "homosexual practice is incompatible with scripture."[9] The day had left both those in favor of recognizing and accepting gay and lesbian clergy and laypeople, and of blessing their relationships in the church, and those who were merely uncomfortable with the tone and spirit of some of the statements in a state of shock. Many no doubt worried about how the news would be received by the faithful among whom they ministered, and among those whom they hoped to reach. Some of those on the losing side of the vote quickly cobbled together "A Pastoral Statement to Lesbian and Gay Anglicans from Some Member Bishops of the Lambeth Conference," released by Bishop Ronald Haines of the Diocese of Washington, D.C., the same day.[10] "We pledge that we will continue to reflect, pray, and work for your full inclusion in the life of the Church," the signatories declared.[11] Within three days this letter had been signed by 142 bishops, including eight primates; by the end of the week, it had gained a further forty bishops from around the world, though signatories from Africa were notably absent (excepting only Botswana and eastern Zambia in central Africa and a number of bishops from southern Africa). There was clearly no consensus on the matter, though a majority position had been demarcated. In some respects, the vote may have served to exacerbate tensions—it certainly did not resolve them. In any case, resolutions passed at the Lambeth Conference have traditionally been only advisory and not binding on the different national and regional churches that make up the Anglican Communion. Homosexuality, however, had become the symbol that marked a divide within the Communion.

The role of African church leaders in this conflict has often been noted, and their conservative opposition to the "sin" of homosexuality in the church is frequently taken as a given. Some attribute this opposition to the greater faithfulness to the message of "biblical" Christianity on the part of African leaders.[12] Others observe that such opposition derives from the fact that homosexuality is unknown or simply unacceptable in African cultures.[13] The church in Africa is treated as a constant, faithful to the "original" Christian teaching in matters of both faith and sexual morality; what has changed are the beliefs of Christians in the Global North and the growing acceptance of homosexuality in North America and Europe. Such an account is far too simple; as we discuss in chapter 3, there has been a great deal of social change in the West, but dramatic transformations have also affected African societies and the churches in these regions, and these form no small part of the story in the global Communion.

It would be misleading to suggest, however, that the only heated disputes have taken place between Anglicans in the North Atlantic and those in Africa. Conflict within the Episcopal Church in the United States (TEC), and to a lesser degree within the Anglican Church of Canada, has been considerable, much of it taking the question of homosexuality as its focal point. In Britain, disagreement on the issue has tended to be quieter, at least until recently (for reasons we discuss in chapter 5). In the United States, the first serious controversy came in 1990, when Bishop Walter Righter ordained an openly gay, partnered man as a deacon. The moderate mainstream within the Episcopal Church was showing signs that it was on its way to being broadly sympathetic to the ordination of gay priests. It was also clear that this was a potentially divisive issue, an impression that was confirmed when ten bishops brought a charge of heresy against Righter, who by then was living in retirement. The church court exonerated Righter of the charges against him,[14] which convinced some conservatives that the church was drifting toward a more liberal position on the question;[15] nevertheless, the church made no major legislative changes on human sexuality at this time. Following the vote at Lambeth in 1998, however, Anglican churches in Africa and Southeast Asia began ordaining "missionary bishops" to the United States, arguing that the "liberal" Episcopal Church had forfeited its right to be seen as a legitimate Anglican, or even Christian, church. Within TEC, this was widely seen as a hostile act, an "incursion" on the authority and jurisdiction of an episcopal colleague.[16] The archbishops sending such missionary bishops to the United States, however, had clearly concluded that the "revisionist" bishops, and the Episcopal Church (U.S.) as a whole, had lost their legitimate authority, even before there were any changes to the church's policy.[17] Dissident conservative TEC parishes then felt that they had the possibility of remaining within the "worldwide Anglican Communion," while declaring their independence from a "liberal" bishop or the unfaithful Episcopal Church.[18] In chapter 4 we tell the story of the consequences of this in one diocese, the Diocese of Pittsburgh, which was split almost down the middle by the demand to choose sides.

The Diocese of New Westminster, in the Anglican Church of Canada, made the next significant move. In 1998, the diocesan synod had voted to authorize public rites of blessing for same-sex couples, but not marriages, which were in any case not to be legal in Canada for another two years. The bishop of New Westminster, Michael Ingham, discerned the divisive nature of disagreements in his diocese. The bishop twice withheld his consent for the resolution to be implemented, until it had passed a further vote in the diocesan synod in 2002. The policy then allowed parishes to apply for permission to use an authorized rite for blessing of same-sex unions in the diocese. The diocesan policy provided guarantees that no parish or priests would be required to perform such services. Further, parishes that felt that the divisions were too deep to allow them to maintain relations with their bishop could apply to have oversight from a "traditionalist" bishop approved by Bishop Ingham (or his successor).[19] Several parishes nevertheless left the diocese, fighting for (and losing) the right to take their buildings and other assets with them.[20] The bishop of Argentina offered to stand in as their bishop, and he did so until a separate organization was formed in 2009 to gather together disaffected Anglicans from across North America.

Events in England and the United States shifted the spotlight away from the Canadian church when the prospect of two openly gay bishops in the Anglican Communion emerged. Both the procedures and the outcomes in the two cases were very different, but both served to mobilize the opposition, following on from the events in New Westminster. The diocese of New Hampshire elected Gene Robinson, a partnered gay man, as diocesan bishop. Though there was considerable controversy both within the American church and from church leaders abroad, the election was ratified by the national church, and Gene Robinson was consecrated as bishop of New Hampshire in November 2003, wearing a bulletproof vest at the service.[21] In the meantime, across the Atlantic, the office of the prime minister announced that the queen had approved the appointment of Jeffrey John as the bishop of Reading in the Diocese of Oxford. A gay man living in a long-term celibate relationship with another man—and hence conforming to the Church of England's own rules for priests and bishops—John had been selected by an appointments committee in the Diocese of Oxford and had secured all the relevant approvals, including a nod from the archbishop of Canterbury. By the time the media storm, largely organized online, subsided, Jeffrey John was no longer to be consecrated as bishop of Reading. In chapter 2, we look at the influence of online mobilization and protest in a shrinking world on the debacle of Jeffrey John's failed nomination.

Each of these events heightened the sense of growing crisis in the church, and this began to harden into a set of divided institutional arrangements over the next five years. By the time the subsequent Lambeth Conference assembled in 2008, an alternate conference had been organized and held. The leaders of this conference, soon to become the nucleus of a rival to the traditional structures of the Anglican Communion, included senior African church leaders and disaffected conservatives from the United States, England, and Australia, who named it the Global Anglican Future Conference, or GAFCON.[22] The following month, when the Lambeth Conference was held, many, but not all, of those leaders boycotted the invitation by the archbishop of Canterbury, Rowan Williams. They claimed that while Williams had not invited Gene Robinson, he had invited those who had consecrated him a bishop. GAFCON in many ways provided the launch pad for a separate "province" of conservative Anglicans in the United States and Canada, who called themselves "the Anglican Church in North America (ACNA)." The ACNA claimed for itself the legitimacy that they argued had been forfeited by the Episcopal Church and the Anglican Church of Canada. The ACNA gathered a somewhat eclectic group of dissident Anglicans and Episcopalians, who not long ago might well have wanted nothing to do with one another, into an umbrella church structure. Members of this new province, like those who attended the GAFCON conference, began to call themselves "orthodox Anglicans."[23]

While the Episcopal Church consecrated an openly lesbian priest as a suffragan bishop in the Diocese of Los Angeles in 2010, the church also continued to hold back developing and authorizing a liturgy that allowed for the blessing of same-sex unions for quite some time; these were not published until 2012. Three years later, the church changed its marriage canons (regulations) to allow for the marriage of persons of the same sex. The recently elected presiding bishop of the Episcopal Church was soon called upon to explain the church's position to the heads of the other churches of the Communion, and even the primate (leader) of the competing Anglican Church in North America was invited to attend the same meeting, held in Canterbury in January 2016. The proceedings themselves were closed and the discussions confidential (after the English fashion), but in the end, the primates announced that since the Episcopal Church, in changing its marriage canons, had taken a decision significantly at odds with "the majority" of provinces, it would suffer certain consequences. The church would be barred from certain kinds of participation in the life of the Communion, and its members would be prevented from representing the Communion in meetings with other churches and faith traditions.[24]

The Episcopal Church of Scotland has since changed its marriage canons to permit same-sex marriages, and Canada looks likely to follow in 2019. Still more churches may opt to follow what looks likely to be New Zealand's proposal when it returns to the issue in 2018, which is to bless same-sex unions but maintain a traditional definition of "marriage" as exclusively between a man and a woman.[25] These situations will continue to arise, particularly in Anglican provinces where the local government regulations on marriage are shifting, as in Australia in the autumn of 2017.[26] The tensions in the global church during the writing of this book have continued to build, and while it is conceivable that an official schism may occur in the global church by the time this volume is released, it is unlikely that this would be the end of the story, even if that should happen. The tapestry in which the story of the global Anglican Church is woven contains too many threads for it to face an abrupt and final end (see chapter 5). Moreover, as chapter 7 discusses, any such decisive schism faces many obstacles and counterpressures.

Anglican organization and terminology are often taken for granted by those who write about, or from the perspective of, the Anglican tradition. Those who are less familiar with the tradition may find some of the terms used, and references to the structures and ideas discussed, in this book unfamiliar.[27] In truth, this may well be the case for many Anglicans as well, given the complexity of global Anglicanism. For that reason, a brief introduction seems appropriate before we proceed to discuss the methods we have used in this study. This can only be schematic here, but we hope it will be sufficient to provide a toehold for such readers.

A Very Brief Introduction to Anglicanism: Structures, Traditions, and Parties

The Anglican tradition was born in the sixteenth century.[28] "The King's Great Matter" (Henry VIII of England's desire for a divorce so as to secure the succession of his line by producing a male heir) may have encouraged his belief in royal supremacy over the church. He contended that the king of England, not the bishop of Rome, should be head of the church in England. This political issue coincided with the movements that were challenging the established beliefs and practices of the Roman Catholic Church across the continent, and that subsequently became known as the Protestant Reformation. While many of the church's foundational documents show considerable emphasis on Protestant thinking, its forms continue to cleave to its pre-Reformation heritage.[29]

Historical Anglicanism, like the Roman Catholic Church out of which it grew, is organized into dioceses, each diocese having a bishop and a cathedral (the *cathedra*, the bishop's throne, is located in the cathedral). Churches with bishops are called "episcopal" (from the Greek word for bishop). It is from this term that the names of a number of Anglican churches around the world derive their names: the Episcopal Church (United States), the Episcopal Church of Scotland, the Episcopal Church of Sudan and South Sudan, the Episcopal Church of the Philippines, and the Iglesia Episcopal de Cuba are all Anglican churches and part of the Anglican Communion.[30] While in many parts of the Anglican world, bishops no longer have as much power as they once did, they remain an essential feature of Anglicanism. Without bishops, the church cannot ordain new deacons and priests (or other bishops), nor can the rite of confirmation (which in some parts of the church still confers full membership in the church) be conducted, and bishops continue to provide leadership, even if they no longer govern alone. Bishops exercise authority within their dioceses, but in practice the power that they exercise over clergy can be quite restricted, though there is very wide variation on this throughout Anglicanism. Because the church nowhere exercises a religious monopoly, its power over the laity (at least as individuals) is extremely attenuated.

The basic logic of episcopal organization is geographical, in that a bishop exercises authority only in his or her local diocese. At some times and places, dioceses could be so large that a bishop's ability to exercise authority over the entire diocese, let alone to visit all the parishes and conduct confirmations, was limited. In many provinces, large dioceses may have assistant, suffragan, or area bishops, who assist the diocesan bishop in his or her responsibilities. Honorary assistant bishops, who are typically retired bishops who reside in the diocese, may also be called upon to help with the bishop's responsibilities in that diocese. Some dioceses may also have other senior clerics who work with the bishop and may take responsibility for an area within the diocese;

these are sometimes called area deans or archdeacons. While a cathedral is by definition the bishop's church, most of the responsibility for running the cathedral is left to the dean (or provost) of the cathedral, who has considerable autonomy; cathedral deans are often quite senior positions within the province, though they are less likely to have the national or international profile and commitments that bishops may have. Deans take responsibility for the cathedral as head of a group of "canons," some of whom will be resident and have responsibility for aspects of the cathedral (the chapter), and some canons are primarily honorary positions, titles granted to clergy or laypeople with roles elsewhere in the diocese (the college of canons).

Dioceses are grouped into a province, usually a national church (such as the Anglican Church of Canada) or multinational regional church (the Province of Central Africa, or the Province of the Southern Cone, which encompasses most of Spanish-speaking South America).[31] In many provinces, significant authority has been devolved (and democratized) in diocesan and general synods (or sometimes "conventions," as in the United States), made up of representative laypeople, clergy, and bishops, which govern in conjunction with the bishop's leadership. This body often has the responsibility for making and changing the church's "canons" (rules). Each province is autonomous and has its own constitution and canons that—at least in theory—work to maintain good order in the church.[32] These need to conform to laws of the nations in which they operate, in areas like charity status, employment policy, and child protection, which differ by national or even subnational jurisdiction. Many synods set policy as to who may be ordained as a deacon, priest, or bishop, and how they are selected, as well as how worship may be conducted in that province, including what kind of rites are permitted. Each province has a primate (from the Latin *primus inter pares,* first among equals), typically an archbishop with responsibility for the province as a whole. Some primates have a great deal of power and authority within their provinces, even being able to appoint and depose bishops (as in Nigeria). In other provinces, the role of the primate is largely outward facing. For example, the primus of the Scottish Episcopal Church represents the church to other provinces in the Anglican Communion, to other churches in Scotland, and to the government; but internally the primus has no more authority or responsibility than the other bishops in the province, who operate collectively as a college.

The Anglican Communion can be dated (albeit somewhat artificially) to the first Lambeth Conference in 1867. This meeting was called in order to deal with particular problems (discussed in chapter 5), but also because of an increasing need for international coordination between bishops, as the British Empire was proving unable (or unwilling) to enforce church establishment and order beyond England. The Anglican churches worldwide in any case already stretched beyond the borders of the empire, perhaps most notably in the United States, but there was a sense in which the establishment and the empire were at a disjuncture even within Great Britain itself. The Episcopal Church in Scotland had never been part of the established church (in Scotland, the established church was the Church of Scotland, which is Presbyterian); in many respects, including in the consecration of the first bishop in the United States, the American church stems as much from Scotland as it does from England, as we discuss in chapter 5.

In addition to the Lambeth Conference, which meets every ten years, three other "Instruments of Unity" have responsibility for holding together the Communion. The Primates' Meeting, which includes all primates from each of the Communion's thirty-eight provinces, meets more frequently "for prayer and reflection" but passes no legislation; the Anglican Consultative Council, to which each province sends three representatives—one bishop, one priest, and one layperson, typically meets every three years; finally, there is the archbishop of Canterbury. Unlike the pope in the Roman Catholic tradition, the archbishop of Canterbury has only moral authority, but no power outside England in the exercise of his office. Some have suggested that the autonomy of the provinces relative to the Instruments of Unity is untenable for an international organization that claims to have 80 million members (for more on the issue of counting the faithful, see chapter 3).[33]

The "Parties" of the Anglican Tradition

Following in the traditions of the Church of England and the Episcopal Church of Scotland, the Anglican Communion is a "big tent." In England, the church has long encompassed a variety of different interest groups, or "parties," an arrangement initially brokered by the "Elizabethan compromise" in the sixteenth century, theorized in Richard Hooker's ecclesiology[34] and cinched into place by acts of Parliament. Since the middle of the nineteenth century, three "parties" have been identifiable in the church, even if all these branches have much deeper roots. Each of the parties has its particular emphases, which distinguish it from the others: Anglo-Catholics emphasize the church's traditions; Evangelicals prioritize scripture and the Reformation;

Liberals tend to emphasize reason and adaptation to modern society. None denies the importance of the elements emphasized by the other parties, but this is more a matter of which of the three sources of authority (tradition, scripture, reason) is asked to bear more weight, at least some of the time.

The Anglo-Catholic (or "high-church") party in its current form owes a great deal to the nineteenth-century revival of "Catholic" spirituality and liturgy, not least as it was given impetus by the "Tractarian" or "Oxford Movement."[35] This group put great stock in recovering and reconstructing the traditions and teachings of the church, in renewed appreciation for and appropriation of the writings of the patristic theologians, and in fostering a "Catholic" understanding of the sacraments and orders of ministry (particularly the apostolic succession and the authority of bishops). Anglo-Catholic services place strong emphasis on "traditional" liturgical worship, often including bells and incense. Some Anglo-Catholics maintain a very "traditional," which is to say, exclusively male, view of the priesthood and have objected vociferously to the ordination of women; some have likewise objected to female clergy because it introduces a further barrier to full communion with the Roman Catholic Church—the restoration of which they long for.

The Evangelical Anglican party likewise owes a great deal to developments in the nineteenth century, and in many ways has positioned itself as a mirror image of the Anglo-Catholic party. The Evangelicals tend to emphasize the most "Protestant" aspects of the Anglican tradition, and place particular priority on the authority of scripture, giving less emphasis to the ceremonial traditions, rites, and structures to which the Anglo-Catholics are especially attached. Because they pay less heed to the church's traditions and structures of authority, and given their focus on individual conversion and their tendency toward liturgically simpler (and sometimes even less recognizably Anglican) worship services, these Evangelicals have often been referred to as "low-church" Anglicans.

The Liberal or "Broad Church" party in Anglicanism has been the least well defined, and undoubtedly the least well organized, of the three parties. The Modern Churchmen's Union (now "Modern Church"), founded at the end of the nineteenth century, is perhaps the best representative of the core of the Liberal party. In its founding "objects" (principles), this group insisted that "dogma is capable of reinterpretation and restatement in accordance with the clearer perception of truth attained by discovery and research." From the beginning, Liberal Anglicans were firmly committed to working toward greater inclusiveness and better ecumenical relations.[36] Because of the strong opposition between Anglo-Catholics and Evangelicals, but also owing to its interest in permitting diverse views and practices in the church, the Liberal party was sometimes able to portray itself, in opposition to the high- and low-church factions, as being "Broad Church."

If the Anglo-Catholic, Evangelical, and Liberal constituencies of the Anglican tradition are identifiable wings, many have also tried to hold to a via media between them; there has also always been overlap, shifting, and blurring of the boundaries, though different borders have been rigidly maintained and defended at different times. Many Anglicans inhabit the borderlands between the Liberals and Evangelicals ("Open Evangelicals" or "Post Liberals"), on the one hand, or between Liberals and Anglo-Catholics (the scholars contributing to *Lux Mundi* or contemporary "Affirming Catholicism"),[37] on the other. These have long been well-populated territories, with relatively porous boundaries in both directions. Though many Anglicans hold one identity to the exclusion of the others, there are many who do not fit neatly into any one category.

For many years, by far the most problematic borderland, relatively uninhabited in many periods of Anglican history and carefully fortified from both sides, has been the frontier between Anglo-Catholics and Evangelicals. The leaders of these two groups have long viewed one another with very deep suspicion, and have run competing associations, seminaries, and mission societies (both home and foreign). Until very recently, the term "Anglo-Catholic Evangelical" would have seemed to many an oxymoron. Evangelicals have often been known to refer to Anglo-Catholics as "biscuit worshippers" for their liturgical sensibilities, and have ridiculed their fondness for Rome and the Virgin Mary, their love of tradition, and their elaborate clerical vestments. Evangelicals have also found the Anglo-Catholics' love of the institution of the episcopacy—even as they regularly fought with their bishops, who seldom seemed to live up to their ideal—puzzling. Likewise, Anglo-Catholics have in turn seen their low-church coreligionists as unsophisticated Bible thumpers. They have found Evangelicals ignorant of the church's history and traditions, and despised Evangelical worship, which appeared to them plainly irreverent. One bishop we interviewed referred to a well-known "chain" of evangelical Anglican churches as the "McDonald's of Christendom"—edible, perhaps, but not especially palatable, and certainly not spiritually nutritious.

Unlike the conflict over women's ordination, the recent tension has given birth to a new expression of Anglican identity that cuts across the differences between Anglo-Catholics and Evangelicals, bridging two constituencies long opposed (as we contend in chapter 1). The new "orthodox Anglican" identity, we claim, is a strategic product of the disputes over homosexuality; it is born of the attempt to suture together elements of the Evangelical and Anglo-Catholic parties, which have previously been in fierce competition and deeply suspicious of each other. This phenomenon is not entirely reducible to the logic of "my enemy's enemy is my friend," but that, in part, is where the alliance begins. Even as we argue in chapter 1 that the recent conflict is not about sexual orientation per se, homosexuality has become the most salient symbol of the conflict, and a marker that is used to widen the chasm that separates more liberal Anglicans from those Evangelicals and Anglo-Catholics who have begun to think of themselves as "orthodox Anglicans." While some of the strategic alliances between Anglo-Catholic traditionalists and Evangelicals that play a role in the later conflicts over homosexuality were born in the crisis over women's ordination, this earlier situation was never able to generate the same broad coalition that opposition to same-sex blessings and openly gay partnered bishops has done.

Methods of Inquiry

We began our research in early 2008 with a small grant from the College of Arts and Social Sciences at the University of Aberdeen. These funds, limited though they were, allowed us to conduct in-person interviews with a number of key bishops in the Anglican provinces of the British Isles. Our goal in selecting our initial respondents was to canvass a range of different positions on the sexuality question, and a range of different church traditions. We wanted to interview the most influential voices, representing differing positions and parties of the church. We sought to listen carefully to all views, and to gain as comprehensive a picture as we could of how the leadership of the Church of England, the Church of Ireland, and the Episcopal Church of Scotland understood the present moment in the church.[38] We initially selected the names of leaders from those we encountered, particularly in the lead-up to Lambeth 2008, in the broadsheet the *Church Times*, and from the people whose views we heard discussed in the growing Anglican blogosphere. We interviewed church leaders in a variety of locations, including the House of Lords, episcopal palaces, diocesan offices, cafés, and once in the bar at St. Pancras station in central London. We asked our respondents at the end of each interview whom they would recommend we listen to, both in Britain and abroad. Here we encountered sometimes less obvious choices, but often these turned out to be figures no less influential or interesting, including episcopal, clerical, and lay leaders in the church.

Our initial attempts to raise the money necessary to travel to other carefully selected areas of the globe were less successful than we had hoped. An Engaged Scholars Fellowship from the Lilly Endowment allowed Chris to make several extended trips to Pittsburgh (first reported on elsewhere, and taken up again in different form in chapter 4)[39] and to gain valuable insight into the conflict "on the ground" at one important local nodal point. In addition to four congregational studies, this research included semistructured interviews and site visits in the Episcopal and ACNA dioceses of Pittsburgh over the course of five research trips to the region between July 2009 and February 2013. In total, fifty-three individuals were interviewed in the Episcopal (47 percent) and ACNA dioceses (53 percent) of Pittsburgh. Of those interviewed, 40 percent were women and 60 percent were men; 45 percent were clergy and 55 percent were laypeople. Chris interviewed eleven of these individuals on more than one occasion for updates and clarifications.

Our "on-the-ground" encounters in Pittsburgh and our ongoing interviews with church leaders in the UK left us convinced that a more global scope would be required if we were to adequately comprehend the dynamics of the conflict. Fortunately, the global communication infrastructures that have so dramatically shaped the crises in the church (see chapter 2) also made it possible for us to interview other global leaders relatively inexpensively. Using Skype, and in a few cases Skype to mobile telephone, allowed us to achieve a much better picture of a global conflict than would have been possible with more shoe leather on the ground in a few select locations. In two cases, we asked our questions by email; in one case, it was all that the church leader's schedule would permit; in the other, the bishop's occasional access to email was the most reliable means of communicating with his remote diocese in the Global South. When possible, we managed to catch other global leaders for in-person interviews as they came and went from London, still the global hub for Anglicans of whatever inclination or alignment. Several trips to London facilitated face-to-face interviews with a handful of international leaders with whom we were particularly keen to speak in person—still preferable, in our view, where feasible, to online conversations. In all, our research involved interviews with 112 individuals, including the case study in Pittsburgh (53) and our conversations with global church leaders (59).

In retrospect, we consider our funding difficulties to have been fortunate. Our initial plans would not have allowed us to consult such a wide range of leaders from around the world; the cost of the methods we pursued, of course, is that we have learned little directly from faithful, "everyday" Anglicans on the ground in most parts of the world, excepting the dioceses of Pittsburgh (chapter 4). We thus cannot say very much about how ordinary parishioners around the world understand the crisis.[40] It was clear from the beginning (and our interviews reinforced this) that the conflict in the Anglican Communion is a dispute between the church elites rather than among the faithful, even if they are sometimes affected by it, as they have been in Pittsburgh.

When we spoke to church leaders, we promised to maintain their anonymity and confidentiality. Some told us that they did not feel this was necessary, and one even suggested that he preferred to shout his thoughts from the rooftops. Others clearly appreciated the ability to speak candidly, and it was not unusual for respondents to remind us of our promise of confidentiality when making points that they clearly felt were more sensitive (this had the added advantage of highlighting such thoughts for our attention). It seemed to us that some even found it helpful to be able to talk through their thoughts on the crisis in the church with someone more removed from the situation, without fear of being quoted (or misquoted) in a blog or newspaper. Given the polemical climate in the global church, in which relations are sometimes not only hostile but also litigious (especially in North America, but potentially also in the UK), the exercise of some caution is called for in this matter, even though the use of pseudonyms will no doubt seem an odd practice to readers not used to the convention. On occasion, we quote an individual but do not refer to him or her even by a pseudonym, to protect a leader's identity that might otherwise be obvious in conjunction with statements quoted elsewhere in the book. Although we have interviewed primates and archbishops in addition to bishops, we generally refer to them all as bishops for the same reason. As there are fewer than forty primates (one per province), this might make them relatively easy to identify. For the sake of simplicity and anonymity, we have referred to both canons and deans as deans.[41]

Our final sample of global church leaders amounted to fifty-nine individuals. As our sample "snowballed,"[42] we continued to attend to a balance of different traditions, though beyond the British Isles and North America one finds fewer Liberals and more Evangelicals (although such terms themselves also become more complicated and less clear, at least from the point of view of the North). This sample is deliberately top-heavy, with very disproportionate representation from primates and bishops, as compared with clergy (and most clergy had significant national or international profiles and leadership roles, more often than not having titles like dean or canon), and laypeople (also recognized as important leaders, experts, or opinion shapers within the global church). In our sample of global leaders,[43] there are eleven primates, representing slightly more than a quarter of the total number of primates at any given time, and these made up one-fifth of the leaders in our sample. Bishops, mostly diocesan bishops and archbishops, contribute a further 57 percent of our interviews, with clergy contributing 11 percent and laypeople 13 percent. Although the gender balance is changing at the highest levels of leadership in the church, the Anglican episcopate worldwide remains overwhelmingly male, and our interviews reflect that. Female church leaders constitute only 7 percent of our sample.

As noted above, online communication facilitated our global reach, although our location in the UK and our North American connections have resulted in a sample somewhat skewed toward the Global North. Of those we interviewed, 24 percent come from the Church of England, and another 10 percent from the rest of the UK and Ireland. Canada and the United States combined amount to 29 percent of the total, with Africa contributing 27 percent of the total interviews. Australia and New Zealand together account for 5 percent, and the rest of the world (all in the Global South) contribute 5 percent.

Our initial response rate to requests for interviews with UK leaders was more than 75 percent; this fell somewhat the further afield we ventured. The response rate to requests for interviews with African church leaders was about 40 percent. There are numerous reasons why this might be. Respondents may be more likely to agree to an in-person interview, especially if the interviewers are offering to travel some distance to conduct it. Our requests for an interview may have been viewed with greater suspicion the further our requests had to travel; it is also possible that church leaders in the Global South were simply less familiar with the aims and objectives of research projects such as ours. It may also be that because the Scottish Episcopal Church is sometimes seen in the Global South as a particularly liberal province, researchers from a Scottish university were ideologically suspect (two respondents who did agree to an interview alluded to this). The following response, from a GAFCON church leader, is difficult to categorize, even in terms of whether the bishop is accepting or declining an interview; it does suggest that a combination of these factors are at play:

——Original Message——
From: [Bishop Athanasius][44]
Sent: 17 December 2010 10:53
To: McKinnon, Andrew; Brittain, C
Subject:
My dear brothers,
Warm greetings in the name of our Lord and Saviour Jesus Christ!

I write to acknowledge receipt of your letter dated 14th October 2010 which I received only 2 days ago. I am sure your expected time is long past but I will email my reply to you.

I have written numerous articles and done several interviews and now may not have any new ideas to share with you. The crisis is an on-going issue and we pray that some day the Church will be united again.
Be blessed.
In His Service,
[+Athanasius]

That the bishop had made his views known was precisely why we wanted to speak with him; we wanted to get him to explain, elaborate on, and perhaps clarify some of his public remarks. We responded to Bishop Athanasius's email assuring him that we would be very pleased to have a chance to speak with him, but we had no further response (so ultimately we have to count it as a nonresponse). Nevertheless, it took two months for our letter of invitation to arrive at the bishop's office (in a sizeable city), and the bishop seems to suggest that he thought he might be too late to respond on that account. It is unclear how many of our invitations and follow-up letters (in cases where a street address was our only contact information) never arrived at their destinations at all. We are inclined to think that the poor infrastructure in parts of the Global South had a negative impact on our response rate, but it is impossible to estimate how much with any precision.

As we conducted our research, we made every effort to listen carefully to what our respondents had to say about the conflict in the church—regarding their own position and those of others. We hope that they will find their positions reflected fairly in what follows. We did not always agree with those we interviewed, particularly since we interviewed church leaders who disagree—sometimes profoundly—among themselves. Consequently, it is probably inevitable that anyone who has a stake in the church, or views on what its positions should be, will find something here to which they take exception.

While we make no claim to impartiality (which seems to us impossible in any case), we have tried to bracket normative questions and positions insofar as possible. We have thus refrained from being prescriptive through most of the book, though in chapter 7, where we review the church's options for the future, we do take a (minimally) prescriptive position on the way forward in light of our analysis in previous chapters. We have, however, made every effort throughout not to confuse prescriptive positions with an empirical analysis of the conflict. The explanations church leaders offered us in our conversations do not always maintain such a distinction. It is appropriate for church leaders to assert specific positions and agendas as they see fit; this is less helpful as analysis. For example, if someone says that the conflict has erupted because a particular group has rejected the authority of the Bible, this seems to us less an explanation than an imperative. Such a position simply asserts that one's opponents should accept a particular view of the Bible. We believe that this is equally true when someone explains the recent conflict in terms of rampant homophobia in another part of the church, or blames it on "fundamentalist" regions of the Anglican Communion. The term "homophobe" may be an effective way of discounting someone with whom one disagrees; it does not strike us as especially useful in making sense of the church's current woes. The same is often true of the rather loose usage of the term "fundamentalist" as it gets thrown around. Even if there may be a grain of truth in all such contentions, the insult typically means that no further diagnosis is called for. A smear attributes blame and thereby seems to stand in place of an explanation.

A Note on Language and Identities

We often found the challenge of getting the language right to be daunting when referring to different identities, both sexual identities and religious identities; at times, we have undoubtedly gotten it wrong. Our challenge was compounded by the fact that these identities have changed over the past twenty years of the conflict, and even over the past ten years in which we did the interviews and writing; further, identities and names for those identities vary by place and time.[45] Thus some of our North American respondents, who have been making a case for greater inclusion of sexual minorities, have begun to talk about welcoming LGBTQ (lesbian, gay, bisexual, transgender, and queer) persons in the church, and we have often used this nomenclature here. The Q itself is a recent addition to the identity politics of sexuality (being added to the LGBT, which began to gain favor in the 1990s). There is no clear global consensus on the acronym, and terminology is likely to continue to change. In Britain, parallel movements tend to refer to the inclusion of LGBTI (intersex), or LGBTI+ persons.[46] One might complicate things even further and observe that in some parts of Africa, men who have sex with men (for example) may be more likely to refer to themselves as MSM, an acronym adopted from the medical literature on sexual practices (and referring more to sexual practices than to identities).[47] The Anglican conversations themselves have often lagged behind wider cultural change, and many of our respondents tended to talk about gay and lesbian Christians (or, very often, given that the central figure in this conflict is a male bishop in a relationship with another man, simply "gay" Christians). Anglicans themselves will often talk about disagreements over "homosexuality," or, somewhat obliquely, as differences over "human sexuality."[48] Where use of LGBTQ is anachronistic, or is far removed from the contexts in which it is being used, we have generally used other terms.

The question of terminology for "Anglicans" themselves has been at certain points no less challenging. This has long been a secondary identity for many in churches that identify themselves as "Episcopal" (the United States, Scotland, Sudan), or for that matter for those who think of themselves in the first instance as part of the Church of England. Referring repeatedly to "Anglicans and Episcopalians" is not only wordy, but it becomes particularly problematic when discussing parts of the church where Anglican and Episcopal have come to mean not only different but also deeply opposed identities (as in chapter 4). The use of this phrase would thus risk sowing confusion about when we are using "Anglican" and "Episcopal" to mean the same thing, and when to mean something different. Thus, when we are talking about global identities, we have opted to use "Anglican" consistently, reserving "Episcopal" for discussions of the United States or Scotland (for example), and for occasions when it is required to distinguish Anglicans from Episcopalians.

I | THE CULTURAL LOGIC OF SYMBOLS AND ANGLICAN "ORTHODOXY"

When we began our research for this book, we started by interviewing a sample of the most influential bishops in the Church of England, the Church of Ireland, and the Episcopal Church of Scotland. We selected them with a view to getting a spectrum of church leaders' views on homosexuality in the days leading up to Lambeth 2008. As we conducted our interviews, however, we were struck by how often the bishops told us that the topic, which everyone knew would soon be on the front pages of the newspapers, just as it had been ten years before, was a secondary issue. Over and over again we heard a variant of the same phrase from leaders, themselves holding a variety of positions on the sexuality debate: homosexuality was a "presenting symptom," "presenting symbol," or "presenting issue" for a much deeper set of issues.

These phrases resonate with important sociological work on intradenominational conflict, particularly two American studies: Mark Chaves's now classic study of the politics of the ordination of women, and Fred Kniss's study of the history of conflict among Mennonites.[1] These books demonstrate the importance of symbols, both as resources deployed in intradenominational strife and as stakes over which religious communities routinely tussle.

Chaves provides an account of just how contentious the ordination of women was in American churches through much of the twentieth century across a number of denominations, and how often it threatened schism. This raises the question why the ordination of women did not divide the Anglican Communion in the same way, or to the same extent, that homosexuality has. From the 1970s through the 1990s, and later in some parts of the Communion, church leaders were concerned that women's ordination might result in a split, but this disagreement has now been largely eclipsed by the homosexuality question.[2] We need to discuss the conflict over women's ordination not just because it is a comparative case but because it is in many respects the precursor to the dispute over the place of gay Anglicans in the church. Comparing the two disputes offers us a better chance of understanding the current one.

The Sociology of Symbols in Religious Conflict

Having noticed that doctrinal disagreement seldom precipitates schisms, sociologists of religion have tended to explain serious conflict that leads to division in terms of structural tensions.[3] Thus they will observe that much depends on the capacity of dissident groups to mobilize resources,[4] and on the political opportunities and constraints afforded by church polity and organization.[5] Churches with a congregational polity are much more prone to splits than those with episcopal leadership, and rapidly growing religious communities are more likely to divide than those that are shrinking. Likewise, studies have shown that attempts by the leadership to centralize power, authority, and decision making often precipitate fractious divisions.[6] Such observations have a fair bit of explanatory power, but they do not tell the complete story. We take up the question of structural tensions of the church in a globalizing world in chapter 5; in this chapter, we build instead upon recent literature on the symbolic politics of church conflict that helps us to make sense of the role of "presenting symbols" in the Anglican conflict.

A number of studies by social scientists have begun to enrich the usual structural accounts, pointing to the role of symbols in intrareligious conflict, both as sources of tension and as resources upon which different contenders draw. Mark Chaves's important "new institutionalist" study of women's ordination in American churches demonstrates that policies regarding women's ordination over the past century have functioned less as a guide for practice than as a marker that allows a denomination to identify itself as either a "liberal" denomination (which ordains women) or a "conservative" denomination (which does not).[7] In practice, such policies have had demonstrably little bearing on the actual leadership roles of women in those churches. Rather, the denomination's symbolic stance on women's ordination allows it to signal its position relative to its allies and competitors for adherents in the religious marketplace. Churches often adopt official stances on this issue as a way to establish alliances with those organizations (churches or otherwise) with which they want to partner. Church policy on women's ordination thus often serves more as a membership card to a club than as a blueprint for the internal gender dynamics within a denomination.

Denominations, like any other institution, have to respond to external pressures (the women's movement, the law, public perception, relations with other denominations) as well as internal pressures (the beliefs, feelings, and commitment of congregants; the availability or shortage of resources, including trained and ordained clergy). Thus the forces that bear on an individual congregation and its leadership will be different from those that bear on denominational leaders, often resulting in a necessarily rather loose coupling between denominational policy and congregational practice. The Roman Catholic Church is a case in point. The church does not ordain women; women nevertheless fulfill many of the functions of a priest in thousands of parishes. Owing in large part to a shortage of (male) priests, there is a large (and evidently growing) number of Roman Catholic churches in the United States that are pastored by "lay ecclesial ministers," the overwhelming majority of whom are women.[8] In large organizations, such loose couplings are not a defect. Rather, they often provide the means by which an organization can flourish in a complicated set of relations and arrangements—or at least they provide a means to survive (more on this in chapter 5).

Fred Kniss's research on the history of conflict in American Mennonite communities offers further insight into the dynamics of church conflict. Kniss provides an important reconception of symbols as both stakes and resources in intradenominational disputes. He suggests that students of social movements have often not paid enough attention to symbols. Sometimes these have been treated either as epiphenomenal to "real" material factors, like resources that can be mobilized or political opportunity structures;[9] alternatively, they have been understood as purely instrumental means for framing preexisting conflicts.[10] For this reason, careful attention to intrareligious conflict has much to contribute to the study of many different kinds of social movements and conflicts; it also enables us to better understand a religious conflict such as that which has developed within the Anglican Communion.

Symbols, Kniss argues, have distinctive characteristics that differentiate them from other kinds of stakes in a conflict, such as material resources or decision-making power. Examining the history of disputes among American Mennonites, he suggests that symbolic markers often make a conflict both heated and intractable. Because symbols are not divisible, the way material resources and power are, it is much more difficult to negotiate a mutually satisfactory compromise. Yet not all symbols are equally likely to provoke conflict. Kniss observes that in religious communities, some symbols will be more salient than others, and the importance of particular symbols changes over time. Crucially, symbols that may be of great theological importance in the history of the Christian tradition may not be particularly salient insofar as contemporary conflicts are concerned; in fact, the bigger and more abstract a symbol, the less likely that religious groups will squabble over it. Relatively abstract symbols and concepts (like "justice" or the Trinity) are frequently more fluid, polysemic, and open to different—even contradictory—interpretations. They thereby often afford many means of diffusing conflict. Conflict is thus most likely to break out over those concrete symbols that Kniss calls "cultural objects" (forms of attire, the organization of space for worship), or "symbolic practices" (the legitimacy of certain forms of rituals or the qualifications for particular offices of authority or honor). These are closest to the "surface of social life . . . [and so] are more likely to be the object of contention."[11]

Despite the many significant differences between Kniss's American Mennonite communities and the cultures of global Anglicanism, the list of recently contentious issues in the Communion does consist of a clearly parallel set of concrete symbols. The Anglican tradition is perhaps most familiar with this pattern through its history of fierce battles over revisions to the Book of Common Prayer, or in the way feuds often break out within congregations over the forms of music employed.[12] In the twentieth century, Anglicans have also wrangled over such issues as liturgical vestments,[13] the rites of marriage for people previously divorced, and whether women can serve as priests and bishops. Seen from this angle, the disputes over the public rites of blessing for same-sex couples and the consecration of openly gay, partnered bishops is simply the most recent in a sequence of skirmishes.

Recent conflicts in the Communion have not tended to focus on the more abstract symbolic codes or points of doctrine; rather, rifts form at the more visible, concrete symbols, which also represent issues of concern to the various parties of Anglicanism. The particular concrete objects of dispute may be linked to bigger theological themes, but these latter tend to lie in the background. Thus, while there are significant areas of disagreement among Anglicans on points of theological belief (the interpretation of the Nicene Creed, the person of Jesus, the efficacy of the sacraments, and so forth), these doctrinal issues are not the primary questions that have brought the Communion to the point of schism. These may well lurk in the background, but in the foreground is the more concrete question of publicly acknowledged and publicly blessed same sex-relationships. A significant group in the church has rallied around this symbol, and its adherents have begun to describe themselves as "orthodox Anglicans." Claiming such a name for themselves, they are setting themselves against those whose beliefs they view as "heretical." They are not indicating an affinity with the Orthodox tradition of churches that broke with the Church of Rome more than a millennium ago. For non-Anglicans, this has the potential to cause confusion, especially as there are far more adherents of that tradition of Orthodoxy than there are Anglicans ("orthodox" or otherwise) worldwide.[14]

Although we did not begin our research with questions framed by the work of either Kniss or Chaves, what we heard in our initial set of interviews with Anglican bishops and archbishops did incline us to turn to this literature on the symbolic dimension of religious conflict. Some translation of Kniss and Chaves is nevertheless required for looking at conflict in the global church, because while a liberal-conservative axis may demarcate the primary fissure in the American religious and political landscape (but see chapter 4), this axis of political contention is much less applicable elsewhere in the world. The American Episcopal priest and anthropologist Miranda Hassett demonstrates in her research that these terms of reference do not make sense for understanding religious and political positions or disagreements in the Ugandan church or society.[15] Likewise, a political spectrum running from liberal to conservative does not even remotely describe the field of political positions in Great Britain, which tend to gravitate around social class, national identity, and one's feelings about immigrants and Britain's place in Europe. Thus, in the UK, the difference between liberal and conservative ideologies does not serve to demarcate the political sphere very well. Within the Anglican churches of the British Isles, there is also no clear affinity between conservative theology and conservative politics, or liberal theology and left-wing politics,[16] which, on the American model, are generally assumed to be part of the same package. There may well be nowhere else in the Anglican world that liberal versus conservative works in exactly the same way, and, for that matter, there is a great deal of debate about how well this describes American political and religious culture, as has been amply illustrated in discussions about the so-called culture wars.[17] This is not to say that there are not political and religious leaders in the United States for whom these terms make a great deal of sense, nor is it to deny that some church leaders elsewhere have found it useful to import the rubric about the hegemony of "liberals" into their own context. Although this may make sense of the battle for some contestants (self-described "liberals" and self-described "conservatives"), it nevertheless makes for a rather poor sociological description of the political culture in which they are situated, and an even worse description of the different parties of the church.

Typologies always risk oversimplification, and that is undoubtedly true of any brief description of the different "parties" in the church that we introduced in somewhat greater detail in the introduction.[18] There is nothing either timeless or absolute about the Evangelical, Liberal, or Anglo-Catholic parties in the Anglican tradition. They are complex identities and sets of affiliations, with considerable variation within each. Within the Anglo-Catholic tradition, there have long been more liberal "affirming" and more "traditional" wings. Within the Evangelical party, some churches (and individual believers) are more "open" and others more "conservative"; some have very strong Calvinist inclinations, while others have been touched by the spirit of the Charismatic revival.[19] Likewise, one can readily identify a wide variety of Anglicans who might call themselves "liberal." Such identities are shifting, and the boundaries between the different parties have often been fuzzy and somewhat porous—except for the rather closely guarded border between the Evangelicals and Anglo-Catholics, particularly in their more conservative versions, where each was long anathema to the other.

One of the significant changes in church conflicts, particularly after Lambeth 1998, has been the concerted attempt to create common ground between these two long alienated parties in the church, and to restyle them together as "orthodox Anglicans." This became the self-identified term used by the GAFCON movement beginning in 2008, signaling a reconfiguration of the map of Anglican identities, one made possible by the new conflict over sexuality; the battles over the place of women in the leadership of the church did not facilitate the same identity construction.

Women in the Priesthood and the Episcopate as a Point of Comparison

In the churches of the Anglican Communion, the ordination of female priests and bishops has been a divisive topic for Anglicans globally and locally; in some places and times it has been every bit as controversial as the later disputes over homosexuality. Those tensions have, however, eased considerably and the center of gravity has shifted: as of 2015, two-thirds of provinces allow the ordination of women to the priesthood and half to the episcopate.[20] There is by no means unanimous agreement in terms of policy across the Communion, but where there are disagreements, there are also agreements to disagree (even if premised on alternate episcopal oversight for those who disagree). This raises the question of comparison: why did the ordination of women not result in the same impaired relations that disagreements over the ordination of gay bishops and the blessing of same-sex unions have engendered? Even if such counterfactual questions permit only tentative answers, we argue that consideration of the question is helpful for providing a point of comparison to the recent conflicts over homosexuality.

Of those provinces that have to date opted to ordain female priests and bishops, the Church of England was one of the slowest in the Communion to permit the practice, ordaining the first women to the priesthood in 1994 and opening the way for women in the episcopate in 2014. Seen from the perspective of the Communion, this has been a long process: in 1944, the bishop of Hong Kong ordained the first female priest as an emergency measure to provide wartime pastoral care—fifty years before the first female ordinands in England. The Hong Kong ordination was initially condemned at the Lambeth Conference of 1948, and the Reverend Florence Li Tim-Oi voluntarily "gave up the title" of priest, even though Bishop Hall of Hong Kong refused to revoke her license. Hong Kong kept pressing the issue, and in 1971, having finally gained a reluctant nod of approval from the Lambeth Conference, ordained two more women as priests.[21] Canada, the United States, and New Zealand all followed suit in the mid-1970s, Kenya and Uganda in 1983, and Australia in 1992; England passed legislation admitting women to the priesthood the same year, though it took another two years for any women to be ordained as priests.

Some groups, and a few dioceses, take exception to the ordination of women, even within provinces where the practice is accepted. The Diocese of Sydney (Australia), for example, does not ordain women, and until they broke away to form part of the new "orthodox" province in North America (ACNA), neither did three dioceses of the Episcopal Church. This disagreement has thus passed over into the ACNA, where one (Evangelical) diocese ordains women as priests, and other (Anglo-Catholic) dioceses do not. As a result, by agreement, none ordain women as bishops. In the Church of

England, Anglo-Catholic traditionalist congregations have special provisions allowing them to be ministered to exclusively by male priests, and now also to have oversight from male bishops who share their objection to the ordination of women as priests. While some nonordaining provinces are quite sizeable (Nigeria and Tanzania), most are numerically small (Southern Cone, Papua New Guinea, and Korea). There is still tension within some provinces over the question. The Diocese of Uruguay wishes to ordain women as priests, though it is blocked from doing so by the rest of the Province of the Southern Cone. Across the Communion, however, the question no longer looks to be a major source of potential schism.[22] Interprovincial tensions over the issue seem to have been contained, although the different policies mean that there is no longer complete acceptance in all provinces of one another's priests and bishops, and it has put a strain on ecumenical relationships with the Roman Catholic and Orthodox churches.[23] The disagreement over the ordination of women forms an important part of the backdrop to the subsequent dispute about homosexuality and feeds into it in a variety of ways, not least because it provided a first opportunity for some Anglo-Catholics to find common cause with some Evangelicals in opposing these developments.

When we spoke to bishops beginning in 2008, we asked them to compare the recent sexuality conflict in the church with other Anglican conflicts (prompting them with the issues of remarriage of divorced people, liturgical change, polygamy, and the ordination of women). The crisis over women's ordination stood out as the first point of comparison in the minds of most. This is perhaps because it was still, until very recently, very much a "live" issue in the Church of England. Debates continued over women in the episcopate as we were doing our field research, and it was on the mind of many leaders in that church, and carefully watched by leaders in other provinces that still did not admit women to the priesthood or episcopate. Much of the heated discussion in this latter debate has been about how to accommodate the minority within the church who cannot accept the legitimacy of women priests, be subordinate to women bishops, or recognize the orders of those ordained by them.

The bishops we talked to took one of three positions—with shades of difference and most with qualifications. Some were in favor of both permitting women in all three orders of ministry and fully including gays and lesbians in the church and its ordained orders. Others supported the ordination of women as priests and bishops but had various degrees of reservation (some to the point of outright hostility) to partnered gay clergy and blessing same-sex unions. Finally, some found both things equally objectionable. It is widely recognized that some Anglo-Catholic clergy have no objection to gays and lesbians in the church but are deeply opposed to women of any sexual orientation in ordained ministry;[24] none of the church leaders we met in the course of our research described their position to us in these terms.

Those who see gay clergy and women clergy as equally objectionable were the least common group among those we interviewed: only three people (all Anglo-Catholics) fell into this category. While Bishop Christopher seemed to insist on giving both issues equal weight, the two other bishops (Newman and Gregory) equivocated somewhat, and it quickly became clear that they were more concerned about women clergy than about gay clergy. Bishop Gregory explained:

> It's sometimes said that the Achilles' heel for Anglo-Catholics has often been the acceptance of homosexual clergy . . . over the years, and I suppose there's some truth to that. I mean, Anglo-Catholics would say that a woman ordained as a priest or bishop is not a priest or a bishop. . . . A homosexual man ordained as a priest or bishop *is* a priest or bishop and the question of the validity of sacraments for that concept for manhood is not an issue, as it would be for a woman holding that office. But nonetheless, the Anglo-Catholics would say that the ordained clergy are held to a standard of sexual ethics and moral conduct that is critical. . . . An immoral bishop or priest is . . . a scandal.

In short, a sexually active gay male priest is still a priest (though this is a scandal), while a woman ordained as a priest is not actually a priest.

We more commonly met bishops who expressed a (sometimes very conservative) evangelical theology, and although they were (again, sometimes deeply) opposed to gay clergy and the blessing of same-sex unions, they had no trouble ordaining women priests, even if some of them had misgivings or reservations about the prospect of women bishops. Bishop John, who resolutely opposes the ordination of partnered homosexuals, has no concerns about ordaining women and sees the question of female bishops as a second-order issue. Christians can legitimately disagree about the issue, he argues—unlike homosexuality, the question of female priests is not a first-order issue, which is a fundamental matter of faith. The question of women in the episcopate becomes a first-order issue, he told us, only if adequate provision within the church is not made for Christians who cannot accept the ministry of ordained women either as priests or as bishops.

Those most deeply opposed to women priests and bishops in the Church of England turn out to be a small segment of the most traditional Anglo-Catholics and a minority of conservative Evangelicals. After 1992, with the introduction of the ordination of women in the Church of England, a group called Forward in Faith (Anglo-Catholic traditionalists) and another called Reform (conservative Evangelicals with strong Calvinist leanings) have represented the views of opponents in national discussions. These two groups have different reasons for objecting to female priests and, subsequently, bishops. Forward in Faith is concerned with the efficacy of the sacraments (in particular, ordination and the Eucharist), while Reform's opposition is grounded on a theology of "headship," whereby, its members argue, the Bible instructs men to be the "head" of the family and to exercise like leadership in the church.[25]

In most provinces that decided to ordain women, some departures of clergy and laypeople followed, though the numbers were not especially large.[26] Ian Jones's *Women and Priesthood in the Church of England: Ten Years On* provides a helpful assessment of attitudes, clerical and lay, to women's ordination. In a sample of current priests, he found minimal change, though on average they have been slightly more likely to shift toward favoring women's ordination.[27] In his sample of clergy, 33 percent of Anglo-Catholic clergy ($n = 161$), 21 percent of Charismatic Evangelical clergy ($n = 24$), and only 7 percent of the larger group of clergy identifying themselves as conservative Evangelicals ($n = 54$; the Reform group would be a subset of this) objected to the ordination of women priests. Only 4 percent of Evangelicals ($n = 68$) who did not identify as conservative or Charismatic objected to ordaining women—a smaller percentage than the 13 percent of self-identified liberal Catholics ($n = 32$).[28] Overall, while Anglo-Catholics and Charismatic Evangelicals are more likely to object to the ordination of women, even among those who hold to such identities this is a minority position, and one that has clearly lost ground since the time of Jones's research.

Homosexuality as a Presenting Symbol

If the issue of women's ordination has been losing its power to divide Anglicans over the past twenty years or so, the question of homosexuality has been gaining force in the same period. In one sense, homosexuality has replaced the ordination of women as the most divisive topic in church life. Responses to women's ordination and to homosexuality do not demarcate the same fault line, however; rather, the symbol of the gay bishop and the rite of blessing for same-sex couples shift the configuration of contending groups within the church around a different presenting symbol, though the meaning of the presenting symbol is different for the different parties involved.

For Bishop John, endorsing the partnerships of people in same-sex relationships is to reject the authority of the scriptures and to abandon the faith of the apostles. He described the conflict over homosexuality as follows: "In a sense . . . the very real issue . . . the debate in the church isn't about homosexuality at all. Homosexuality is the presenting problem. I think we all wish it was a different one but it's the presenting problem of how seriously we take the authority of the Bible and especially of how seriously we are committed to the faith of the apostles." The bishop argued that those within the church who advocate blessing same-sex unions, and who permit practicing gay and lesbian priests and bishops, are effectively changing the Gospel itself. Saint Paul, he explained, included homosexual sex on a list of sins for which Christians need to repent. Some modern church leaders are, in his view, therefore undermining the church's teaching about what it means to live rightly before God, and are blessing in the church a practice that God condemns.

By no means, however, do all the bishops who share Bishop John's view that the homosexuality question is a presenting symptom agree with him on the nature of the disease. Bishop Luke, for example, is entirely in favor of the full inclusion of LGBTQ persons; he sees the basic questions as having to do with pastoral, rather than doctrinal, matters. In his view, many Anglicans in Britain and North America get very upset about the question of homosexuality because it suggests to them that

> the church is abandoning its historic traditions. And so, all the other issues about the authority of scripture, what the church has historically taught, the understanding of marriage. . . . It seems that suddenly in giving way pastorally to the needs of gay and lesbian people, you're running a coach and horses through the whole tradition, so people get very anxious about it. So, apart from the personal issues, you get both positive and negative reactions because people have got agendas of their own. . . .
>
> You've got all those other issues. So it's become a political issue. It's a campaigning issue. So it's the presenting issue for a battle for power in the church.

Bishop Luke, like many others with whom we spoke, recognizes that the question is deeply personal for individuals, including both LGBTQ people and some of those who oppose blessing same-sex marriages in the church. Bishop

Luke expresses a great deal of sympathy for the very real and deeply felt anxieties and pain surrounding the issue, but he argues that these things alone do not account for the intensity of the conflict as a whole. Rather, the intensity has much more to do with how the sexuality issue has become "political" and a "campaigning issue." It is a symptom of a "battle for power in the church."

Bishop Timothy compares the tensions in the Anglican Communion to the conflict in Northern Ireland; there, he argues, tough legislation swept away political patronage and resulted in very substantial social change after 1998, but the importance of the symbolic divide (between "Catholic" and "Protestant" communities) remains. He explains that for people living and working in the north of Ireland, "what trips you up is the symbolic stuff because that's the enduring stuff. [Speaking of the marches:] 'I have walked down that road for the last 150 years.' . . . [These may not be issues of substance but] they have a visceral connection with identity . . . with who people are. So they're not negotiable. And I guess that in some elements the gay issue has become symbolic, which means that they're not negotiable." Bishop Timothy encouraged us to think about the "symbolic" as opposed to the "substantial" nature of the conflict; this certainly helped make sense of the seemingly intractable nature of the positions. This was a realization, however, that begged a question. In Northern Ireland, the religio-political groups that embody and identify those symbols are clear; in the Anglican Communion, with its several distinct "wings" and thirty-eight provinces spread around the world, the meaning and use of a presenting symbol is contested from different angles, and is put to use for different, often opposed, purposes. The presenting symptom of homosexuality needs to be understood not simply as the marker of a preexisting divide between "liberals" and "conservatives." It is a symbol that contributes to the reconfiguration of the traditional parties of Anglicanism (Evangelicals, Liberals, and Anglo-Catholics). The question of homosexuality has deepened divides within and among these communities and contributed to a "realignment" of the political/theological parties that have long constituted Anglicanism—and the division of the Anglican world into those who are and those who are not "orthodox Anglicans" is a product of this conflict.

Homosexuality and New Divisions in the Evangelical Party

Most English Evangelicals have come to accept the ordination of women as priests (and many even as bishops); the symbol of the gay bishop, or the rite of blessing for same-sex couples, has created a rather different, and by many accounts rather deeper, divide. Bishop David describes himself as an Evangelical in the spirit of the Keele Congress.[29] In our interview, he lamented the way in which the Evangelical wing of the Church of England has become increasingly divided between the "open" or "generous" version of evangelicalism, to which he is firmly committed, and what he sees as the hard-line conservatism that has coagulated around the question of sexuality. A few of his fellow Evangelicals, he argued, have long seen themselves as heirs to the Puritans, who never got their chance to "complete the Reformation." He described some of them as having long been "itching for a fight," and as being quite explicit that the sexuality question was their chance for a "call to arms" that could be taken up by a broader constituency. The sexuality question was thus from the start embroiled in longer-standing issues, concerns, and politics, including the question of how the Bible operates as an authoritative text in the church—something of central importance for Evangelicals. Bishop David explained that while

> all Anglicans will say that the Bible is our fundamental authority, . . . Evangelicals will almost stop there, even though they are paying lip ser-vice to tradition and reason. . . . And then classic Anglicanism will talk about the Bible interpreted through tradition and with the use of reason and taking into account experience. . . . There are a number of ways of configuring that ground . . . but all of us would start with the Bible.
>
> But of course the conservative Evangelical will be suspicious of what everybody else means by the authority of the Bible. And that suspicion eventually has led to: "okay, let's test it out; let's see what they mean by this." And the feeling of having perhaps retreated and been sucked into the church as a whole has now been challenged: "okay, let's see what the color of their money is and what they really mean by the authority of the Bible." And then you run into the hermeneutical questions. . . . You've got this one issue taken as a litmus test for . . . "liberalism."

Bishop David does not support the public blessing of same-sex unions, nor does he advocate consecrating partnered gay priests or bishops. He does, however, see the question of how the church should respond to homosexu-ality as something over which Christians can legitimately disagree.[30] When we suggested, in response to his consternation about how some Evangelicals treat one's position on homosexuality as a "litmus test for liberalism," that it is often most challenging to hold a position in the middle as an issue becomes increasingly polarized, Bishop David expressed his exasperation:

I think that's right! Of much more concern, and this is part of that, is that we don't seem to be able to discuss in that area now. A banner is raised, a word is said, a phrase is used, and you know immediately which side of this divide you're on. And people listen out for trigger phrases, for symbolic phrases and words. So that middle area of intellectual debate, of real honest grappling, is getting evacuated as people just make it into a political scrap instead of a theological debate. I think Rowan Williams is classically one of those people who gets castigated from both sides as he tries to hold us together. What I'm saying is that we need to be able, within Anglicanism, to have the big tent that allows us to have the same tools and reach different conclusions with integrity and to live with that integrity of difference. Why this issue, for instance? There are seven texts on this issue and two thousand verses on poverty in the Bible. So I say, "For heaven sake, don't make this a Communion-breaking issue."

Bishop David explains how the symbol of homosexuality constructs a sharp boundary between those who "really" accept the authority of the scriptures, and those whose orthodoxy, and even the authenticity of their Christian faith, is questionable. By making the question of how opposed you are to gays in the church the "litmus test" of orthodoxy, the Evangelical wing of the church divides itself down the middle. Things become very difficult for Anglicans who consider themselves Evangelicals but who view homosexuality in less negative terms, or who do not see the question as a threat to the integrity of the Gospel.

On a number of occasions in the course of our research, Evangelical leaders shared their private doubts about their own publicly "conservative" position on homosexuality. Reverend Dave, a well-known Evangelical leader in North America, began our interview by criticizing the church's drift toward a "liberal" position on homosexuality, which he described as symptomatic of caving in to a liberal culture. As our conversation progressed, however, he began to open up somewhat. He admitted that his children, whom he described as Bible-believing Evangelicals like himself, did not share this view. Having had a long-standing friendship with an openly gay priest in the diocese, he told us that his children, now grown, experienced that priest as a caring pastor and an influential role model of a life faithful to the Gospel. Asked if this made a difference to his own view, he responded, "Honestly, I'm not always sure that history will show us to be on the right side of this issue." He even wondered whether people who hold the current conservative position will end up looking to Christians of the future like those who once justified slavery with theology—"I just don't know." This was certainly surprising ambivalence coming from someone who is publicly known for his "conservative" defense of Anglican orthodoxy. We have not followed up with Reverend Dave, but one wonders both what will grow from this seed of doubt and how many other conservative Evangelicals are quietly entertaining similar reservations about the party line. We certainly met more of them than we expected to in the course of our research. Often, but not always, these were priests in conservative parishes (we even met them in "realigned" ACNA parishes, or in churches with strong GAFCON connections); such clergy are sometimes concerned about the repercussions if their softening views were to become widely known, or if their parishioners were to start having reservations about the theological trustworthiness of their priest.[31] Age certainly seems to be one factor here. Reverend Dave's reflection on the position of his own children points to a wider shift, which is affecting Evangelicals as much as other Christians. Compared with their parents and grandparents, younger Christians are much less likely to see homosexuality as in any sense problematic for a Christian.[32]

When we interviewed Evangelicals who are resolutely opposed to gay blessings and gay bishops, and who do see this as a Communion-breaking issue, some found it difficult to comprehend how "real" Evangelicals might take a different view of the seven New Testament texts thought to refer to homosexuality. Bishop John even seemed a bit surprised when we put the question to him. Although he expressed a desire to be conciliatory, a different view from his own on this issue was a bridge too far:

> I think the issue is that I can cope with somebody that is a Christian seeking to be equally faithful to the Bible as I'm trying to be, and who comes to a different conclusion but really wants to take the Bible seriously, and argues on the basis of the Bible, and says that I haven't understood it properly. I might disagree with them but I can take that. But what I think is very difficult is for them to say, "I am a Christian and I respect the authority of the Bible," but in a very cavalier manner, "I'm willing to dismiss the plain teaching of the Bible and two thousand years of the history of the church on holiness."

Although he knows other Evangelicals, including some of his fellows on the Episcopal bench, who do not see homosexuality as an issue that divides the sheep from the goats, Bishop John is only able to see such a position as "cavalier," a dismissal of both scripture and tradition. In his view, it is not a point over which Evangelicals themselves can disagree. Rather, Bishop John contends, a gulf separates the "two religions" one finds within the Church of England and the Anglican Communion at present, and these are best identified as "Christianity and liberalism."

Bishop John's reference to "Christianity and liberalism" struck us as a possible reference to a book by the American fundamentalist Presbyterian leader J. Gresham Machen, who published *Christianity and Liberalism* in 1923 and who makes much the same argument (though with no reference to homosexuality). When we asked if he was alluding to Machen's book, the bishop seemed pleased to have the book recognized, and proceeded to pull a copy of Machen's book out of his briefcase! Needless to say, this is an unlikely book to be carried around by an Anglican bishop, but it does indicate how far the wings of the church may spread beyond the church's traditional denominational center of gravity, even in the episcopate. It suggests that for Bishop John, the issue of homosexuality marks a very deep chasm; those who sit on the other side of the question belong to the faith of "liberalism" and not to the Christian faith.

Anglo-Catholics, Sex, and Gender

Over the past several decades, while some Anglo-Catholics have objected vociferously to women priests and, more recently, to women bishops, Anglo-Catholics have tended to make very little noise about homosexuality in the church. There is good reason for this. One Evangelical bishop (Bishop Mathew) described much of the Anglo-Catholic tradition in England as "all a bit camp," and another (Bishop Luke) suggested that, in England at least, "the [Anglo-]Catholic wing is absolutely riddled with" homosexuality. "This is an agenda," Bishop Luke explained, "that they just don't want to talk about, for obvious reasons. Women are the issue. They can't deal with the gay issue, because the gay issue comes right close to home."

While this is undoubtedly true in Britain,[33] it is probably less so in Anglo-Catholic majority provinces like Tanzania or west Africa, and possibly also less true in the United States, where traditionalist Anglo-Catholics seemed somewhat more troubled by the election and consecration of Gene Robinson as bishop of New Hampshire. Three of the four dioceses in which there was fierce opposition to the "liberal domination" of TEC (San Joaquin, California, San Antonio, Texas, and Quincy, Illinois) are strongly Anglo-Catholic; these were the last holdouts to women's ordination (before most of the parishes in these dioceses left the Episcopal Church in 2008).

Over the past fifteen or twenty years, Anglo-Catholics have increasingly divided between "affirming" Anglo-Catholics and their more traditionalist fellows. "Affirming" Anglo-Catholics in general now tend to be in favor both of women in the priesthood and episcopate and of the full inclusion of gays and lesbians in the church. Traditionalist Anglo-Catholics tend to be deeply opposed to women priests and bishops, and are likely to express ambivalence about openly gay, sexually active (male) priests. Their reasoning about matters of faith and practice is generally quite different from that of Evangelicals: for traditionalist Anglo-Catholics, the Evangelical's emphasis on scripture is inadequate. "It's not just scripture," Bishop Christopher, a GAFCON-affiliated Anglo-Catholic, explains, "it's how the apostolic teaching is passed on and received in the church and what role scripture has to play in that process that are going on all the time, of course." If conservative Anglo-Catholics object to gay bishops and blessing same-sex unions, their objections are more likely to stem from their understanding of the church's traditions, the theology of marriage, and what such a theology of marriage has to say about God. They also worry about driving a further wedge between the Anglican and Roman Catholic churches.

While he is not in favor of authorizing public rites for the blessing of a gay couple and does not condone homosexuality, Bishop Newman told us, he would never ask one of his priests what goes on in his bedroom. "That's between them and God," he explained. "It's none of my business." That seems to be a view shared by some parishes, where the priest's (same-sex) partner has been given the unofficial title within the parish of "Father's friend."

As Father Peter, an "affirming" Anglo-Catholic, explained, there have long been divisions among Anglo-Catholics, though this was less obvious until well into the second half of the twentieth century. Previously, what held the Anglo-Catholics together was their commitment to the celebration of the Eucharist, which set them apart from most Church of England parishes, where Holy Communion would often be celebrated only four times a year. There have long been markers of difference between traditionalist Anglo-Catholics, or, as he describes them, "Anglo-Papalists," but these are just as likely to have been about the dress code for priests celebrating the Eucharist—a penchant for beards and birettas, say—as about matters of belief and practice.[34]

The ordination of women to the priesthood later became a serious issue of disagreement within Anglo-Catholic communities, some supporting it enthusiastically and others keeping one foot in the Tiber as they fought a rearguard battle against women in the episcopate. At present, as Dean Roger observed to us, one of the great ironies is that with the ordination of women to the priesthood, a significant number of lesbians have been ordained in the Church of England, and a disproportionate number of them have found a home in (affirming) Anglo-Catholic parishes.

Constructing "Orthodox Anglicanism"

A number of the bishops we interviewed talked about their surprise at the recent alliance between Anglo-Catholic and Evangelical leaders. This phenomenon has gone beyond the occasional strategic alliances between conservatives in both communities that have been temporarily formed in the past. For example, in the Church of England, some Evangelicals and Anglo-Catholics collaborated in opposition to union with the Methodists, and against women in the priesthood. In recent years, however, the leaders of the two parties have become much closer, particularly in North America, but also, though to a lesser extent, in England, where strategic partnerships have formed because of shared opposition to what they identify as "the liberal agenda."

Despite their alliance against Liberals, however, Bishop Peter suggests, "they're very, very different in the concerns they have about the liberal agenda." Not only are their specific anxieties different, but so too are their respective styles of being Anglican. The GAFCON experience in Jerusalem, a meeting in 2008 of bishops from the Global South and conservative dissidents from around the world, was marked by "the astonishment of Evangelicals, who are not used to any liturgy, or robes, or anything like that. Suddenly they find themselves in a high-church liturgy, both conservative African and high-church Catholic and others, where the host is being elevated," said Bishop David. Among the ACNA- and GAFCON-aligned or affiliated participants whom we interviewed, there is much evidence of a subterranean rift between conservative Evangelical and traditionalist Anglo-Catholic leaders. Some Evangelicals in particular emphasized the great unity among the "orthodox Anglicans," or "historic, orthodox Anglicans," who participated in the GAFCON events. Conservative Anglo-Catholics tended to be somewhat less sanguine. One such Anglo-Catholic, who was at GAFCON in Jerusalem in 2008, suggested that among the conservative dissidents, "I think there is tension. For instance, there were people [at GAFCON] who ordained women and people there who didn't ordain women. And the declaration itself recognizes it and says that you work through those kinds of things. Whether the tension will be greater than the need for unity is the question. I don't know the answer to that. But yes, undoubtedly, people who are in some ways unlike each other now see the need to hang together." The Jerusalem Declaration referred to above was the key statement emerging from the GAFCON conference in 2008. Rather than simply an expression of self-evident Anglican orthodoxy, this is an attempt to *create* Anglican orthodoxy by means of compromise between conservative Evangelicals and conservative Anglo-Catholics, both of whom have historically emphasized different (and even contradictory) elements of the Anglican tradition.

The fourteen points of the Jerusalem Declaration, which is formulated as a statement of faith for orthodox Anglicans, include apostolic succession and the four ecumenical councils for the Anglo-Catholics, and the thirty-nine articles for the Evangelicals. The declaration's statement on the Bible in particular betrays this attempt to suture together the two traditions: "The Bible is to be translated, read, preached, taught and obeyed in its plain and canonical sense, respectful of the church's historic and consensual reading."[35] It is far from obvious that the Evangelicals' "plain sense" and the Anglo-Catholics' canonical, historic, and consensual readings mean the same thing, or are so readily reconciled with each other.

Most significantly, the statement of faith inserts a declaration intended to exclude same-sex marriage, sandwiched between the GAFCON position on clerical orders and one on the "Great Commission" (that is, to "go . . . and teach all nations, baptizing them in the name of the Father, the Son and the Holy Ghost" [Matthew 28:19]). Many Anglicans undoubtedly could agree with the statement as a whole but might take a different view on the question of sexuality, or might at least not see it as an issue that is worth a schism. Without opposition to homosexuality, "orthodox Anglicanism" still lacks internal coherence as a theological statement or a religious community; shared opposition to the church's recognition of gay and lesbian relationships and leadership roles holds the alliance together. The movement does achieve some further, much needed coherence, although it is again in a negative sense, by positioning itself against the "spirit of the age," which orthodox Anglicans identify as "liberalism" (in the theological and cultural rather than the economic sense). In this way, the unity of the moment is defined by what it opposes, rather than by clear tenets held in common.

Constructing the Opposition

What "orthodox Anglicans" lack in terms of internal coherence they make up for by constructing a coherent enemy, typically presenting liberalism as a self-evident and commonsense category. For those who are so marked, it is not always quite so obvious what it means to be a "Liberal." Bishop David, who describes himself as an Evangelical, feels that his fellow religionists often discredit him because he sees homosexuality as a matter of *adiaphora*, an issue over which there can legitimately be disagreement in the church. Describing the response of some of his fellow Evangelicals to his attempt to avoid the polarizing terms of the debate on homosexuality, he often finds himself dismissed as a "Liberal," a label that he rejects unequivocally.

Bishop Timothy, who does identify himself as a Liberal, finds that what this means is typically caricatured by critics (though he admits that the caricatures are sometimes adopted in the "knee-jerk reactions" of those who think of themselves as "Liberals"). Critics, he says, often treat Liberals as if they simply accommodate whatever the culture dictates. Therefore, by setting themselves against whatever they see as "accommodating" (or Liberal) positions, they can think of themselves as standing "in a position over and against the world," and as taking a principled stand. To be a Christian, then, means to produce a mirror image of your understanding of the culture in which you find yourself, and in opposition to the position of those within the church who seem to represent it.

Interestingly, Bishop Kevin suggested that within the parameters of the current conflict, the category "Liberal" has actually been constructed by the new alliance of conservative Evangelicals and traditionalist Anglo-Catholics. "To what extent," he asks,

is "liberalism" an invented category that allows these folks to gather, and ignore their own differences? Hmmm. To what extent is it the straw man that they've erected to legitimize their own struggle for control of the church? When I ask people, "What is a Liberal, in your view?" I get a thousand different answers, except that they're bad people, and not real Christians. We've placed ourselves outside the church, and all this. Now, if I were just to speak personally, I would be, I suppose, a Liberal on the sexuality issue, but I'm not a Liberal on a *whole* [*laughing*] lot of other things. I'm not a Liberal liturgically. . . . I'm not a Liberal—I get letters from priests in the diocese wanting to throw the communion table open to everybody, baptized or not. And I say, "You cannot do that. The Eucharist is the meal of the baptized." And there's a lot of pressure on language, and language change, and I am not Liberal about that. So I don't really know if I am a Liberal, or what one is. So I suspect it's a kind of invention, and one of the difficulties in this discussion is stereotyping, and it, of course, it happens in all directions. I'm not saying that only Conservatives do stereotyping.

Conservatives might provide "a thousand different answers" for why they would identify Bishop Kevin as a Liberal, but there is one clear point of agreement between Bishop Kevin and his conservative interlocutors: that the distinction between the groups has become most clearly marked by where one stands on the question of homosexuality in the church. This has become the most salient symbol of the conflict, a hook on which the new orthodox Anglicans have hung a number of different complaints, and which liberals use to oversimplify the concerns of conservatives.[36] In the view of "orthodox Anglicans," it separates the wheat from the chaff.

Sometimes this symbolic marker operates even in the absence of the actual positions on the sexuality question. Bishop Martha, for example, describes how misinformation and misunderstanding have characterized relationships between different churches within the Communion. She recalled a conversation with an African bishop at Lambeth 2008:

> [He] said at one point, "I don't understand how [your province] thinks it can approve same-sex relations!" I said, "We haven't." And he said, "Yes, you have!" To which I answered, "No, actually we haven't." So I asked him, "Why does your church accept that bishops can have more than one wife?" He answered, "It doesn't." So I added, "Well, I have been told that your church does!" He said, "I have been told that your church accepts gay weddings!" I said, "It doesn't." He exclaimed, "Why would someone tell me if it wasn't?" And then he stopped and said, "Oh . . ."

The way the conflict within the Communion has been constructed, with two inherently opposed and mutually exclusive positions, is far from an accurate description of the situation, though responses to the symbol increase the polarization.

Why Homosexuality and Not Women in Leadership?

Although there is no way, at present, to know with absolute certainty, the impact of the "homosexuality conflict" seems to have been much more significant in the Anglican Communion than the fallout over the ordination of women as priests and bishops. It is easy to forget, however, that from the 1970s until well into the 1990s, church leaders worried that the conflict over ordaining women might well result in schism, and in its day it seemed every bit as significant a disagreement. The ordination of women was the initial impetus for the Eames Commission, which produced the *Virginia Report* in 1997.[37] By the time a second commission chaired by Archbishop Eames produced the *Windsor Report* in 2004, the overriding presenting symbol had definitely become the question of homosexuality. The report had been overtaken by recent events, including the election of Gene Robinson, the controversy over the appointment of Jeffrey John, the authorization of the blessing of same-sex partnerships in the Diocese of New Westminster, and crossborder episcopal incursions in North America.[38]

It is worth asking, therefore, why the difference in fallout between the two issues? Granted, the two cannot be entirely separated from each other, as we have argued in our assessment of "Anglican orthodoxy" as an attempted, and partially successful, synthesis of Anglo-Catholic and Evangelical opposition to "liberalism," and the—admittedly unstable—cooperation between the two groups in the ACNA Province of North America. Nevertheless, the issues, the people who take sides on them, and the consequences are different and at least partially comparable.

The argument that the conflict over homosexuality has been more fierce because homosexuality is a more serious moral issue than women's ordination is not viable. Some of our respondents made this claim, which of course has been contested by other bishops who would agree neither with the normative claim nor with the sense that this accounts for the risk of schism. More important, while moral claims may tell us how someone *should* act in a particular situation, they are not a very good guide to understanding how or why people *do* in fact act.[39]

Different groups are upset by the prospect of full inclusion of gays and lesbians in the church and the prospect of women priests and bishops, and even find these prospects contrary to the essence of their faith. Some Anglo-Catholics find the idea of women clergy deeply troubling, whether because they (like Bishops Newman and Gregory) see women priests as simply illegitimate, or because they think that women priests (and even more so bishops) would make full communion with Rome impossible. As Bishop Michael observed, this was one reason why some of the more self-consciously "Protestant" members of the Church of Ireland voted for women priests: even if they had theological reservations, at least women priests and bishops would provide some measure of insulation from the bishop of Rome.

In the end, only a rather small segment of the Anglican Evangelicals we interviewed were deeply opposed to women priests, and this became too small a base for the battle against liberalism in the church. Homosexuality has long been of less concern to Anglo-Catholics, but their concern about women as priests made them strange bedfellows indeed with Anglicans who objected strenuously to gay bishops or same-sex blessings. Coming on the heels of the conflict over women priests and bishops, where traditionalist Anglo-Catholics felt increasingly isolated, they were probably more receptive to conservative Evangelical overtures than if the one had not followed the other. While there is little doubt that Anglicans take a variety of positions on homosexuality and the church, and do so in good faith, the contests between leaders of the Anglican Communion have not been only about sexuality. Rather, the issue is a presenting symptom of deeper, long-standing rifts, and public positions are taken in accordance with one's own party, and in opposition to those of different camps within the church. The constitution of the two groups representing the "two sides" of the homosexuality question was not already given at the outset of this dispute, nor are the two groups likely to remain static. The symbol of the "gay wedding" or "gay bishop" has become the rallying point around which two groups of church leaders, not long ago deeply opposed to each other, have begun to form what may be more than a strategic alliance, and perhaps even a new identity as "orthodox Anglicans."

Yet there are significant challenges to such a unifying identity, comprising traditionalists and Evangelicals, and it is far from certain whether it will hold, let alone be transmitted to a younger generation. The many issues that could divide the two groups include the ordination of women, lay presidency, and friction generated by the emerging structures of power and authority themselves. For younger Anglicans, of whatever stripe, it is unlikely that this will be an issue over which they wish to fight as they move into positions of authority and influence in the church.

"Anglican orthodoxy" seems not only to have been developed by leaders of the dissident movement but is also more or less restricted to it, and it has less than firm traction among leaders in the areas supposedly best represented by its ideals. When visiting local churches politicized by recent conflicts, and participating to one degree or another in the protest against liberalism and homosexuality, one seldom finds much evidence that the synthesis of Anglo-Catholic traditionalism and Evangelical Biblicism has taken root. Rather, the seeds of "Anglican orthodoxy" seem more often than not to have fallen on "stony places where they had not much earth" (Matthew 13:5). It is usually evident that such churches are firmly committed to their identities as either Evangelical or Catholic.

On the other hand, there are still many parishes, far from the heat of contemporary conflicts, where one finds symbols of Evangelical, Catholic, and Liberal Anglicanism commingled. Such churches are seldom without their internal tensions, and it is true that parishes very often lean in one direction or another, but a recent visit to a parish church in the southwest of England strikes us as not atypical of the holy muddle of Anglican life. The signs were all there, even though there was no one in the church to tell us about the life of that community. The pew Bibles were all in the New International Version (NIV), the clear choice of Evangelicals; at the same time, a crucifix hung on a wall not far from a banner featuring a female saint who bore an uncomfortably close resemblance to the Virgin Mary for many of those who prefer the NIV. Lest the other Catholic markers be overlooked, a burning red candle indicated the reservation of the sacrament, driving the point home to any observer sensitive to the symbolism (as many, if not most, Anglicans would be). Finally, among notices for church suppers, committee meetings, and antipoverty campaigns, we found several notices associated with the Liberal wing, among them an advertisement for an upcoming local interfaith dialogue event and, tacked up by one corner that showed the wear of having been removed and replaced several times, a photocopied recent issue of *Signs of the Times*, the bulletin of the Liberal parachurch organization Modern Church. Nothing in this church made any reference to questions of homosexuality, for or against, though it seems likely that a range of views are held on this matter as well.

2 | GLOBALIZATION, COMMUNICATION, AND THE REDISTRIBUTION OF RELIGIOUS AUTHORITY

In a conversation by Skype from his diocese in sub-Saharan Africa, Bishop Benjamin disagreed with our description of the Anglican Communion as being in a state of "crisis." "Of course we can say that it's a 'crisis,'" he explained, "but if you do understand the polity of how the church operates, then one would say, it's not a crisis, but it's a different way of operating . . . [unclear]. If you think about TEC, strictly speaking, in TEC the deputies are more powerful than the bishops, which is very different than in Africa, where the bishops are more powerful than the laity. So, unless you understand that difference, one would say that we're in a crisis." The bishop told us of the visits he has made in his own attempts to encounter in person, and to understand, provinces where they do things differently:

> I've made visits to the States to try and understand . . . the way they operate, and they operate within their own constitution . . . unless you say, "Well your constitution is wrong," which I can't do, because I don't belong to that province. And one also has to look at the countries where we come from—what the law of the country says. For instance, one would say that, in South Africa, they passed a law allowing gay relationships, which is not the case in [my country. Here,] it's actually criminal to be in a gay relationship.

So, if I have to compare myself with a South African, it would be like comparing mangoes and pawpaws [papayas], which are not the same, because the environment in which we operate is totally different. So, unless we understand the landscape in which we are operating, that will influence the way we are looking at the events that are happening in the Anglican Communion.

Bishop Benjamin is himself theologically conservative, and he insists emphatically that same-sex unions and marriages have no place in his own diocese. However, having spent time visiting provinces where they do things differently, he has become much more understanding of those differences. He argues that some of the Communion's difficulties arise from the different contexts in which the church operates, from the different constitutions and canons of different churches, and from the resulting complications in inter-provincial relationships. One should not compare mangoes and papayas, or province and province, he says, though such comparisons are difficult to avoid in the age of global communication.

The Anglican skirmishes of the past few years have been inescapably global, even when they are at their most local. The disputes about the legitimacy of same-sex relations and the incursions of bishops into the affairs of other provinces have shown that local church conflicts are now inevitably imbricated with their relations to Anglicans in faraway parts of the globe, as we show in chapter 4. In this chapter, we draw upon our interviews with church leaders to show how the time-space compression[1] of recent globalization has made conflict between leaders in the Anglican Communion increasingly unavoidable, even if the conflict that has erupted and threatened to split the church was itself largely contingent, as we argued in the last chapter. Here, we demonstrate how the networked world of global, new-media technologies and fast, relatively inexpensive long-distance travel can exacerbate—but also moderate—the conflict, depending on who uses these media, how, and to what end. We argue that the forces of globalization have redistributed the capacity to exercise authority in the Communion; new means of communication and modes of travel have made the exercise of local authority more challenging and the exercise of transnational religious authority increasingly possible. This is part of the reason for the increasing centralization of decision-making power, even if there are at the same time real attempts to apply the brakes and insist on local autonomy.

The Anglican Communion and Globalization

There is a basic contradiction or paradox at the heart of Christian thought and practice: the Gospel is for all people everywhere, but this universal good news nonetheless needs to be expressed and lived in particular ways appropriate to the specific places, cultures, and times in which people live their faith.[2] Such local expressions of faith inevitably look very different from one another, often raising the question of whether it is in fact the same faith being practiced in different contexts. This dialectic of the universal and the particular[3] is a tension found in all the Abrahamic faiths, though it is particularly acute in the Christian tradition, with its belief in the universal significance of the incarnation and its long-standing practices of inculturation.[4]

Different Christian traditions have attempted to manage this tension in various ways, including via ecclesiological structures and decision-making procedures. The Church of Rome centralizes decision-making power and the capacity to define the faith in a magisterium, insisting on the universal truth of the Gospel as it is seen from the vantage point of the Vatican. While local options for taking a different position are limited, the tensions are often reduced by the response of the faithful to the teachings of the magisterium. On many issues, the *sensus fidelium* diverges from the church's official teaching: in most parts of the world, the Catholic Church's teaching on birth control clearly has little measurable impact on Roman Catholics, for example.[5] This is not the only sense in which official teaching is selectively, if routinely, ignored even by devout Roman Catholics, a phenomenon Mary Jo Bane has dubbed "the Catholic puzzle." At the other extreme, in many Protestant churches, the authority to make decisions about matters of faith rests with the local congregation, though this often entails the implicit assertion that the local beliefs and practices ought to be universal. The resulting discrepancy may be part of the reason why churches in the congregational and Presbyterian traditions are more prone to schism than others.[6]

Anglicanism's response to this dialectical tension (which takes neither a magisterial nor a congregational form) is an important part of the story of the recent conflicts in the global Communion.[7] The forces of globalization have heightened the contradiction between the whole and the parts, the universal and the particular. Globalization entails the shrinking of the globe, the compression of space and time, and the increasing speed with which goods, people, and ideas travel long distances. This has had dramatic implications for local economies now inextricably linked to the capitalist world system,[8] as well as for nation-states and their interrelations.[9] As Roland Robertson argues, there is an equally significant cultural aspect to globalization, which entails above all the globalization of consciousness, including religious consciousness.[10]

The world is shrinking, and people, both as individuals and as groups, are increasingly aware of their place within it in relation to the plurality of global cultures. We know that we now live in a "global village," to use Marshall McLuhan's oft-quoted though undoubtedly overly bucolic metaphor. Popular accounts of globalization often wrongly suggest that globalization means that the world is simply becoming homogenized—or, in a somewhat more political version, Westernized—as exemplified by the ever proliferating archetype of the golden arches.[11] Robertson, however, rightly argues that globalization may homogenize in some limited senses, but the same forces of increasing proximity also encourage, even demand, the heightening of cultural difference and distinctiveness at the same time. "Westernization" and "anti-Western" reaction are part of the same process (Robertson himself uses the term "glocalization" to describe the globalizing/localizing process).

One can find examples of the global dialectic of particular and universal in many different fields. The nation-state has spread throughout the globe over the past two hundred years; a person is no longer permitted *not* to have a national identity.[12] But national identities are built out of differences from other nation-states, and in some cases these can be deeply antagonistic to one another. Much the same is true of the modern concept of "religion": it is an umbrella term under which a mind-boggling variety of beliefs and practices can take shelter, guaranteed by global conventions (such as the UN Declaration of Human Rights), which provide everyone the right to his or her own religion, or to no religion. In that sense, the concept may be homogenizing, but particular, often local, religious identities are as likely to set people in opposition to one another as to unify them.[13] Likewise, the era of globalization has seen the massive proliferation of recovered (and indeed invented) local cultural traditions, often seeking protection under the aegis of global auspices, such as UNESCO, or asserting the right to maintain local cultural traditions as fundamental (that is, as universal) human rights.

The Anglican Communion has been both a product and a carrier of global processes and is itself an exemplar of the inherent tensions of globalization. While the Church of England has its origins in Henry VIII's declaration of independence from the bishop of Rome (and hence as a particular church within the church universal), it has long been both less and more than the religion of the English.[14] Likewise, while the colonialist stereotype of the Church of England abroad has more truth to it than many contemporary Anglicans might like to admit, the tradition has long recognized the importance of particular expressions of the Gospel, even those that are not English. The Church of England translated the liturgy into Welsh for the use of its four dioceses in Wales in the sixteenth century; the Episcopal Church of Scotland, by contrast, has always been independent of the Church of England throughout its long and complicated history.[15] With the American War of Independence, Episcopalians in the newly declared United States had their first bishop ordained by the Scottish Episcopal Church at Aberdeen to avoid the requirement of the oath of loyalty to George III (which would have made the bishop a traitor at home). One could argue that the process of ecclesiastical decolonization began well in advance of the slow collapse of the British Empire. Roughly a quarter of the provinces that are now part of the Anglican Communion have never been part of the British Empire—they chose to become Anglican, and their communion with the See of Canterbury has always been a matter of the "bonds of affection," rather than of obedience to a colonial master.[16]

It has long been Anglican tradition to encourage local autonomy and indigenous adaptations as both appropriate and conducive to evangelism. The Lambeth Conference of 1920, for example, articulated this clearly when it recognized "the practical steps which missionary societies and boards have taken towards the realization of the ultimate aim of all mission work, namely, the establishment of self-governing, self-supporting, and self-extending Churches, from which outside control has been withdrawn at the earliest moment, so as to allow the free expression of their national character."[17] The conference then suggested that, this imperative for local and autonomous expressions of the Gospel being especially urgent at that historical moment, further development in this direction should be encouraged. It therefore emphasized the need to give "the widest freedom to indigenous workers to develop the work in their own countries on lines in accordance with their national character" (point no. 4). We contend that, however appropriate for the mission of the church, and however significant a factor in the church's growth this policy has been, it has also heightened the basic tension between the local and the global. In a shrinking world, it has become increasingly difficult for "indigenous workers to develop the work . . . in accordance with their national character" in different contexts at the same time. Contradictions emerge as church leaders seek to meet the different pastoral needs of parishioners in different contexts, while electronic communication and high-speed global travel mean that church leaders in very different contexts are increasingly looking over one another's shoulders.

The tension between the particular expressions of faith in the different provinces of the Communion has long been a source of worry and disagreement within a church on which the sun never sets, and has been the impetus for the development of "instruments" to keep the whole bound together. One could argue that the Colenso affair, which gave urgency to the first of the gatherings of bishops that have become the decennial Lambeth Conference, involved just this issue. Bishop John William Colenso (1814–1883) wrote his treatise on Saint Paul's Epistle to the Romans—a commentary that was a scandal for many Anglicans—"from a missionary point of view." Much later, the emergency wartime ordination, in Hong Kong in 1944, of Florence Li Tim-Oi, the first female priest known to have been ordained in the Anglican tradition, sparked much disagreement. The tensions continued to simmer in part because Bishop Hall of Hong Kong refused to revoke Tim-Oi's license, and the church in Southeast Asia continued to press for women's ordination after the war—long before many took the case for the ordination of female priests seriously in the United States, Canada, or New Zealand. The issue became an impetus for the development of the Anglican Consultative Council.[18]

Globalization and the Compression of Time

The church leaders we interviewed were keenly aware of the global mediascape in which they speak and act and through which they relate to distant parts of the church; many were also sensitive to how instant communication has compressed time as much as it has space. Indeed, for Bishop Jordan, who spoke with us in Scotland from Australia by means of Skype, a great deal of the recent tension in the Communion can be attributed to the speed of communication worldwide. As he put it:

> I think that this is probably the first Communion-wide tension that's been played out in our kind of instant communication period. So we're not really good at that, 'cause you know, in times when things took longer and people wrote letters and wait[ed] for answers, a whole lot of stuff might happen in between. . . .
>
> Now, people will expect an ultimatum; they'll expect that, from whatever perspective, there will be immediate action, they'll want to hear someone's live commentaries, the archbishop of Canterbury on every little thing, which is . . . [unclear][19] would have been unknown apart from

the immediate circle of such people, in a previous, even in one previous generation.

The church had generations to get used to having dialogue, debate, and disagreement when the pace of communication was slower; Anglican leaders attuned themselves to the more unhurried deliberations of occasional interpersonal conversation and long-distance communication by post. For Bishop Jordan, the controversies over partnered gay bishops and blessing same-sex unions have been exacerbated by the fact that the church has not yet learned how to have these conversations at Twitter speed, or how to cope with the fact that many people expect a speedy rejoinder to every latest event, statement, or controversy. The slower pace of the debates about women's ordination was, at least in part, a function of the slower media in which the dialogue and debates unfolded.

While Bishop Jordan expressed no aversion to electronic communication per se, Bishop Paul was less enthusiastic about its potential, particularly about the widespread use of blogs in the Anglican debates of the past few years. He argued that the speed of a response to the latest events is often indicative of the amount of thought that is put into formulating it. He told us about an institution he once watched destroy itself over an increasingly heated set of email exchanges on a listserv. The participants, he said, were given to "reacting quickly, reacting sometimes—maybe often—without pause for reflection, without pause for consideration about what analysis or what else might have been said and reacting in a way that is significantly unhelpful."

A "hot" medium can certainly raise the temperature in an already heated discussion on a listserv, but it can also reconfigure how we communicate.[20] Albert Thomas, a layperson whom we interviewed because of his expertise on Anglican communications both online and in print, argued that the increased speed of all kinds of communication was a factor in the recent tensions over homosexuality. He explained that there has been a revolution in the processing and disseminating of information that is not limited to the blogosphere but affects the way that both the "mainstream" press and the church press cover events, and that this has changed the whole nature of disagreement within the Anglican Communion. "There's a huge shift to electronic," he explained,

> and, of course, what that has meant is a huge speeding up. So, you know, you learn things much, much faster. I mean, just as a simple example, this week . . . you know, there's this debate coming up [in the Church of England]—women bishops. And in the space of a week, the archbishops announced they were going to publish an amendment . . . they're going

to put in an amendment to this legislation, they put out a press release, or a so-called press release . . . [unclear] and then yesterday they actually published the text of what the amendment is to be. And now, today, on the blogs, people are discussing this amendment and saying whether it'd be a silly, not helpful—well, that all within, you know, twenty-four to forty-eight hours of a cycle.

Albert Thomas contrasted the one- to two-day news cycle in which the archbishops of Canterbury and York found themselves spun with the slower pace of the weekly *Church Times*. But even that has had to speed up in recent years in response to the pressures of high-speed electronic communication, although it is still one of the slower media for debate and discussion of church affairs. He explained:

> Previously, [a news item] had to wait for the *Church Times*; it takes two days. . . . Now, it's supposed to be [a] Tuesday [deadline] and published on the Friday, but it goes to press on Wednesday and gets published on Friday.
> So [the *Church Times* is] actually speeding up printing on the distribution a little bit and the technology of doing this changes, so it's all much, much faster. But even so, that's a weekly cycle and that was the best you had, and so, yes, I mean, the whole method of communicating has changed. And so there's no doubt at all that that raises the temperature on the debates. People follow on statements, you know, without a lot of reflection. If you're on a weekly publishing cycle, for example, and you just missed the deadline and you know there's no point in writing it in three days, you can wait and see what else happens together. And that's not true on the internet, because the publishing cycle is actually zero. So, yes, that does alter the nature of the discourse.

The speed of communication makes a direct contribution to how a discussion unfolds, and the speed has now increased to the point that there is virtually no time at all—the publishing cycle is "zero"—between one leader's making a statement and another's responding to it.

Globalization and the Compression of Space

It is not just the speed, however, but also the reach of the new media world that has changed the context in which dialogue and dispute take place. The new mediascape means that local churches are always making decisions about how to be the church within earshot of church leaders who live, minister, and have their primary responsibilities in other contexts; these other leaders often see the world, and understand the faith, differently. Of course, church leaders typically do not hear, or overhear, about the goings-on in other parts of the world directly. Rather, much communication is mediated by bloggers and journalists who shape the story of what is happening—sometimes, though of course not always, with malicious intent. The mediascape increasingly feeds on itself, halfway independent of the events being reported on themselves: bloggers respond to journalists, and journalists increasingly use bloggers as news sources;[21] blogs become news and news becomes the foil for blog posts. Because of the enormous reach that the internet makes possible, events and statements have ripple effects that travel the globe. Space has become so compressed that comments or events in one part of the globe can, like the proverbial butterfly flapping its wings, cause a tornado in a distant land.

In our interviews with leaders in the Global North, we sometimes heard tales (some of which bore the clear marks of exaggeration) about the consequences of "liberal" policies in the United States or Canada for Anglicans living as minorities in parts of the Global South. For this reason, we asked a church leader in a majority-Muslim part of the world about local reactions to the election of Gene Robinson as bishop of New Hampshire and the blessing of same-sex unions in the Diocese of New Westminster. We wanted to hear firsthand about the impact of these events on his ministry, many miles away from New Hampshire and Vancouver. Bishop Elias insisted that these distant events did have direct repercussions in his local context. As he spoke, we could hear the tones of the *adhan* (the Islamic call to prayer) in the background.

> I can't tell you how much we suffer at the ordination, because these news are the news that the media brings. They don't bring the news, the good news of the church planting or serving the community, or some of these wonderful things—what the church did after Hurricane Katrina and all— they don't care about these things. They care about the bad news. So we were hurt and we still, I said to you last week that is, after seven years from the consecration of Gene Robinson. Let me tell you one thing. . . .
>
> I had a friend who is a bishop in the States and he came over. He wanted to see for himself, and that during this visit I invited the family, just [to] welcome him. And what I have never imagined [is] that this fifteen-year-old child started to talk with the bishop. I would never think

that this issue of consecration of Gene Robinson would affect a fifteen-year-old . . . boy. . . . And he said, "My classmates said to me, you go away, we should not speak with you because your church ordains homosexuals." This is among the new generation, fifteen-year-olds, and the children knew from the internet what's going on. And they wanted to marginalize this boy. And the boy said with the American bishop who was visiting me. And this is the first time the boy ever came and spoke with me, and said, "My classmates say this: we don't want to play with you because you are a gay church."

Even if minor elements of this story may have become distorted in the retelling (would young boys in a predominantly Muslim context understand the concept of "ordination"?), it nonetheless has the ring of truth about it. Put into the mouth of a child, innocent of the politics of the Anglican Communion, the account has a certain poignancy, and it conveys how the current crisis could feed into the undoubted everyday difficulties of minority Christians in lands where homosexuality is *haram* (forbidden)—at least in theory, if not quite so consistently in practice.[22]

Messages, of course, are shaped by how they are conveyed by new media, just as they are in the old media of print, radio, and television; messages may in fact journey from origin to destination via both new and old media, either sequentially or concurrently, and sometimes this resembles children's games of "telephone." While Bishop Elias suggests that the local boys got the information from the internet, the reach of internet news need not be direct. Bishop Jeremiah, whom we interviewed by telephone because he does not have good internet access in his diocese, told us that the local radio conveys information evidently gleaned from the internet, by means of which even illiterate people in the countryside hear news about "the gay church."

A few church leaders told us horrifying stories of Anglicans in Africa being subjected to violence by Muslims because of their association with "the gay church." These stories have generally been unverifiable, as in the case of a well-publicized account by Justin Welby, the archbishop of Canterbury, standing at a mass grave of Christians reportedly killed as a result of TEC policies on human sexuality.[23] In any case, even where attackers might be explicit about the reasons for their actions, in areas of extreme interethnic, interreligious tension, it is nearly impossible to identify the ultimate, or even proximate, causes of violence.[24] There is little doubt that in a number of contexts around the world, some Muslims who already have tense relations with their Christian neighbors may find it convenient to slander them by association with "the gay church." In our interviews, however, we heard much more frequently about Pentecostal preachers exploiting the "bad press" the church gets along these lines.[25] Bishop Jeremiah explained the situation in his diocese, which is rural, poor, and (at the time of our interview) had little internet access.

> CHRIS: You've explained how people think and operate in your diocese, and how they're traditionally minded and so on. But before that, you said something about how the controversy has made ministry in your diocese challenging; is that because people in your region and diocese hear about what is going on and get upset and think about other churches? Is that the challenge?
>
> BISHOP JEREMIAH: Yes, because the world is now a global village . . . and all the time, the news on the telly, on the radio, they are attacking the Anglican Church. So people just think that we are the Anglican Church, and so when . . . people are hearing us, they are thinking of this, and it makes it difficult for us in our preaching the good news . . . so we are very much under attack. And the Pentecostals, they especially say that we are "the homosexual church."

Indeed, given the intense competition from international and indigenous Pentecostal churches, and the real losses to Anglican churches, it is not surprising that church leaders in some parts of Africa have begun to find their association with "the homosexual church" a cause for concern. It may well be an obstacle to the church's evangelism, and may make it more difficult to stem the flow of young people into the Charismatic and independent churches, which Bishop Benjamin told us was one of the greatest challenges of the Anglican Church in his part of central Africa. This is an important part of our overall story, and we discuss it in the following chapter.

Relative Anonymity in the New Media Environment

The ability to communicate almost instantly across great stretches of space raises another challenge for the Anglican Communion. A number of bishops described the challenges of disagreement in the church via long-distance communication in terms of its relative anonymity or "facelessness" and the way this changes the dynamics of interaction and dialogue.[26] Bishop Kevin described the anonymity of global new-media-shaped technology and how it has contributed to the current instabilities in the Communion.

> The internet makes it possible for you to live in a private world. You don't actually have to deal with another person face to face. That's why Rowan [Williams] was quite right to call us all to Lambeth, and quite right also in lifting the legislative burden from the assembly so that we wouldn't have to vote each other down or off the island. When you have that face-to-face encounter, it becomes quite a different matter. The internet provides the technological equivalent of drive-by shootings. You can just say what you want about anybody, without any knowledge or knowing them.

The internet's capacity for permitting us to live in our own private worlds may be largely unrelated to the compression of time, but it is certainly not unrelated to the virtual compression of space. The internet has made it easier for people to be in dialogue—or in a dispute—with one another without ever looking one another in the eye. Face-to-face presence facilitates dialogue and encounter, not just with ideas but with other people, something that Bishop Kevin values deeply.

Face-to-face conversations are also important to Bishop Simon, an American bishop who sees in-person encounters as mitigating, though not eliminating, the potential for participants to want to "shoot" each other.

> One of the things about the shrinking communication world is that you can enter into and hear one another instantly, without knowing the other's context at all. And one of the harder pieces of work is actually meeting face to face, and entering into a respectful relationship, which you need . . . you have other points of contact besides your controversy. My experience has been visiting east, central, and south[ern] Africa, and visiting with bishops from various places right around the world, is that actually when you get to know the people, you discover you do have a lot in common, and you use that commonality to build a relationship, and you can then discuss the tough and difficult questions without trying to shoot each other.

Of course, the capacity to meet, to build face-to-face relationships, and to understand the life and faith context of others, is no less a component of the shrinking world of globalization than are the global electronic communication networks. Rather than satellites, relay towers, and fiber-optic cables, global networks of relatively inexpensive airline travel facilitate such encounters.

Undoubtedly, there needs to be a measure of goodwill before a face-to face meeting is even possible. Nonetheless, face-to-face encounter is clearly different from electronic communication, and more conducive to having difficult conversations and building trust. Bishop Simon speaks of face-to-face contact as a means of understanding the context of one's interlocutor; studies of face-to-face communication compared with mediated communication have also shown that face-to-face communication is the most information-rich means of communication, because it allows participants to communicate with body language, facial gestures, and eye contact as well as speech. All of these are useful for building and maintaining trust, even if the signals do sometimes become confused in cross-cultural communication.[27]

Political Uses of Time-Space Compression: The Challenge to Religious Authority

The impact of lightning-fast communication technology with global reach does not only affect Christians, whether lay or clergy, in provinces of the Global South. These communication mechanisms have demonstrated clearly that the flow of information—and protest—travels well in either direction, and can be put to use within the ecclesiastical politics of any province. Church leaders were undoubtedly not habituated to the fast pace at which global Anglican disagreements unfolded, and key institutions of the Church of England and the Anglican Communion were also slow to develop the necessary infrastructure for working effectively in this new world.

Describing the events that followed the announcement that Jeffrey John, a celibate partnered gay man, would be appointed suffragan bishop of Reading in the Diocese of Oxford, one of our respondents, who had seen the events transpire at close quarters, described how the Church of England was caught on its back foot.

> The thing that caught Lambeth [Palace, the office of the archbishop of Canterbury] with its trousers down, shall we say . . . napping completely . . . was the web. And they were utterly and totally unprepared for an immediate worldwide mobilization of opinion by electronic means. And I think that caught up a little bit and there is now a press officer at Lambeth

Palace whose expertise [is] with electronic communication and not press releases. But at the time, what we had was the sort of old-fashioned paper-pushing, newspaper-type press office. And, I mean, I know that their whole computer system crashed because they couldn't handle the incoming messages. So . . . they were completely in the dark and then very, very startled by this highly organized, highly international, highly prepared and mobilized onslaught. So that's another new element that . . . is . . . as it were, brand new to ecclesiastical politics.

Indeed, one of the organizers of conservative Anglicans who had objected to Jeffrey John as bishop of Reading offered us an account of how the opposition organized its campaign. The first priority was a sophisticated media strategy that relied heavily on electronic communication, including new websites, and the effective use of electronic networks that had already been established. Some of the participants had been involved in the networks of Anglicans who were concerned with what they saw as the liberal drift of certain provinces, which had begun to form before Lambeth 1998 and were built up in person at the conference and associated events. They were thus able to take advantage of established relationships and already had lists of email contacts, including those of Anglican leaders in the Global South. These activists were far better prepared and equipped to influence the course of events than was the office of the recently installed archbishop of Canterbury, Rowan Williams. As the church leadership found itself fighting fires on a number of fronts, mainstays of church conversation like the *Church Times* struggled to keep apprised of events. A website called Thinking Anglicans began to pick up some of the slack, offering a more effective electronic communication hub to counterbalance (and, arguably, to provide more reliable information than) conservative outlets like Virtue Online and Anglican Mainstream, which had stepped into the gap left by the failure of the church's own organs of communication.

The Oxfordshire clergy and laypeople who, along with well-placed allies, challenged Jeffrey John's appointment as area bishop for Reading in 2003 proved that they were able to shout down both their diocesan bishop and the archbishop of Canterbury. In the end, Canon (and now Dean) John revoked his earlier acceptance of the appointment, clearly under significant pressure to do so, apparently by that time as much from within Lambeth Palace as from without.[28] Not surprisingly, one activist involved in organizing this highly successful campaign described this new situation as much more democratic. These dissenting Church of England faithful were able to force Lambeth

Palace to take notice of their strongly held views, overturning the recommendation of a diocesan bishop and his advisory committee, which had been approved by the archbishop of Canterbury and by Her Majesty the queen. This activist argued that this was the voice of the faithful prevailing over the liberal views of church "elites."[29]

Many, though by no means all, of the bishops we talked to tended to describe the new global mediascape in terms of the ways in which it undermines episcopal authority. We quoted Bishop Paul earlier on the dangers of overly hasty electronic communications, about which he is somewhat ambivalent; but he reserved particular contempt for blogs:

> I detest blogs. I don't read blogs. I don't write blogs. The only ones that I have ever read, a total of five in nature, was after I was elected . . . and people said, "You need to read what people are saying about you on these blogs." So I read those five because they were about me. So that's me and blogs . . . again, on blogs, I believe people are giving themselves—and are being accorded—an authority because of what they say in the blogs that they don't deserve, nor should be given recognition, which is why I don't read them. You may write blogs very avidly—whether you do or not is immaterial to me—but if you did, I would say, "Why should I read your blog and take what you say with a level of authority beyond that which I might find after reading Adorno[30] or something like that?" Blogs are a medium for unsubstantiated and unjustified authority on the part of the writer. And that's why they have their power. And I think that power is quite insidious.

The bishop's views do not simply reflect old-fashioned distaste for new technology; rather, he objects to blogs primarily because they usurp authority. If authority is "legitimate power," as Weber tells us,[31] the bishop's repeated emphasis here reinforces that point by claiming that people promoting their views on blogs are being granted an illegitimate ("unsubstantiated and unjustified") power by those who read them. This seemed to be his view irrespective of the content of the blogs (which he has seldom encountered directly), and their position on questions of sexuality or theology.

Communication scholar Heidi Campbell has looked at the question of whether blogging undermines religious authority.[32] Initially, many researchers suggested that it would, since the blogosphere is widely accessible, and anybody with a computer and enough time on their hands can share their views with the world. Authority rests in what people say, not in having access to the means of distributing their ideas. Interestingly, Campbell found that this assumption is too simple: the blogosphere is full of authority talk—some critical of authority but most asserting authority, particularly the authority of God or the Bible, but also of particular religious leaders.

If blog-land is indeed full of talk of religious authority, perhaps this points toward a slightly different question. Perhaps we should be asking not whether religious authority is undermined but "what does the internet *do to* religious authority?" Bishop Kevin suggests a preliminary answer in his description of what is different about the current crisis: "Technologically, [this is] the first internet war that the church has had to fight, and that has changed all of the parameters of the conflict, and redistributed authority, as the internet does." Provided we do not take this assertion in a technologically determinist fashion, the suggestion that the internet tends to "redistribute" authority seems to us a helpful one. It remains to be seen, however, *how* it does so.[33]

Not all of the bishops we interviewed took such a strongly negative view of the authority of bloggers as Bishop Paul did, and not all were quite as critical of the redistribution of authority as Bishop Kevin was. A growing number of bishops and other church leaders now engage in blogging, or use Facebook and Twitter. For Bishop Timothy, the medium and its potential for democratic discourse are directly related to how he hopes to exercise his own episcopal authority in his province, which he described as a basically "liberal" province in our discussion about the role of a bishop in a liberal church:

ANDREW: I had a thought the other day: do bishops still send pastoral letters to be read in all the churches? Or have the blogs replaced that?

BISHOP TIMOTHY: That's a nice question [*laughter*]. I think, in general, the answer is probably no [blogs haven't replaced pastoral letters from bishops], because they see themselves as being embodiments of moral and spiritual authority. But I think it's a very interesting question because it emerged just within issues of how bishops function in a liberal church. So how do bishops function in this church? I suppose the question came down to, I don't particularly want to be an organizational/managerial figure within the church. So what am I really about? What I really want is to project into that situation moral and spiritual authority and integrity. How do I do that?

Acknowledging that pastoral letters are one way in which bishops have exercised moral and spiritual authority, such letters do not sit well with Bishop

Timothy's vision of the kind of bishop he wants to be. He asks, "How does one drip-feed theological and spiritual depth?"

> How do I drip-feed that so that the answers that people give, particularly through democratic and representative structures, are not . . . instant theology-light, which they tend to be? And sometimes that will come through what, in ministry terms, we often call prophetic challenge, which is the critique; it's where you operate outside the church, at the sharp end, you do as the Old Testament prophets did and you say, "Thus says the Lord, and I don't care whether you like it or not. Thus says the Lord."
>
> But it's not like that nowadays. When you're getting the sharp end of the antigay stuff and you say, "It's interesting that Jesus spent time with the woman taken in adultery. What do you think about that? How would he have reacted to a gay person?" And you bring in a critique of what people are saying, which is about trying to make sure that the way in which the church reacts to these issues is scripturally rooted, is theologically valid, is expressive of an internal dialogue of the church which recognizes the difficulty of the issues.

For Bishop Timothy, the pastoral letter embodies a top-down authority in which communication flows in only one direction, from the shepherd to his or her flock. Blogging offers another way to encourage the growth of "theological and spiritual depth" in a church that, in part because of its "democratic and representative structures," can, without leadership, drift toward what he calls "instant theology-light." It is the job of the bishop to encourage deeper reflection in the "internal dialogue of the church"; this includes fostering a respectful conversation with those with whom one disagrees. For this reason, Bishop Timothy insists emphatically that a "liberal" church needs to be a broad church with plenty of room for those who disagree quite adamantly with his own liberal positions.

Bishop Timothy does not deny that global electronic communication has deepened the crisis in some respects, but he also finds it a useful resource for maintaining unity in the midst of disagreement within his own diocese. His connections to other leaders in other parts of the world sometimes give him a better handle on how to respond to local activists, who are themselves part of their own transnational networks of communication. "The whole internet-driven world," he says, does hugely ratchet up the speed with which the conflict intensifies. On the other hand, there are mitigating dimensions to that. I get emails from people in mainstream Anglican congregations in America and they talk about what it's like, and their sense of where the point of balance is, is partly influenced by me. Or, to take another one, I meet the gay lobby here, [the] Changing Attitude lobby, which expresses its views, I think, in quite a difficult, uncompromising way. I spent two and a half weeks sitting in a Bible study group with [names withheld; two American bishops, one of whom he identified to us as gay]. I now know what language they use to talk about the same issues, and I could ring them up and ask them how it is for them today. So once again, that world consciousness within Anglicanism makes it much easier for me to handle the local dimensions of the conflict here. So in some ways it ratchets it up, but in some measure it can also be helpful. I could ring them up and say, "this is what it's like for me," and say, "how is it for you?" It's a huge help.

Bishop Timothy was not the only church leader who suggested that the internet can be used to facilitate helpful conversation and dialogue, even as it offered possibilities for those who want to foster division. Nor was he the only one whose electronic correspondence on church matters often grew out of friendships that began and developed in face-to-face conversations. Many of the bishops who went to Lambeth in 2008 in particular, whether or not they liked the philosophy of *indaba*[34] conversations, and whether or not they were happy with the general direction of TEC (U.S.) or the Anglican Church of Canada, spoke of the importance of these meetings for building their relationships with other bishops from across the globe.

The Diversity Lost in the Global Reorganization of Authority

Of course, the movement of bishops around the globe, and their interconnectivity, is not always seen as a positive development. The recent incursions of bishops into other provinces reflect capacities only possible within the structures of modern global information communication technology and global travel. In some cases, Canadian Anglicans or American Episcopalians who saw themselves as a beleaguered "orthodox" remnant suffering under a heretical bishop sought out like-minded primates in faraway Africa, Southeast Asia, or South America. These primates, they hoped, would replace their diocesan bishops for such essential functions as the ordination of priests and conducting confirmations, while also giving parish churches a claim to still be part of the Anglican world, even as they severed ties with their own provinces.

In addition to being fast, travel is now relatively inexpensive (seen in historical terms), but it is not free, and there have been a lot of meetings at hotels, conferences, and networking events. There is little doubt that these meetings have been underwritten by rather large sums of money from wealthy benefactors, particularly from the United States,[35] although some of the funds have evidently also come from disaffected American and Canadian parishes that have joined the churches of Rwanda, Nigeria, or the Southern Cone. As Manuel Castells has demonstrated in his many books on the global networked society, not all social groups are equally well positioned to use the power of networked communication to their advantage.

Bishop Kevin expressed his deep concerns about the consequences of these incursions of bishops from other provinces for the church as a broad tent, able to encompass difference within dioceses. He was particularly uneasy about the possibility that the Anglican Consultative Council or the archbishop of Canterbury might officially recognize the Anglican Church in North America (ACNA), granting it legitimacy as a province in the Anglican Communion, even though it overlaps geographically with the Episcopal Church and with the Anglican Church of Canada. He explained that, in his view,

> if Rowan [Williams] or the Anglican Consultative Council recognize the Anglican Church of North America, then historic Anglicanism is *over*. One of the four pillars of the Lambeth Quadrilateral is the historic episcopate in the Catholic tradition, which is geographical. The bishop is pastor to a whole collection of different people.
>
> In fact, Rowan made a big deal about this at the pre-Lambeth retreat in 2008. And Rowan is brilliant, really masterful in his description of the bishop as the shepherd to all. Well, then, you can't be, if you move away from the geographic boundary of the dioceses. Who's going to be part of the nongeographic boundary? It's going to be the self-selected collection of the like-minded. You then turn dioceses into theological parties, and bishops become party leaders, no longer shepherd to all but only to those who agree with them, so far as the internet diocese can reach. Historic Anglicanism won't survive that. It won't be containable to North America—there will be a new province under Michael Nazir-Ali in England, and in New Zealand and Australia . . . in Australia there is

such resentment against the Diocese of Sydney that there would likely be a split there. . . . It will go through the whole Communion.

Thus far, neither Canterbury nor the Anglican Consultative Council has recognized the ACNA, although some of the divisions seem to have become increasingly entrenched, and the ACNA was represented by its archbishop, Foley Beach, at the gathering of primates in January 2016. At that meeting, Beach's status was somewhat ambiguous, though he was, at least according to a story in the *Church Times*, given the opportunity to vote on measures taken at the meeting.[36] What is at stake for Bishop Kevin, as for many Anglicans who value the tradition's comprehensiveness, is the church's ability to maintain unity without uniformity (a theme to which we return in chapter 5). A bishop might no longer be understood as a "shepherd to all" or as the "focus of unity," but rather as someone from whom congregations feel the right to expect agreement.

Many Anglicans of a centrist or Broad-Church inclination see the diversity of parties and views as one of the virtues of Anglicanism, perhaps even as Anglicanism's gift to the Christian Church at large. This view may be increasingly under fire from conservative Evangelicals and traditionalist Anglo-Catholics alike, who feel as if they have one foot outside the big tent. Many nevertheless celebrate the notion of comprehensiveness or the inherent tensions between different currents in the church. Globalization has undoubtedly contributed to these tensions, making it impossible for church leaders in one part of the world to ignore the very different, but undoubtedly sincere, attempts to live and preach the Gospel in very different contexts around the world. Comprehensiveness is much easier, though very much less real, when the different traditions can share the same tent without having to confront those differences.

The forces of globalization have now shrunk the world to the point where such avoidance is no longer possible; perhaps this means that the Communion can now begin to learn how to actually live with its differences and disagreements, as it aspires to do. And while the churches of the Global South are beginning to develop a greater understanding of the churches of the Global North, misunderstandings still abound. It is equally true that deep misconceptions about Africa abound within Anglicanism, not least in the debates and discussions about the church and homosexuality in the Communion and its provinces.

3

THE GLOBAL SOUTH AND
THE COMMUNION

Africa as the New Anglican "Center of Gravity"

In February 2013, the British prime minister's office announced that the queen had approved the appointment of Justin Welby as the 105th archbishop of Canterbury. Many commentators suggested that Welby was the perfect choice to confront the contemporary challenges facing the Anglican Communion. As an Evangelical, many presumed, he would enjoy greater sympathy and trust among conservative Anglicans than his predecessor, Rowan Williams, had. Moreover, having previously worked for an oil exploration company that operated in west Africa, the new archbishop, some observers suggested, would be better equipped to foster positive relations with the African provinces of the Communion. Finally, others hoped that Welby, as a former business executive, would be able to administer an institutionally complex church with efficiency and finesse.

When Archbishop Welby traveled to Nairobi, Kenya, to attend the second GAFCON Conference in October 2013, it quickly became clear that the tensions within the Communion were not going to be resolved simply by changing the principal occupant of Lambeth Palace. The archbishop had originally planned to send a prerecorded message to the gathering because, he explained, other obligations, including the baptism of Prince George, prevented his attendance.[1] However, the archbishop made a sudden scheduling change so as to attend the first part of the conference, and he delivered a homily at the opening worship service. According to the online journalist George Congar, "It was a disaster!" The former primate of Nigeria, Peter Akinola, declared the sermon "outrageous!" because it sounded to him like a homily on "moral equivalence." At least some of Welby's GAFCON audience took him to be saying that two parties were equally responsible for the tension in the Communion—the American Church for blessing same-sex relationships, and the GAFCON leaders for their irregular crossing of episcopal jurisdictions. The archbishop was understood to be presenting himself as above the fray, trying to reconcile two sides of the Communion at war. By all accounts, this message was not well received.

The reports that came out of GAFCON II—the less than warm reception of the archbishop of Canterbury but also the fact that he apparently felt compelled to attend in the first place—were further signs that the ground had shifted in the global church. The leadership of GAFCON was asserting that Canterbury and the Church of England would no longer be setting the agenda for the "majority" of the Communion. The "Nairobi Communiqué" issued after the conference made it clear that traditional authority structures in the church would no longer be decisive for the future of the Communion: "We commit ourselves to defend essential truths of the biblical faith even when this defence threatens existing structures of human authority."[2] Archbishop Welby appeared to get the message. When the 2018 Lambeth Conference was "postponed," almost no one was surprised.[3] The business of the church at the international level could no longer carry on as usual.

This chapter examines the role of Anglican churches that identify themselves as part of the "Global South" in the recent disputes in the Communion. The concept of the Global South originally emerged out of discussions over international development, following a 1980 publication that identified a "Brandt line" dividing the rich and politically powerful North from the poorer and less developed South. The term intends to distinguish between relative levels of wealth, health, quality of life, political autonomy, and influence.[4] According to the Center for the Global South at American University in Washington, D.C., the Global South is made up of "157 of a total of 184 recognized states in the world [in Latin America, Africa, and Asia], and many have less developed or severely limited resources."[5] Replacing the notion of the Third World (outdated after the Cold War), the concept does not refer to geographical space, as clearly illustrated by the fact that Australia and New Zealand lie to the south of countries like Afghanistan and Ethiopia. That "South" is more than a reference to a compass point was further emphasized by the church leaders from the Global South we interviewed. While often referring to their location in the "Global South," they were more likely to refer to North America, Europe, and Australasia as "the West" than as "the North," although both terms appear in our transcripts. We have followed their practice and used the terms interchangeably.

Both popular and scholarly accounts of the situation in the Communion use events such as Archbishop Welby's ill-fated journey to meet with GAFCON leaders to show that the growing Anglican churches of the Global South are flexing their muscles to resist the authority of the shrinking churches of the North. Some imply that the tensions in the Communion are exacerbated by a global shift in the balance of power in Christianity; cultural changes in churches in the North, which have grown more theologically liberal and more accepting of sexual minorities in church and society, increase the strain. The churches of the Global South, by contrast, are seen as faithful "to the essential truths of the biblical faith" (as suggested in the Nairobi Communiqué, mentioned above).

The past thirty years have undoubtedly witnessed a sea change in the acceptance of homosexuality in Britain and North America, and this has provoked much reflection and a change in thinking and practice in some parts of the church. What is seldom considered, however, is how the Anglican churches of Africa are also responding to this change in their own contexts. The meaning of "homosexuality" has also changed in sub-Saharan Africa over the past twenty to thirty years, and political elites have often both encouraged and exploited these changes, further heightening the social significance of the topic. Anglican churches have also increasingly faced pressures and competition, particularly from the growth of Pentecostal and Charismatic churches, which have given their responses to events in faraway lands greater urgency.

To explore how the recent conflicts in the Communion have been understood in the Global South, we conducted semistructured research interviews with fifteen significant church leaders from the region, including eleven archbishops and bishops from the Anglican churches in Africa and four nonepiscopal leaders from, or with extensive experience of, the Anglican churches in the region. This sample certainly does not represent a comprehensive portrait of Anglicans in Africa; we make no claims to statistical representativeness in the technical sense, but we have interviewed leaders with a wide range of views who represent ten of the region's thirteen provinces. We have interviewed only leaders, and so our grasp of how these issues may be understood by the faithful is derived entirely from conversations with the leadership; we have also benefited from recent ethnographic "shoes-on-the-ground" studies, which have helped us set the views of these leaders in a more grounded context.

A Critique of Two Popular Theses: The "Proxy Army" and the "Missionary Hypothesis"

As we interviewed global Anglican leaders, and heeded commentary on the Anglican disputes, we heard two arguments proposed with some frequency. We were told on numerous occasions that the leaders of the Global South churches are simply acting as a "proxy army" hired by northern conservatives to fight in the so-called American culture wars. Others, by contrast, emphasized the role of Anglican missionaries who brought Victorian sensibilities to Africa, which live on there even as they died off in England. In their weaker form, these arguments have some merit; in their stronger form, as proposed explanations for the breakdown of recent years in the Anglican Communion, we find them theoretically problematic. We also found little evidence for them in our interviews, while other forces tended to stand out more clearly.

Conservatives in the United States (and in England), feeling beleaguered by the drift to what they see as heresy and the corruption of Christian morals, undoubtedly played a significant role in informing and organizing southern conservatives in the lead-up to Lambeth 1998, where the conference passed Lambeth 1.10, affirming the church's "traditional" teaching on sexuality. They have continued to play an important role in resourcing, supporting, and shaping the GAFCON movement. To this extent, it is legitimate to talk of American conservatives trying to "export" the so-called culture wars.[6] Conservative organizations like the American Anglican Council and Anglican Mainstream, and educational institutions, including the Episcopalian Trinity School for Ministry (U.S.), the Oxford Centre for Mission Studies (UK), Moore Theological College (Australia), and, much more marginally, Regent College (Canada), provided channels of communication and networks of relationships that included northern Evangelicals and African church leaders. Sometimes, such organizing by the northern Evangelicals seems to have extended to putting words in the mouths of African bishops. There have been numerous accounts of this, although one of the most widely discussed came when the *Church Times* reported that a communiqué from Archbishop Peter Akinola had been largely written on Martyn Minns's computer (in Virginia, U.S.) and subsequently edited on Canon Chris Sugden's word processor (in England).[7]

Bishop Micah, a leader from central Africa, expressed his concern about what seemed to him the disproportionate influence of leaders from the North in the GAFCON movement and even at the Council of Anglican Provinces in Africa. "There is a lot of money involved in this," he said. "Where is it coming from? . . . The African bishops, they're just puppets. . . . They're not the strategists; they're not the thinkers." Many of our interview subjects raised the intertwined questions of money and influence. It is undoubtedly true that, in the mirror image of TEC's long-standing role as chief financial backer of the Anglican Communion,[8] conservative American funders have played no small role in bankrolling conservative movements within TEC and the broader Anglican world.[9] In other words, both liberals and conservatives have undoubtedly been channeling funds to their friends and allies, some of them likely at the expense of those with whom they disagree.

Several of our respondents observed that the organizing and logistical work provided to Global South leaders by northern Anglican dissidents goes well beyond financial assistance. This often leaves other participants with the sense that someone else is pulling the strings, even in the midst of a face-to-face encounter like the Primates' Meeting. As one primate told us:

> The meeting took place in a conference center. The handlers were all in a hotel, eight or ten miles down the road. And there was constant to-and-fro between the conference and the handlers. They couldn't come into the meeting but they were within easy access. They were allowed phone contact. They were deciding whether or not the decisions being made were acceptable. They were massaging the media presentation of those issues. And certainly the sense that the primates . . . who would have been either in the mainstream or the liberal world were saying that it was unnerving because when you were speaking to people you weren't quite sure who you were talking to, and you could, as it were, come to an understanding and then find that that understanding was swept away in terms of what was in the media. So it was a very unreal, very uncomfortable meeting. I heard [the same thing] expressed last week by one of the primates who I know and respect greatly, saying, "I dread the Primates' Meeting because it's not a real encounter."

While there is no doubt that this kind of backstage management has a real effect on these meetings, we do need to be careful not to overstate the role of American and English conservatives and their considerable financial and organizational power. As John Anderson has warned, to attribute all of these developments within the Communion to the work of northern conservatives would be to deny African church leaders agency.[10] In its strongest form, such an argument would reflect paternalistic and imperialist assumptions about Africans, as if to imply that they have no reasons of their own for acting as they do, or that the viewpoints they defend are not genuinely felt. Moreover, we might just as well ask: who is using whom? If African or Asian church leaders are happy enough to accept financial, logistical, or copyediting support from English or American churches, does this necessarily mean that they have not actively recruited such support to help them further their own agendas?

Similar difficulties bedevil arguments that overemphasize the role of missionary activity during the nineteenth and early twentieth centuries in shaping reactions to the current controversies in the Communion. After her experience at Lambeth 1998, Bishop Barbara Harris of Massachusetts, the first woman in the episcopate in the Anglican Communion, argued that "the vitriolic, fundamentalist rhetoric of some African, Asian and other bishops of color . . . was in my opinion reflective of the European and North American missionary influence propounded in the Southern Hemisphere nations during the eighteenth, nineteenth and early twentieth centuries."[11] Explanations for the behavior of differing national churches in the Global South often make reference to the influence of particular mission societies, which encouraged particular versions of the Anglican tradition in the regions in which they operated. The Church Mission Society (CMS), for example, generally embodied a low-church and evangelical ethos, and was very active in countries like Nigeria, Sudan, Rwanda, and Burundi.[12] When the CMS split in 1922 (because some members thought the organization had become too liberal), the more conservative element formed the Bible Churchmen's Missionary Society. This organization was subsequently very active in Kenya, Uganda, and Ethiopia.[13] Given that some of the leading critics of the contemporary Anglican Communion have emerged from the regions where such missionary societies were most active, the ways in which such agencies taught the Christian tradition might well have influenced the local understanding of Anglicanism. Likewise, where other missionary societies were prominent, the local churches have often been less critical of the Communion. For example, the CMS suspended its activities in South Africa in 1899 and was replaced by the more Broad-Church approach of the Society for the Propagation of the Gospel in Foreign Parts (SPG), which was also influential in west African nations like Ghana, as well as in the West Indies.[14] The Universities' Mission to Central Africa is partly responsible for the Anglo-Catholic ethos and character of the churches in central Africa.[15] The churches in these provinces have generally been less antagonistic toward the traditional structures of the Communion and more muted in their criticism of developments in the United States, Canada, and Britain.

Recent studies of African Christianity provide good reason to be cautious about accounts that trace everything back to the values of the missionaries who brought Christianity to Africa, however. These studies highlight the significance of the efforts by Africans themselves to shape their own Christian identity and theology.[16] African churches have developed in response to their own particular contexts and challenges. For this reason, we cannot assume that an Anglo-Catholic from Malawi will share the same views, or even the same practices, as an Anglo-Catholic from Fort Worth, Texas; nor can we take for granted that an Evangelical from Birmingham, England, and one from Uganda will understand the world or their faith in the same way.[17] The identities of African Anglicans are as multifaceted and complex as the identities of Anglicans elsewhere in the world.

Emma Wild-Wood's study of Anglican identity in L'Eglise Anglicane du Congo offers a useful insight here. Congo was initially part of the Anglican mission to Uganda, Burundi, Rwanda, and Boa-Zaire, in which the CMS was the principal missionary agency. Beyond the missionary influence, however, the country has experienced considerable internal migration, war, and fluctuating contact with a variety of international aid agencies. More immediately, a lack of clergy, communication, and infrastructure has often prevented the church from establishing a uniform identity among its members. Thus, according to Wild-Wood, "Congolese Anglicanism became increasingly hybrid as a result of members' mobility."[18] A broad range of beliefs and practices are contained within the one church, a situation necessitated by frequent internal migration, multiple ethnic and linguistic groups, and a variety of cultural norms. Such situations of "translocality" undermine the presumption that the identities of African Anglicans are determined primarily by the heritage of a specific missionary society.

Ethnographic studies of how African Anglicans actually live out their faith, such as that of Wild-Wood, caution against the tendency to reduce African Christianity to simplistic stereotypes, including the thesis that the opinions of contemporary African Anglicans are determined by which missionary society first introduced the Christian Gospel to their nation. As the missiologist Lamin Sanneh suggested decades ago, "the African, as an agent of religious adaptation, has played a far more critical role than his [*sic*] missionary counterpart whose role as historical transmitter has too often been exaggerated."[19]

Anglican Christianity in the Global South

The dramatic growth of the church in Latin America, sub-Saharan Africa, and, more recently, Asia greatly altered the global composition of Christianity over the course of the twentieth century. In 1900, 68 percent of all Christians lived in Europe and 14 percent in North America. Other regions contributed only 18 percent to the globe's total number of Christians. The twentieth century saw a marked shift in these numbers; by 2000, only 27 percent of the world's Christians lived in Europe, and only 13 percent in North America. Sub-Saharan Africa's share of the world's Christians, by contrast, grew from 2 percent to 20 percent. Latin America's share grew from 11 percent to 24 percent.[20] Anglicans are very much in the minority in Latin America and Asia; as a proportion of the world's Anglicans, these regions likewise make a small contribution in terms of numbers. For this reason, the remainder of this section focuses on the churches in Africa.

The period of Christianity's greatest growth in sub-Saharan Africa occurred between 1950 and 1970, during the period of decolonization when many African nations achieved independence. In 1950, only about 15 percent of the population of the region was Christian. By 1970, the proportion had almost tripled (to 43 percent), and it continued to grow to 53 percent of the population over the next forty years. While the growth in the number of Christians in the region relative to other faith traditions (principally Islam and traditional African religions) has leveled off and stabilized since the end of the twentieth century, the proportion of Africans in the global number of Christians has continued to rise, due principally to massive population growth. The population of Africa is nine times larger than it was in 1900, and North America's is two and a half times larger, while Europe's population has remained relatively stable.[21]

The historian Philip Jenkins has famously pronounced that these demographic trends suggest that "the center of gravity in the Christian world has shifted inexorably southward."[22] According to Jenkins, northern Christians, when they have even noticed this new reality, have often responded to it by seeking to deploy it for their own purposes. He adds that this tendency has generally taken one of two forms. Christians on the left have often suggested that the emergence of the Global South calls for a liberationist agenda focusing on economic justice and the celebration of diversity. More politically and theologically conservative Christians, Jenkins continues, have instead celebrated the supposedly "traditional" doctrinal and moral views of southern Christians, and have argued that their witness calls upon northern Christians to return to a more "orthodox" pattern of belief. As Jenkins phrases it, "A Liberation Dream confronts a Conservative Dream."[23] He understands the conflict in the Anglican Communion as the paradigmatic example of such tensions within contemporary Christianity.

The changes to the Anglican Communion over the course of the twentieth century mirror, to some extent, the changes in global Christianity as a whole. According to figures from the World Christian Database, presented in the *Atlas of Global Christianity*, in 1900 there were approximately 26 million Anglicans in Britain and northern Europe (80 percent of the world's total), compared with an estimated 400,000 in sub-Saharan Africa (1 percent of the total).[24] By 2010 the figure for Britain (and northern Europe) had remained constant, but that number now represented only 30 percent of the world total of identified Anglicans, assuming for the moment an unlikely total of 86 million nominal Anglicans worldwide. African Anglican churches have grown explosively in the same period, according to the same figures, to somewhere in the neighborhood of 50 million, which would make them 58 percent of that hypothetical world total. At best, these numbers should be treated as educated estimates. There are very good reasons to doubt their accuracy, even if the overall demographic shift of the center of gravity that they describe is, in the broadest possible brushstrokes, correct.[25]

The leaders of the churches of Nigeria and Uganda have put the weight of recent demographic shifts behind their challenges to the authority of the archbishop of Canterbury and to the status quo within the Communion. In 2005, Peter Akinola, then primate of Nigeria, while reacting against a proposal to accept celibate gay and lesbian bishops, uttered a harsh warning: "If England adopts a new faith, alien to what has been handed to us together, they will walk apart."[26] In 2007, the primate of Uganda, Henry Luke Orombi, asserted that "the younger churches of Anglican Christianity will shape what it means to be Anglican. The long season of British hegemony is over."[27] These primates represent two of the largest Anglican provinces in the Communion, with the Church of Nigeria claiming 21.5 million Anglicans (nearly a quarter of the world's nominal Anglicans), and the Ugandan church claiming 12.1 million Anglicans (approximately one eighth of the nominal global total).[28]

A number of Anglican provinces in Africa have thus directly challenged the more traditional modes of exercising authority in the Communion. This is exemplified by the significant presence of African church leaders in the GAFCON movement, and the willingness of the Anglican churches of Nigeria, Rwanda, Kenya, Congo, Uganda, and the Southern Cone to actively offer support and episcopal oversight or "hospitality" for dissident conservatives in the United States, Canada, and, more recently, England. These activities have been deeply troubling to many northern bishops, and serve as fuel for ongoing conflicts between different provinces of the Communion. The future of these "reverse missionary" activities remains uncertain, however, and they have often run into their own internal complications. Whatever the future of these initiatives, they signal clearly that the leaders of Anglican churches in the Global South are no longer content to wait for leaders in the Global North to propose solutions to challenges in the wider Communion.

GAFCON leaders have long argued that the official statistics may mask an even more dramatic reality, given the fact that the decline in church attendance in England is such that only about 4 percent of self-identified Anglicans are in church on Sunday morning.[29] The working assumption has been that active participation in the Anglican churches of Africa is much higher than in, say, England or the United States, but recent research has begun to call into question whether the difference is quite that dramatic. Daniel Muñoz has used a range of available statistics (from provincial, diocesan, and parish sources), as well as more unorthodox methods, like using parish photographs to estimate the extent of the demographic shift from north to south. On the basis of available data (considerable inference is required to approximate missing data), he concludes that the contrast is much less striking than both academics and church leaders have assumed. He argues, using the best available data, that the proportion of "active participants" in the Church of Nigeria, for example, is similar to that of England, at about 6.3 percent of those who identify as Anglican. Likewise, looking at Kenya, Muñoz finds that there is an "outer circle" membership (those who identify as Anglican) of about 3.3 million, and an active membership of about 388,000 Anglicans, or about 12 percent of the outer circle of membership.[30] While some of his methods reflect the skill set of an amateur demographer, he makes an interesting case, and one that is not without merit.

Of course, it is possible to make a more positive case, such as that found in David Goodhew's recent *Growth and Decline in the Anglican Communion: 1980 to the Present*. Goodhew suggests, in response to Muñoz's article, that "a wide range of researchers, including the team behind this volume, offer substantial evidence to the contrary."[31] Two chapters in Goodhew's volume are particularly relevant here. One does not provide much evidence that would counter Muñoz; the other does, but the case it advances points to much more modest growth than those who celebrate a "global shift" in African Christianity generally assume.

Richard Burgess (chapter 4), despite offering an interesting and knowledgeable history of why the church may have grown in the period under consideration, simply assumes the dramatic growth of Anglicans in Nigeria. He makes no attempt to engage with even the most basic demographic questions or considerations that might allow us to assess the growth itself. While it may be possible to make a more positive case than Muñoz does, Burgess offers nothing more than anecdotal evidence. Joseph Galgalo's contribution (chapter 6), on the other hand, is a much more careful examination of available figures for another of the Anglican "success stories" in Africa. He provides good reasons for why he thinks the Church of Kenya's official diocesan counts of the faithful, which would suggest a church in rather steep decline relative to population growth, are themselves much too low. He argues that the church's assertion of 5 million members nationally (which is made without reference to evidence) is in fact closer to the mark than the figure one arrives at by adding up the listed diocesan totals. While many of Galgalo's points are well taken, the estimate of between 4 and 4.5 million members nevertheless appears optimistic. Moreover, even if we were to accept this figure, his estimate of the number of Anglicans would mean Anglican church growth that has been only marginally faster than that of the population of the country as a whole.[32] Further, Galgalo gives little attention to the question of where the growth in church membership might be coming from: what is the relative contribution of "natural" growth (births/deaths) in the Anglican Church of Kenya compared with conversion and defection? Finally, the questions Muñoz poses about nominal versus active membership are not addressed.

Given the exceedingly poor quality of much of the data on nominal and active Anglicans throughout most of Africa, we are in the realm of competing educated estimates at best. Even if Muñoz's estimates seem rather low, there is good reason to think that Anglican growth beyond population increase has been much more modest than many assume. None of this is to say that the Anglican churches in Africa have not grown dramatically over the past sixty to eighty years—there is plenty to suggest that they have. For the most part, however, they have been riding a demographic wave for the past thirty years. This is not, of course, to dispute that the churches in much of the West have declined in the same period. In that sense, the balance has indeed shifted.

As we argue below, there is plenty of evidence that in much of sub-Saharan African, the Christian slice of the demographic pie has grown no larger, and that within the Christian population, Anglicanism is being outcompeted by Pentecostal and Charismatic churches. There is also good evidence to suggest that such competition is making African Anglican leaders feel increasingly threatened. In this sense, the primary difference between England and much of Africa may be that in England nominal Anglicans are not likely to be in church on Sunday morning, while in much of Africa they are as likely to be found instead in a Charismatic or Pentecostal church down the road.

Interreligious Tension and Competition: Islam and Pentecostalism

The demographic changes within Anglicanism in Africa constitute an important part of the backdrop against which we need to set the recent rifts in the Communion. As we have seen, Christianity has grown dramatically in Africa, though this growth has now more or less stabilized relative to Islam and traditional religions. In other words, the number of Christians in Africa is now growing at the same rate as the population. The sands continue to shift, however, within the various Christian churches, and although we began our research with the expectation that conflict with Islam would feature in the narratives of African Anglican church leaders, we found that most were more preoccupied with competition from Pentecostal and Charismatic churches. While we see tensions between Christians and Muslims as important in particular regions, we have come to think that these tensions are dwarfed by the challenge that Pentecostalism poses to Anglican churches in Africa, at least in its impact on the sense of urgency with which African church leaders respond to the question of homosexuality in the Communion as a whole.

Since the election and consecration of Gene Robinson, a number of Anglican leaders have argued that the acceptance of same-sex relationships by the churches of the Global North endangers the lives of Anglicans in Africa. In June 2008, Cyril Okorocha, the bishop of Owerri, Nigeria, suggested that African Christians face "severe persecution [from] our Muslim neighbors because they keep accusing us of maintaining relationships with those who deny the Scripture."[33] Such concerns have been picked up by a number of leading conservatives. Peter C. Moore, then dean of Trinity School for Ministry in Pennsylvania, argued that Bishop Robinson's election "exposes Christians in those countries [with large Muslim populations] to persecution."[34] Bishop John put the relationship in even more dramatic causal terms: "If the Anglican Church says, 'Sexual relationships outside marriage are okay so long as they're loving or faithful, within whatever terms they are, if it's serial monogamy or faithful within the serial or whatever,' then a Muslim turns around and says, 'We always knew you were a hopeless lot.' And the persecution gets worse. Churches are being burnt down, people being beaten up, and raped and killed. That is honestly no exaggeration. I can give you stacks of evidence for that." It is difficult not to find such warnings both chilling and worrisome—although the evidence Bishop John invokes is much harder to come by. Although terrible accounts of violence between African Muslims and Christians continue with tragic regularity, one might ask: to what extent is it accurate to connect such violence with decisions by churches in the West?

Among the bishops we interviewed, it is not surprising that the greatest concern in this regard was expressed by bishops in areas where Muslims far outnumber Christians. In the previous chapter we recounted our conversation with Bishop Elias, who told of a child whose Muslim friends accused him of being part of a church that ordains homosexuals. Similarly, when we spoke to Bishop Joel, he told us that TEC's acceptance of homosexuality "affects the way people [here] look at us." Though he denied that such tensions include violence, he suggested that these developments do "sometimes become a hindrance to our efforts to witness."

Most of the bishops we interviewed from parts of sub-Saharan Africa plagued by ongoing tensions and periodic violence between Christians and Muslims did not tend to blame it on northern churches. One bishop, whose diocese is in a very troubled region where Christians are in the minority, admitted facing interreligious violence between Christians and Muslims. However, he blamed political corruption and a dire economic situation, insisting that the violence is not fueled by religious disagreements, much less dissension among Anglicans. When we asked him whether media reports of church decisions in the United States intensified Muslim-Christian tensions in his diocese, he replied, "What we are dealing with, right here, now: our concerns are bad governance."[35] By contrast, he told us that when he himself criticized local proposals to legalize prostitution, he found that this built bridges with the Muslim community: "You won't believe it: it was more the Muslim youths who . . . [supported] my call."

In other contexts, we were told that attempts by church leaders to establish better relationships between Anglican Christians and Muslims have been viewed with considerable suspicion. Bishop Isaac told us that his efforts to participate in positive dialogue with leaders of the local Muslim community led some Christians to criticize him: "[They say] I am Muslim, I'm no longer Christian, because of my engagement with my Muslim neighbor."

Nevertheless, some news stories have continued to suggest that the acceptance of homosexuality by some northern Anglican churches has been used as a rhetorical device to criticize Christians in Africa. Our interviews suggest, on the contrary, that although such instances are troubling, they may well be far less frequent than some Anglican leaders imply, and many popular reports appear to omit a great deal of nuance, which our informants were at pains to emphasize.

The bishops we interviewed spoke more often and at greater length (and with more obvious hand-wringing) about the way Pentecostals used the "scandal" of homosexuality in the Anglican churches to belittle African Anglicans, even if homosexuality is not considered acceptable practice in their provinces. As Bishop Jeremiah put it, "The Pentecostals, they especially say that we are the homosexual church." The more we heard this refrain, the more clearly a more general issue began to come into view: the challenge of Pentecostalism in Africa for the Anglican churches. When we asked Bishop Justice to share some of the general challenges in the local diocese, the reply we received surprised us: "the exit of young people to Charismatic churches and ministries." When asked to explain this phenomenon, Bishop Justice said that this exodus was largely due to "the Pentecostal style of worship," which the youths found more attractive than an Anglicanism that "is very traditional in its approach." Bishop Benjamin offered similar concerns when describing the challenges facing his diocese: "Meeting the needs of our young people, especially in the form of our worship—that has been a big challenge." Given the age structure of most of Africa, the "young people" to whom Bishop Benjamin refers may well mean more than half of the people living within his parish.[36]

Our interviews suggest that competition from Pentecostal churches is important for understanding African Anglican responses to events elsewhere in the Communion, a fact that only gains more credence when we look at the estimated numbers of Anglicans relative to Pentecostals and Renewalists from 1910 to 2010 from the *Atlas of Global Christianity*, bearing in mind the difficulties with these numbers noted above.

TABLE I ANGLICAN AND PENTECOSTAL/CHARISMATIC GROWTH IN AFRICA

	Anglicans 1910 (% of general population)	% Anglicans 2010	% Pentecostals (Renewalists) 1910	% Pentecostals (Renewalists) 2010	Total Growth Anglicans (% of general population)	Total Growth Pentecostals (% of general population)
Eastern Africa	0.4	7	0	14.5	6.6	14.5
Middle Africa	0	0.4	0	23.2	0.4	23.2
Northern Africa	0	1.1	0	0.8	1.1	0.8
Southern Africa	3.8	5.3	14.5	42.7	1.5	28.2
Western Africa	0.2	7.1	0.3	19.1	6.9	18.8

Source: Johnson and Ross, *Atlas of Global Christianity.*

Looking at the growth of Anglicanism compared with that of Pentecostal/ Charismatic churches in Africa over the hundred years from 1910 to 2010 as a proportion of the population, we see that Anglicans rose from roughly half of a percent of the population in Africa to just under 5 percent (table 1). This is a dramatic tenfold increase, most of it coming in the period of decolonization, 1950–1970. Pentecostals and Charismatics (including Renewalists) grew from just under 1 percent in 1910 to almost 16 percent a century later (a sixteenfold increase). The growth of Pentecostal and Charismatic churches is particularly dramatic if we consider that these have predominantly grown over the past thirty years, much more recently than the bulk of Anglican expansion.[37] Even if we allow for overlapping membership, the contrast is striking.

Looking at the continent as a whole masks important variations. In western Africa, the numbers of Anglicans and Pentecostals were relatively similar (well under 1 percent of the population) in 1910; Anglicans are estimated to have grown to 7 percent of the population, but Pentecostals and Charismatics now make up roughly 19 percent of the population. While Renewalists in southern Africa were a much larger group than Anglicans in 1910 (roughly 15 percent versus 4 percent), they now amount to about 43 percent of the population, against Anglicanism's 5 percent. Discussions within the Communion often focus on the comparative decline of Anglicans in the Global North relative to the rapid growth in the Global South, and in Africa in particular. What they have missed is the severe pressure on Anglican churches in Africa due to the growth of Pentecostal and independent Charismatic churches, a pressure also faced by other "mainline" Protestant churches and, to a lesser degree, the Roman Catholic Church.[38]

This growth of Pentecostal and independent Charismatic churches must be understood in the context of what has become essentially a zero-sum game within Christianity, as the expansion of Christianity has slowed to (more or less) match that of natural population increase. According to population estimates from the World Christian Database, "births and deaths have now become more significant than conversions or defections in the overall growth of the Christian Church in Africa."[39] In other words, the church has continued to grow dramatically since the beginning of the twenty-first century, but the growth is driven by the high birthrate in sub-Saharan Africa. The percentage of Christians relative to the total population has stabilized (at roughly 48 percent Christian, compared to 41 percent Muslim). Better demographic data (fertility, mortality) for different religious groups and denominations would give us a more accurate and comprehensive picture, as would reliable data on the rates of affiliation, defection (and how these are constrained by ethnicity), and overlapping membership.[40] This information is simply unknown. Given the well-documented problems with even basic economic data in much of sub-Saharan Africa, we should not find this surprising.[41] Nevertheless, the big picture is clear—and it fits well with the concerns raised by our African informants about the loss of young people to Charismatic groups. Some successful Anglican missionary work aside, the general demographic figures suggest that other developments (the rise of Pentecostal, Charismatic, and independent African churches) have clearly become the dominant trends in African Christianity.

In some instances, the popularity of the Charismatic and Pentecostal movements is changing the Anglican Church from within (and indicating that these are somewhat flexible identities).[42] As Bishop Benjamin described his diocese, he told us that most of his "young clergy" are Evangelical or Pentecostal in style and outlook:

> When you go to their churches, they're basically Evangelical, maybe even Pentecostal if we have to be precise. So sometimes I do wonder whether . . . I am in an Anglican church, or if I've got lost and ended up in a different church. That has helped, because a lot of the churches, the numbers,

the attendance, it's very good. But I have one church where the priest is Anglo-Catholic, is Conservative, and he is struggling. Although the population in that particular area is big, he is struggling to get people to come to church, and I think that shows that most of the young people would like to attend the Evangelical type of services.

While the story is often told in terms of the great growth of the Anglican churches of Africa, it is clear that these churches are being outcompeted (in some regions, dramatically) by Pentecostals and Charismatics. This may help us understand the strident declarations of opposition to homosexuality by some church leaders from the region. Rather than expressions of moral triumphalism from numerically successful churches, the posturing of some of these leaders makes more sense if it is understood as coming from a church that (implicitly, at least) is under threat. Northern Anglican churches' inclusion of gays and lesbians may make evangelistic outreach in the African context more difficult; it may also make it more difficult to stem the tide of defections to Pentecostalism, with its elective affinity[43] for local cultures and worldviews, exuberant worship, and clear "traditional" moral jeremiads against the threats of homosexuality.[44] As homosexuality has become a signifier for Western decadence and a threat to the social fabric in much of Africa over the past twenty years, this is not an unimportant factor. Strongly antihomosexual claims give Charismatic, Pentecostal, and other independent churches a rhetorical advantage over churches tainted by the accusation of being a "gay church."

Homosexuality and Christianity in Africa

Africa is a vast, populous, diverse continent, and it is therefore exceedingly difficult to make generalizations about beliefs and attitudes about homosexuality across the different faiths, religions, cultures, ethnicities, and nations of the continent. In an atmosphere of generalization and stereotyping, however, Bishop Jeremiah's account of the reception of visitors to his diocese may sound very familiar: "When I brought these people [here] . . . for a . . . conversation, I took them across the whole diocese. Some people rejected [the visiting delegation] because they were people who ordain women, and so they said, 'They are not the right kind of people.' About [other visitors], people complained, 'They are the ones who ordain homosexuals, so they are not the right kind of people.' This is the problem!" But these visiting Anglican delegations, representing practices rejected by many of their hosts, were not from the distant Global North. The first group was from eastern Africa, while the second was visiting from South Africa. South Africa has a reputation for being more liberal on the question of rights for LGBTQ persons (rights that are enshrined in the country's constitution, even if the rights of sexual minorities are not consistently protected). Indeed, we encountered a wide range of views in the course of our interviews across the continent, and not only from respondents in South Africa. While some church leaders expressed views largely consonant with the public statements of the GAFCON primates, we interviewed church leaders with a diverse spectrum of opinions. Some who believed that any sexual relations outside heterosexual marriage are wrong also thought that this was a question on which Christians could legitimately hold different views (*adiaphora*); a few maintained, or were open to the idea, that same-sex relationships could legitimately be accepted by Christians.

Bishop Benjamin wondered aloud why homosexuality had become such a source of disagreement in the Anglican Communion, and why some of his fellow African prelates insist on excluding homosexual persons from the church. Using an evocative metaphor, he told us that "there are certain sins that have horns . . . horns, like that of a cow, which you can see from very far. But then there are certain sins that you cannot see." He asked, "Are visible sins more serious than other sins, such that the bishop should not even engage them in dialogue? Why don't we say that I cannot talk to the adulterers that are in our churches? Why don't we say, uh, those who are involved in financial scandals in our church? Why don't we say that I cannot talk to people who are polygamous? I've got, in my diocese, one part of my diocese where polygamy is the cultural way of living. So I think for homosexuality the issue is [one of] those sins that has got horns. And yet, we leave these other things [alone]." In this bishop's view, homosexuality may be a sin, but it is one sin among many and is far from the most serious or relevant issue in his diocese. What, then, accounts for the visibility—and the sense of danger—of homosexuality, making it the sin with "horns"? Why has it become the presenting symbol that preoccupies African critics of the northern churches?

Over the past few years, a scholarly literature on beliefs and practices related to homosexuality in Africa has begun to emerge, undoing the previous assumption that Africa is "the heterosexual continent."[45] This literature provides helpful explanations of why homosexuality has become such a hot-button issue in a number of African countries, paying particular attention to the roles of religion, politics, and culture. This is very much an emergent literature, with many remaining gaps, but it includes important research on countries, regions, and cultures relevant to our study of the Anglican Communion (including Nigeria, Ghana, Uganda, southern, and southern-central Africa),[46] and provides the beginnings of comparative research between different African regions, nations, and cultures, as well as attempts to understand the question in Africa as a whole.[47]

Westerners long viewed Africa as a continent in which the sin of sodomy was unknown, a view actively promoted in the early nineteenth century by opponents of the slave trade to reinforce their claim of African moral superiority—in contrast to the decadent slave-owning and slave-trading cultures of Europe and the Americas. This view was subsequently adopted and promoted, albeit more passively, by anthropologists, missionaries, and other colonial officials, who turned a blind eye and generally avoided asking questions the answers to which might have indicated otherwise. Given the rich social and cultural diversity across sub-Saharan Africa, and the ambiguous and often incomplete historical record, generalizations are difficult. Nevertheless, the characterization of "heterosexual Africa" clearly elides the very widespread desires and practices (some hidden, some semi-overt, and some explicit) that would be understood in the West as "homosexual" or "bisexual." Until recently, such practices have not commonly been understood locally as markers of LGBTQ identities, as they would be in Europe or North America.[48]

These concepts and identities are relatively recent in the West as well. Only from about 1870 did homosexuality begin to be understood as a sexual "orientation" (to use a term adopted later still), "homosexuality" (which began to include same-sex attraction between women) thereby displacing "sodomy." The latter term had generally been thought of as a distinct and occasional act, and one that could be a temptation to any man. Partly for this reason, it was widely viewed as sinful and was subject to legal sanction, including capital punishment in some jurisdictions.[49] Explaining the nineteenth-century understanding of sexuality in Britain, Jeffrey Weeks writes that it "seems likely that homosexuality was regarded not as a particular type of *person* but as a potential in all sensual creatures."[50] Terms for revulsion or hostility toward LGBTQ persons, like homophobia and heterosexism, are much more recent still, emerging in the late twentieth century, coined by the movements for the decriminalization of homosexual acts beginning after the Second World War, and for gay rights in the aftermath of the Stonewall riots.

Same-sex desires, practices, and affections have always been present in Africa as elsewhere,[51] even if until very recently there was no assumption that these constituted a sexual orientation called homosexual, gay, lesbian, or LGBTQ; correspondingly, there was also no attempt to claim rights for these persons—particularly as a class. Such desires and acts were generally not perceived as a threat to the social fabric, even when and where they were frowned upon and/or subject to punishment. More commonly, they were largely ignored in Africa, as in much of the history of the West, and the subject not discussed at all if it could be avoided. This is still the case in parts of the African continent. As Bishop Jeremiah puts it, speaking about most of the rural areas in his diocese, "When you come to homosexuality, nobody's even heard of it!"

Why, then, has there been so much concern about homosexuality in a number of African countries recently, with political leaders striking dramatic poses and enacting internationally controversial legislation about a problem that they claim is fundamentally "un-African"? This is an undoubtedly complicated story with interrelated cultural and political dimensions. The political dimension is easiest to delineate; the history of this "political homophobia" begins with Robert Mugabe in Zimbabwe and with the postindependence SWAPO government in Namibia making political capital out of a campaign against homosexuality, beginning in 1994 and 1995. The reason for a campaign against homosexuality as "a threat to an idealised patriarchal culture and national values, frequently and explicitly linked to Western Imperialism and 'reactionary forces,'" is clear.[52] This threat provided a much needed refocusing of popular attention away from the government's failure to deliver the social, economic, and political goods that it had promised.[53] Such campaigns have subsequently been used to generate political capital in a number of other countries across the continent.[54] It can be argued that some Anglican leaders have followed suit in using this strategy,[55] and as we show below, postcolonial concerns certainly animate the dynamics of the conflict within the church. We defer to the following section the more complicated question of *why* a campaign against homosexuality would be an effective means of gaining or maintaining political capital in particular times and places.

Our conversations with Anglican leaders in the Global South were permeated with postcolonial themes and arguments, and these informants commonly made claims that sometimes conflated religious and political leaders from "the West" as co-conspirators in a common "agenda." Many of the African bishops we interviewed expressed their desire to challenge lingering paternalism and imperial authority, particularly within the churches in the North, but also in the way the Communion is structured. This included questioning the assumption that the archbishop of Canterbury, with his see in England, should lead the Communion. As Bishop Amos (from the Province of Southern Africa) explained, the great outcry by bishops from the Global South at Lambeth 1998 "had little to do with homosexuality as an issue [but rather] with questions of power and authority. It seems to me that it was in part a manifestation of growing resentment against church leaders in rich, Western countries who feel that they have the right to set the agenda." Neville Hoad, a scholar studying the politics of sexuality in postcolonial Africa, has noted that Lambeth 1998 inadvertently reproduced an imperialist logic in the way it was organized, a contention that supports Bishop Amos's claim.[56] Hoad recalls how Resolution 1.10 had originally been presented as a proposal by the American church for the full inclusion of LGBTQ persons; "had that first resolution not been put forward, no . . . condemnatory resolutions would have been passed."[57] This conjecture fails to account for the fact that conservative Evangelicals had been organizing their response well before Lambeth 1998 in order to counter any gay-positive agenda.[58] Hoad is nevertheless right to emphasize how the anger of bishops from the Global South toward those in the North fueled the confrontation. Many southern leaders were convinced that their northern colleagues intended to use the meeting to set the agenda of the Communion, and that they assumed that they were on the side of the angels.

We asked Bishop Joel why homosexuality seemed to have become a hot-button issue in the politics of a number of African countries, as well as something discussed by church leaders in recent years. In asking the question we referred to Uganda (not his province), where the parliament had days earlier proposed antihomosexuality legislation that had been making international headlines. Bishop Joel explained:

> What is upsetting to us is when governments in the West come to us and say, "Unless you take a certain position on the issue of homosexuality, we will cut off aid." And then you begin to wonder if there is an agenda here. Because, as we said before, you need to look at the context, and where this is different, and not just impose your context on the rest of the world. But there may be some who have their own agenda, and push how things should be . . . come up with some sorts of requirements. It makes people harden their positions. So that those who take a more moderate view are forced to take a more extreme view because the others will say that you're taking a position in favor of homosexuality.

Indeed, in response to the legislation in Uganda, Western political leaders had been making both implicit and explicit threats about the funding of aid programs,[59] just as they had done in other contexts—British prime minister David Cameron had made similar threats at the Commonwealth Heads of Government Meetings with reference to Malawi, Ghana, and Uganda in 2011.[60] Such a rhetorical context creates the sense that "the West" as a whole has an agenda, and this hardens opposition to human rights for sexual minorities, as it erodes the position of moderates on the issue in Africa. Showing that he was not himself unsympathetic to laws protecting sexual minorities, the bishop returned to the question about Uganda, where we had begun: "I cannot comment on Uganda. . . . But what Western governments need to avoid is imposing their own view on other countries. This is very offensive to us. But then, if there are issues that are not fair or not just, and laws that oppress people who have a different orientation, then it is important to check on that, but otherwise . . . if they cut off aid because of our position on homosexuality, this affects all the people, including the homosexual people, if there is no aid." Given the importance of aid, not only for development but also for the very survival of many of Africa's poorest people, such threats are taken as particularly heavy-handed, if not downright cruel.

Paul Gifford has noted that since the second half of the twentieth century, a prominent focus within African theology (Anglican or otherwise) has been concerns for African self-reliance and authenticity. He suggests that African theology "came to revolve around two poles: first, to rehabilitate African culture and religion, and second, to critique the Western impact on Africa, including that of Christian missionaries."[61] The reaction by leaders from African Anglican churches to the current situation in the Anglican Communion needs to be understood in this context. Regardless of their position on homosexuality, the primary issue that angered many of our African informants was the perception that the priorities of the North continue to set the agenda for the Communion. African church leaders often used the word "impose" when they spoke of how they felt about the dominance of Western churches in the Anglican Communion—they felt that churches in the North were imposing their values, beliefs, and practices on churches in the rest of the world.

We heard such accusations leveled not only against leaders in faraway rich countries but also at other African leaders. Bishop Micah criticized some of his fellow African church leaders for acting as "pawns" for northern conservatives. Likewise, Bishop Isaac recalled how, when he spoke in favor of attending

Lambeth 2008 and the Communion's subsequent "continuing *indaba*" process, other leaders accused him of being a "Western stooge" who was promoting "Western values." Similar rhetoric seems to have characterized the dispute over the election of the primate of Tanzania in February 2013 (at least as it was reported abroad and online). Rumors abounded that opponents of the initial victor, the bishop of Mpwapwa, Jacob Chimeledya, had alleged that his supporters had been bribed with funds provided by TEC. Bishop Chimeledya denied the accusations and suggested that his opponent, Archbishop Valentino Mokiwa, had been funded by overseas conservatives. To thicken the plot, it was reported that one issue of difference between the two bishops was the extent to which the Anglican Church of Tanzania (ACT) would continue to align itself with GAFCON.[62] Official spokesmen for ACT, however, subsequently denied that the election process was anything but fair and transparent, and the election of Bishop Chimeledya was upheld.

Culture, Connection, and the Salience of "Homosexuality"

If opposition to homosexuality has become a means of generating political capital in a number of African countries since the mid-1990s, we need to ask why this might be the case. Given that it is a relatively recent development—and one that depends on having a conception of "homosexuality" to begin with—it would be especially unwise to simply assume that a negative disposition toward gays and lesbians is somehow innate in the cultures of Africa. In addressing this question, we will consider the case of Uganda, which is a useful example because of its importance in the larger story, but also because of useful secondary literature. The (Anglican) Church of Uganda has played an important role in the leadership of the GAFCON movement worldwide (including in interventions abroad), and is a key player in public discourse about homosexuality within Uganda,[63] even if some of the key pace-setters in the antihomosexuality campaigns have come from Pentecostal and Charismatic churches.[64] Very helpful research on Uganda, which has yet to find parallels elsewhere, gives us some purchase on the cultural logic of disputes over sexuality in that context.

Sadgrove and colleagues have studied why homosexuality has such political salience in Uganda, such that the draconian Anti-Homosexuality Bill of 2009 (which included the death penalty for "aggravated homosexuality") seems to have received so much support. They conclude that there are two primary reasons why homosexuality is perceived as a threat to the social order in Uganda. First, they argue that since procreation is considered "a core social responsibility" and source of respectability, "individuals who appear unwilling or unable to produce offspring cannot help but transgress fundamental social norms." Second, they argue,

> In a social context where the individual is defined in terms of the community of which he or she claims to be a part, people who fail to adequately embed themselves in reciprocal social relations are viewed as presenting insuperable challenges to notions of personhood and identity. Homosexual relationships and those who claim homosexual identities force Ugandan society to confront the prospect of a new kind of modern individual—one who does not submit his or her will to that of the group, and does not meet the expectations of the community by which the interests of the individual are in turn defined.[65]

In a culture where individuals are defined primarily with reference to a group to which they have responsibilities, those who claim a different identity, based not on relations to kin and community but on individual sexual proclivities, are seen as a threat to the social order.

Anthropologist Lydia Boyd has also studied the implicit cultural logics of antihomosexual rhetoric in Uganda, arguing that it is not just homosexuality (in its modern configuration as an identity) that is experienced as threatening, but also the way in which rights for sexual minorities are conceived. She argues that "much anti-homosexual rhetoric in Uganda is animated by a conflict between two frameworks for ethical personhood: one related to the local value of *eketiibwa* or 'respect/honor' and the other based in a discourse of rights, autonomy, and freedom" promoted by NGOs and foreign governments, as well as local activists. For many Ugandans, rights claims are premised on individualism and freedom, over against deeply held values of respect for one's elders and community, interdependence, and mutual obligation. "Ugandans I spoke with," Boyd continues, "expressed the idea that certain rights could be anti-social, a means by which individuals may erode or directly challenge accepted modes of authority and standards of conduct in society. At the core of this conflict over human rights lie divergent models of moral personhood, one predicated on interdependence and obligation, the other on the neoliberal ideals of autonomy and self-empowerment."[66] This kind of interrelatedness is helpful for thinking about popular Ugandan responses to a new and potentially threatening conception of personhood based on autonomy; we have also found it helpful for understanding the sense of hurt and disappointment we encountered among African church leaders when they spoke about their relations with the broader Communion.[67]

Bruce Kaye suggests that many African cultures tend to think of human beings as inherently relational, an argument that he develops with reference to the theology of South Africa's archbishop emeritus, Desmond Tutu. Tutu uses the Xhosa word *ubuntu* to explain how many African cultures conceive of individual identity in communal terms. Kaye quotes Tutu on this point: "Unlike Westerners, Africans have a synthesizing mind set as opposed to the occidental analytical one. . . . Westerners have a very strong sense of individualism. We have a strong sense of community."[68] The concept of *ubuntu* describes a sense of relationality in which "a person is a person through other persons." It stresses that "I am human because I belong. I participate. I share."[69] This conception of identity as interrelated and essentially communal is quite distinct from the emphasis on individual identity and autonomy that often characterizes the cultures of the Global North.

Building on this strong conception of relational personhood, many of our African informants used familial metaphors to explain to us the sense of connection that they feel toward Anglicans worldwide; Bishop Isaac went so far as to say that he preferred to think of Anglicanism as a family *rather than* as a communion. Either with or without direct reference to Tutu or his conception of *ubuntu*, many articulated a similar sense of how African Anglicans understand themselves and, significantly, their expectations of others. For Bishop Isaac, "family really brings people together, the more it has a sense of commitment and belonging." He told us that he could not understand how Anglicans in another part of the world would make decisions without taking seriously the churches in Africa and elsewhere in the Global South. These northern churches might "make up their own mind," but, in his view, they were not behaving like a member of the "family." Bishop Elias also emphasized the difference between what he saw as the reality in the global church and his expectation that the church should behave as a family: "In my own family . . . we keep talking, we wait for each other. We do not go ahead and make decisions that can affect the members of our family."

While it was common to hear concerns about the state of the Communion, and while some of our respondents expressed deep disappointment with their "brothers and sisters" in the distant West, most expressed an abiding commitment to the global church family.[70] Bishop Ezekiel, for example, told us that although "the churches in Africa are growing very fast . . . we cannot ignore our brothers and sisters from the North and from the West. We need one another. I think that is the reason that it is necessary for us, especially for Canterbury, for us to stay together whatever the costs." Some of this commitment is deeply rooted in gratitude for the heritage of the faith that Western missionaries brought to their region, but the fondness goes deeper still. The very identities of African Anglicans have been shaped with an awareness of brother and sister Anglicans across the oceans: "The idea of separating from our parent church is very difficult for us," stressed Bishop Jacob, an Anglo-Catholic. After telling us of his deep sadness upon hearing that some English Anglo-Catholics had left the Communion for Roman Catholicism, he said, "I could not do that. My heart wouldn't be in it, because I was born an Anglican."

None of these expressions of commitment minimize the serious tensions in the church family, particularly of late. A number of our informants were not convinced that all of the parties were equally committed to making the relationship work. Bishop Simeon thought that the different behavior of provinces in the global church reflected changing assumptions about how family relations should work. "Like all relationships," he said, "there is an assumption about what the relationship is about and how it is carried on. And over time, I think, those assumptions have changed. . . . For example, how connected do we feel to one another? . . . The rest of the Communion, outside of what's generally known as the West, feels a very strong sense of kinship with the Western side of the church and the Communion. . . . I don't think the West feels [this] with the same level of identification that the rest feels." And therein lies a great deal of hurt, disappointment, and anger.

When Bishop Isaac described the state of the Communion as a "family crisis," we asked him whether he thought the church could still continue to be a family. He seemed almost surprised by the question: "Yes. Oh, yes!" Probing a bit more, we suggested that in some parts of the church, leaders were acting as if some family members had already filed for divorce. In response, the bishop became very animated:

> This is thought by some people. . . . [But] the divorce has always been there. Because the Anglican family began as a family with two basic traditions: the Catholic and the Reformed. And neither the Catholic nor the Reformed has ever taken hold of the entire family. So if people today get up and say there is a divorce, as a student of history—church history— I believe we have always lived together as a divorced family. So it's not

new. . . . If we're talking about a divorce, the family has always been divorced from the word go.

The common familial metaphor does not, however, suggest any straightforward solutions to the family troubles, perhaps because of different understandings of "family" and how it ought to be structured and understood. A metaphor means different things in different contexts, and different leaders drew quite different conclusions from thinking about the Communion as a family.[71] In particular, some understandings of family are more hierarchical than others, entailing warmth of feeling, devotion, and commitment but also respect for authority and reluctance to disagree with one's elders.

Bishop Jeremiah described his diocese as being extremely diverse, and thus as presenting challenges not unlike those he sees in the Communion: "In my diocese, you have traditional worshippers, you have Pentecostals, you have people of the Muslim religion—all in one household, and with the same father (although they may have different mothers because of polygamy)! So, in our region, we know about being in relationship with people you disagree with. You disagree with one another, but you cannot fight with your brothers." Although he was willing to participate in the Communion's "continuing *indaba*" conversations, Bishop Jeremiah conveyed a sense of unease with the process. Part of this seemed to stem from the fact that the church did not meet his expectations of what families look like and how they work: "In a family, there is an authority, and so of course you can go on talking, but at the end of the day, there is an authority. . . . So to talk about not having a central control, some of us are afraid it may result in conflict." For Bishop Jeremiah, that authority belongs to the archbishop of Canterbury, implicitly the parental figure of the Anglican Communion, though he recognized that this view was not shared by many of his African episcopal colleagues, who saw themselves as fathers of their own households. Some of them felt a sense of hurt and betrayal, often directed at the archbishop of Canterbury; some thought that such responsibility is a burden impossible for any single individual to bear.

In our interviews with church leaders, from Africa and elsewhere, we often heard about the culture of respect for authority in Africa, and in the African church in particular. Some (in particular Bishops Luke, James, Micah, and Jacob) noted that this made it more difficult for younger church leaders to criticize their elders, or even for clergy to disagree publicly with the bishop, or bishops with the primate. This is not unrelated to differing models of the church, both explicit and implicit, as we discuss in chapters 5 and 6. Respect for authority may inform one's sense of interconnectedness and commitment to the "family," but it may also contribute to tensions as much as it resolves them—particularly when the church's senior leaders are at odds with one another. Conflicts between different authority figures (such as the primate of the province and the archbishop of Canterbury) will inevitably heighten tensions. It has long been noted that churches with episcopal forms of governance seem less prone to schism—unless bishops fight among themselves, particularly over territory or authority.[72] Misunderstandings, such as those discussed in chapter 5, certainly do not help.

In contrast to more hierarchical understandings of the church and family, Bishop Micah made the case for a communal and democratic approach to the question of how one resolves the problem of difficult relationships. He described the global church as being involved in a long process of learning, despite the "false prophets" who proclaimed the end of the Communion. "You need to have patience," he told us. "God never lets go of his church, and the church, which is at the grassroots, just carries on, while the false prophets come and the false prophets go. The church is at the grassroots, and that is where I see God, not in one or two primates who are traveling around the world staying in five-star hotels. And that's how it comes to pass." Clearly a bit exasperated, he inverted the hierarchical family metaphor by describing some of his episcopal colleagues not as fathers of the church but as "crying like little babies. Sometimes I just want to say to my fellow bishops, 'Oh, grow *up*,' you know." In Bishop Micah's view, the squabbles in the Communion have "become a power struggle. Politics and domination—our Lord was not about that! Who is generating the politics?! And another thing is, it's not really an African battle, [it's] a Western battle. . . . This idea of *ubuntu*, this sense of humanity in Africa . . . we need to recover that." For Bishop Micah, resolution of the tensions in the Communion need to draw on the African conception of interrelated persons (*ubuntu*) and the rich Anglican tradition of spirituality, both of which he sees getting lost in the polarizing contests for power:

> Part of this getting to know Christ in ourselves and in others would deal with a lot of these issues. I'm talking about the spiritual dimension—to get to know God more and more . . . as an experience of God, that I come to see myself and to see others the way that God sees us. . . .
>
> There's too little prayer, and too much temptation to become managers, and not mystics. We are dealing with diverse, ah, polarized positions and we see contradictions—we do not see how A and B connect. But the

mystic does not see contradictions, does not see from a point of view, but sees points of view, how we all together contribute to the building of Christ.

For Bishop Micah, this mystical sensibility allows Christians to overcome the polarization of different views, seeing how they all contribute, despite their differences, to the body of Christ. This, of course, is not easy, but Bishop Miçah is convinced that in this respect the churches of Africa—at the grass-roots in particular—have much to contribute.

4

LOCAL DISAGREEMENT IN THE MIDST OF A GLOBAL DISPUTE

The View from the Pews in the Diocese(s) of Pittsburgh

Over the course of our interviews with leaders across the Communion, we sometimes encountered the view that conflicts and tensions at the global level have little impact on individual Anglican or Episcopalian local congregations, despite the loud confrontations between global church leaders. Bishop Mathew, for example, suggested that "congregations don't really seem demoralized by this whole conflict; they mostly ignore it and get on with the worship and work of the church." Bishop Mark echoed this point when he said, "Most people in the parishes, in my experience, want to get on with the job of being the church . . . running the church school, doing youth work, ringing the bells, worshipping on Sunday, helping with voluntary work in society."

This is not an uncommon attitude. We noticed similar reactions to the "gathering of primates" organized by the archbishop of Canterbury in January 2016, a meeting called to discuss the festering tensions in the Anglican Communion. Like a number of our episcopal informants, many observers dismissed the significance of what happened at the gathering for individuals in the pews. The English priest and *Guardian* newspaper columnist Giles Fraser, for example, suggested that "these sort of grand, transnational agreements are actually a bit of a vanity project really. If I'm a parish priest . . . it makes absolutely zero difference."[1]

Remarks like this suggest that even as the tensions and political posturing within the Anglican Communion are intensifying at the transnational level, such developments are of no real consequence to average Anglicans. What happens at the Communion level, in other words, has little impact on the local congregation.

This chapter challenges that assumption. It argues that local church communities are sometimes profoundly affected by transnational conflicts between leaders in the Communion. Whereas the previous chapters have explored the global character of the contemporary conflict in the Anglican Communion, here we look at one example of what can happen to local relationships when a global (and national) conflict over salient symbols forces people to choose sides. We are less concerned here with explaining the causes of such a division than with understanding the *local consequences* of a global conflict. To explore the impact of global tensions on local churches, this chapter focuses on the Diocese of Pittsburgh, where a significant schism emerged when the local bishop—who was also a global player—forced local Episcopalians to declare whether they were "with us" or "against us."

The two opposing camps in the Pittsburgh region used local symbols to portray their opponents as the "moral other." These symbols revolved around two strong individuals who came to personify all that was wrong with the church: the presiding bishop of the United States and the bishop of Pittsburgh. We demonstrate the elasticity of key unifying concepts employed to rally resistance to TEC (opposition to homosexuality, "orthodoxy," and the authority of scripture). These plastic concepts permitted the leaders who employed them to include a wide range of constituencies, while at the same time masking the extent of the diversity among them. Our analysis reveals that the conflict in Pittsburgh was not a dispute between "liberals" and "conservatives," for the ways in which many individuals responded to the split that emerged in their diocese do not break down into such a tidy ideological binary.

In light of what we learned in Pittsburgh, we find ourselves at odds with those who claim that local churchgoers are insulated from wider Anglican Communion politics.[2] To the contrary, we show how the parishes in Pittsburgh were unable to escape the tensions that had built up and the polemics that were unleashed elsewhere in the global church. On any given Sunday morning, a priest there might be confronted by an angry parishioner demanding to know what the rector thinks about a statement made the previous day by an archbishop in a province thousands of miles away. The emergence of the so-called global village, one might say, means that we must begin to think in terms of a "global parish." The local Anglican or Episcopal congregation is no longer merely a self-contained entity, if it ever was, but often experiences waves of tension and polemic flowing through it that originate far away. To demonstrate this presence of the global in the local, let us turn now to the southwestern corner of the American state of Pennsylvania.

The Dispute in Pittsburgh

On 2 November 2007, after a history of tension with the national church, the Diocesan Council of the Episcopal Diocese of Pittsburgh voted to change its constitution so that it would no longer be bound by the canons of the Episcopal Church of the United States (TEC). In response, the national House of Bishops deposed Bishop Robert Duncan on the grounds that he had effectively abandoned communion with TEC. The Convention of the Diocese of Pittsburgh subsequently declared that it was formally withdrawing from TEC to "realign" itself with other dissenting Episcopal churches, and temporarily put itself under the authority of a South American province, the Province of the Southern Cone. The following year, Bob Duncan was instrumental in creating the breakaway new province, the Anglican Church in North American (ACNA), and was elected its archbishop and primate. The congregations that opted to remain in TEC reorganized to form the "continuing" *Episcopal* Diocese of Pittsburgh. Those who left the national church referred to themselves as the "realigned" *Anglican* Diocese of Pittsburgh.

The situation in Pittsburgh is sometimes described as an instantiation of a supposedly inevitable clash between "liberals" and "conservatives" of the sort described by James Davison Hunter's "culture wars" hypothesis. Such an explanation, however true (and in this chapter we will suggest reasons to be skeptical about Hunter's argument), provides no insight into how the global conflict in the Communion affects a local region, or into the many different concrete ways in which such an impact is both fueled and suppressed by local factors.[3] In what follows, we highlight some of these, including the use of the Global South by a conservative minority to reframe itself as part of a "global majority" view in the Anglican Communion, the influence of local leadership, and the pressure exerted upon such leaders by laity demanding a response to events elsewhere in the global church.

To dig deeper into these issues, we conducted ethnographic research in the greater Pittsburgh region. This activity was structured in the first instance around four congregational studies.[4] We selected for study two congregations that took a leading role in shaping the direction of their divided diocese (one remaining within TEC [which we will call St. Bylsma's] and one deciding to "realign" itself [which we'll call St. Gonchar's]), and two congregations where the decision over which direction to follow was much more controversial and led to divisions within the congregation (St. Malkin's and St. Sydney's). Using this focus, we interviewed clergy and laypeople from other congregations and made numerous other site visits. These semistructured interviews and participant observations occurred during five research trips to Pittsburgh between July 2009 and February 2013. For each of the four primary congregations studied, Chris interviewed at least two members of the clergy and at least five members of the congregation. In addition to the interviews, he engaged in participant observation at worship services, parish meetings, and diocesan synods (referred to locally as "conventions"). In total, we interviewed fifty-three individuals, 53 percent of whom were members of the "realigned" ACNA diocese of Pittsburgh, and 47 percent of whom were members of churches that remained within TEC (the "continuing" Episcopal Diocese of Pittsburgh). Of those we interviewed, 40 percent were women and 60 percent were men; 45 percent were clergy and 55 percent were laypeople. Eleven of these individuals were interviewed on more than one occasion for updates and clarifications.[5]

Presenting Symbols and Local Tensions

At the outset, it would have been easy to quickly surmise that the reasons for the conflict between the Diocese of Pittsburgh and TEC were relatively straightforward and largely to do with the "presenting symptom" of homosexuality (see chapter 1). The specific case, argued by ACNA Archbishop Duncan and his supporters, to advocate a withdrawal from TEC emphasized several elements: the Episcopal Church disregards the authority of scripture; it is unable to discipline those who violate its doctrines; conservatives have long been marginalized by the dominant "liberal" ethos of TEC; and the consecration of Gene Robinson was inappropriate and disrupted relations with the Anglican Communion. Archbishop Duncan often summarized the matter this way: TEC compromises "the Gospel imperative for Truth."[6]

Presented in such terms, Archbishop Duncan's position shares much in common with the rhetoric employed by GAFCON in its criticism of the situation in the Anglican Communion (see chapter 3). It is also notable that this way of framing the dispute establishes a sharp division between conservatives and liberals, which would seem to correspond with Hunter's concept of the "culture wars." Both of these initial impressions suggest a close correspondence with the ways in which the conflict in the Communion is understood at the global, national, and local levels. Even such preliminary observations call into question claims that the local congregation remains unaffected by disputes in the global Communion.

As Chris began to meet with members of local churches in the Pittsburgh region, however, the interconnection between the local and global churches began to look much more complicated, and it became clear that the situation required a more nuanced description. Details on the ground revealed that after Robert Duncan required that every parish in the diocese hold a vote on whether to leave TEC, four in ten congregations voted to stay in TEC.[7] This not only surprised the bishop of Pittsburgh; even international observers had imagined that this diocese was the one most likely to withdraw from TEC in a united protest against the national church.[8]

More striking still, many of the clergy who had decided to remain within TEC emphasized that they were "conservative Evangelicals." This was often the first thing they wanted to communicate in their interviews, to avoid being either misunderstood or misrepresented. In other words, they wanted it to be clear that they did not understand themselves to be "Liberals" who agreed with all of the policies of TEC. It was important to them that we recognize that they had not decided to remain within TEC out of sympathy with its dominant moral or theological positions.[9] Other considerations, they insisted, informed their refusal to realign themselves with the Province of the Southern Cone. The headlines framing the parameters of the conflict in Pittsburgh were not accurately capturing the decisive issues informing the decisions of Episcopalians and Anglicans in the region.

The dispute in Pittsburgh cannot, therefore, be collapsed into a simple narrative of "liberals versus conservatives." What happened on the ground was more complicated than such dichotomies imply, and the nuances of local issues need to be better understood. We also recognized something very important to many Anglicans and Episcopalians at the local level, who found themselves caught up in the dynamics of the dispute in the larger Anglican Communion: a desire not to be misrepresented or to have their actions reframed in terms of the dominant politicized rhetoric surrounding the conflict. Anglicans and Episcopalians in Pittsburgh resented some of the ways in which their words and actions were described and interpreted outside their local area.

This concern about being misrepresented illustrates a prominent dynamic often found within church conflicts and in political disputes more generally: a propensity to construct one's opponents as a "moral other" and to frame the struggle as a battle between "us" and "them." Listening to the protests of individual priests in Pittsburgh regarding how they were represented by their opponents demonstrates how local disagreements and tensions can quickly become reframed along the lines of wider national or transnational disputes and storylines. Much to their frustration, the story these individuals wanted to tell about themselves and their motivations was often translated into rhetorical language and symbols that originated at some distance from Pittsburgh. Many felt that the dominant narrative of the conflict was imposed upon them. Evangelical Episcopalians who remained in TEC resented being labeled "liberals" or "traitors"; Anglicans who left TEC complained about being dismissed as "fundamentalists," "homophobes," or "un-Anglican."

This phenomenon was most obvious in the prominence of two rhetorical symbols employed during the dispute between the Diocese of Pittsburgh and TEC: the personas of Robert Duncan, archbishop of the realigned Anglican diocese, and the presiding bishop of TEC, Katherine Jefferts Schori. This dynamic was introduced to us in striking ways during two of Chris's first encounters with local congregations in the region.

After Chris attended a midweek evening service at St. Bylsma's (a congregation that voted to remain in TEC), members of the congregation were naturally curious about who he was. Upon learning the purpose of his visit to Pittsburgh, Fred, a member of the choir, became very animated: "That Bob Duncan! Well, he is really manipulating what he can! The guy is a real player. . . . He wants people to fall in line. . . . There are some real mental issues there!" Don, a senior layperson from the same congregation, also commented on the bishop's personality: "Bob Duncan was a very ambitious man. He wanted to be an archbishop." Don then leaned closer and added, with emphasis, "He wanted to be *admired*." For many members of congregations that remained in TEC, Bishop Duncan was a focal point of criticism and suspicion.

Chris had a similar experience the next day while meeting with Reverend Victor, a priest at St. Gonchar's Anglican Church, which had voted (more or less unanimously) to leave TEC and become part of the ACNA. When asked to explain why he and his church withdrew from the national church, Victor's reply began with reference to the presiding bishop, Katharine Jefferts Schori. He pulled out his smartphone and read a list of the "most heretical" things the presiding bishop had said. She "talks about Jesus as our 'vehicle to the divine,'" he said, "which falls far short of Jesus' statement, 'I am the way, the truth, and the life'!"

What is particularly striking about both of these encounters was not so much the content of the criticism but its emotional intensity. It was evident that Fred and Don did not merely disagree with Robert Duncan, any more than Victor was simply offering constructive criticism of Katharine Jefferts Schori; rather, these two figureheads had come to symbolize to them something profoundly threatening. The presiding bishop and the failings of TEC seemed to be one and the same in Victor's mind, in the same way that Fred and Don largely equated anyone desiring to withdraw from TEC with the personality and views of Bishop Duncan.

A number of sociologists argue that the way in which people define a situation shapes the outcome.[10] Rhys Williams argues that in order to mobilize like-minded people to support a social movement, leaders must frame a situation in such a way that they are spurred to action.[11] Beyond establishing a general sense of grievance, Williams continues, a key component of effective social mobilization involves shaping a collective identity constructed in opposition to a clear enemy.[12] Such definitional work often involves establishing a clear boundary between *us* and *them*. The creation of this "moral other" relies upon highly polemical rhetoric: "One way of accomplishing this identity distinction is to create *demons*—identify another social group as the moral other against which one's own group stands as a bulwark."[13] The philosopher Eric Hoffer describes this dynamic in the bluntest of terms: "Mass movements can rise and spread without belief in a God, but never without belief in a devil."[14]

This was the function of the two primary rallying symbols of Robert Duncan and Katharine Jefferts Schori in the conflict in Pittsburgh. It was evident in the way that Bill, a lay member of St. Gonchar's, explained why his church voted to leave TEC: "We have to make a stand for this [realignment]; otherwise, it's another stronghold that the other side will gain!" When asked to clarify what he meant by "the other side," he replied: "The Enemy. Satan." In Bill's view, the devil had taken over TEC. Thus, when he thinks that someone like the presiding bishop is denying the uniqueness of Christ, for him it is a sign that the entire church itself has walked away from the core of his faith.

That Bill's way of framing the situation had been encouraged by his leaders is evident in the similar rhetoric employed in sermons by Archbishop Duncan: "The distortion of Anglicanism in the West—the deceit the Enemy has sown . . . is soon so badly distorted and quickly compromised that those who begin to cross [that bridge] are soon not recognizably Christian anymore."[15] In this view, not only is TEC seen as flawed and in error; it is no longer Christian and is in league with the devil. For many in Pittsburgh, Jefferts Schori came to symbolize all that is wrong with the Episcopal Church: increasing centralization, lack of theological rigor, unacceptably compromised teachings on traditional "orthodoxy" and "biblical truth." This development was encouraged by the leaders who advocated withdrawal, as well as by sympathetic leaders in the Global South (Duncan's remarks quoted above were first delivered at the opening plenary of the first meeting of GAFCON).

If the leadership mobilizing to withdraw from the national church constructed the presiding bishop of TEC as the "moral other," Archbishop Duncan was often a figure of derision among those advocating that the diocese should remain within TEC. Echoing Fred and Don from St. Bylsma's, Reverend Eric at St. Malkin's remarked, "Duncan is a megalomaniac; . . . he is simply about power and ego, and this has taken over his agenda." Reverend Sam at St. Sydney's noted that many "think [Robert Duncan is] arrogant, and everybody said he's out to become a primate. He won't be happy until he does that." Although he did not employ the technical term "moral other" to describe Archbishop Duncan, Reverend Sam aptly observed that he served as the "whipping boy" of many who decided to remain in TEC.

The tendency to frame local disagreements in such terms illuminates the ways in which polemical rhetoric can alter intimate relationships at the local level. As the figures of Jefferts Schori and Duncan came to symbolize the boundary of the dispute within the Diocese of Pittsburgh, not only were these two leaders demonized, but so too were many others who found themselves associated with one of these two symbols. Reverend Eric, for example, lamented the treatment he received at an event where most people in the room had sided with Archbishop Duncan: "They called me disloyal. That I was a traitor. [They were] very angry." He continued, "I'm brokenhearted. I've got great friends on both sides. I have a lot of hurt that people could be so judgmental. This group—they've taken it upon themselves to purify the church! We no longer debate our differences. We shout at each other. This is a group within the group—it's very extreme and a symptom of the situation." Similarly, Reverend Gino told us that "the realignment supporters in the diocese pretty much denounced us as traitors against the bishop." Such accounts of feeling demonized were common among those we interviewed who had decided to remain within TEC, particularly among the clergy.

Members of the ACNA Diocese of Pittsburgh also shared feelings of marginalization with us, but their stories usually focused on their general experiences within TEC, rather than on the events following the division of the diocese. They conveyed the feeling of being looked down upon and ridiculed—because they were "Evangelicals," "fundamentalists," or "homophobes." Mark Vasey-Saunders argues that the use of such terms to describe Evangelical Anglican opposition to the ordination of gay clergy or to ecclesial acceptance of same-sex marriage is frequently misleading. Although the term "homophobia" may helpfully emphasize the harm done to those on the receiving end of anti-LGBTQ rhetoric, the way it psychologizes the opinions of Evangelical critics is often merely polemical rather than analytical. The same is true of the term "fundamentalist," which Vasey-Saunders suggests is so broad a category as to encourage misunderstanding of contemporary Anglican conservatives.[16] What stands out in his analysis of Evangelical theological writing on homosexuality is the way his conclusions resonate with the observations of the social movement theorists we cited above. In the wake of fierce conflicts over an authentic "Anglican" identity, opponents tend to depict each other as "monstrous."[17]

Marginalization and Fear of Centralized Authority

A conversation with Reverend Marc, the rector of St. Jordan's church (ACNA), offered some context for the frustration felt among leaders of the "realignment" camp in Pittsburgh. When Chris first met him in his office, the conversation soon turned to his understanding of the historical tensions between his congregation and TEC: "St. Jordan's joined a movement back in the '60s whose passion was to change the Episcopal Church . . . through the transformation of Episcopalian parishes, and to bring back to the church classical Reformation affirmations of faith and spirituality, combined with an appropriate partnership of modern evangelicalism with all of its breadth." After describing the Episcopalian identity that appealed to him, Reverend Marc explained why he thought the atmosphere within TEC made it difficult for someone like him to stay: "Then resistance to that [Evangelical renewal] movement began to harden . . . in a clarified direction with a progressive agenda that was clearly antithetical to some of the core values of the renewal movement. . . . That really began to happen when we got to the 1990s."

After elaborating on the resulting sense of marginalization and disrespect felt among Evangelical Episcopalians, Reverend Marc clarified why he no longer thought it tolerable to remain within the structures of TEC; he and others had lost confidence in their "ability to control who [our] next bishop is going to be." Events in the church convinced him that the national church would increasingly interfere in episcopal election processes. Reverend Marc told us how, previously, he had been confident that "no one was going to mess with our clergy. No one was going to mess with our bishops." But when TEC leadership rejected a call by the primates of the Anglican Communion in February 2007 to reverse the national church's position on homosexuality, or at least to allow for the episcopal oversight of aggrieved congregations by other provinces, this was "the straw that broke the camel's back." From then on, he shifted from being an insider who was critical of the status quo and trying to change it, to pursuing an outsider "realignment" strategy that involved exploring ways to leave the structures of the national church.

Such a fear of being socially marginalized has been documented in other studies of evangelicals in the United States. As the sociologist Nancy Ammerman observes, American evangelicals often paint "themselves as an embattled minority, fighting a hegemonic culture."[18] Such rhetoric, she continues, is generated by a conviction "that they might lose the ability to preach [their understanding of] the gospel and preserve their way of life." This interpretation resonates with the feelings that Reverend Marc shared with us. The issue was not simply that he and others like him felt like a minority within TEC (what Ammerman calls "status discontent"); rather, he had come to the conclusion (rightly or wrongly) that a minority position such as his would not be permitted much longer by the power structures of the national church.

Reverend Marc's fear of the centralizing power of TEC is an example of how local congregations do not feel insulated from developments (real or imagined) that take place at the denominational level of their church. The conflict in Pittsburgh was thus thoroughly entwined with issues at the national level of the institution. Whether the suspicion that he and like-minded church members in Pittsburgh felt toward TEC was justified, the belief that external forces threatened the autonomy of their congregations fueled their desire to withdraw from the national church. Reverend Marc shared with us some of the specific interference he feared: "You get it done by controlling most of the seminaries; then you get it done by controlling the calling processes for bishops." His reasons for suspecting that TEC would try to control his bishop, and through the bishop his congregation, subsequently came more clearly into view:

> In order to become a bishop or priest now in the Anglican Communion
> . . . you don't have to personally consent . . . to the presence of people

who are in active sexual relations outside the covenant of marriage. . . . You don't have to consent to that in your parish. . . . But you do have to consent to it [existing] in the diocese, and you have to consent to it nationally, and you have to consent to it in the House of Bishops. . . . Once you do that, then you are creating room for something that the Bible quite clearly forbids and prohibits. It's not the sexuality issue, but it's the authority of the Bible that has been put in the secondary place. . . . [Because] in the end, it will be mandated. . . . It will become a civil rights issue, and it will be, in the end, enforced by canon law. . . . That's exactly where this whole thing is heading.

These remarks illustrate how a fear of encroaching institutional control over the diocese and its congregations was a key feature influencing Anglican clergy on the ACNA side of the divide in Pittsburgh. Sociologists of religion have argued that church schisms typically have more do with organizational issues than with doctrinal matters,[19] but they have also found that episcopally led denominations are less prone to schism.[20] Indeed, an Anglican congregation cannot withdraw itself from the authority of a bishop and remain "Anglican," nor can a diocese simply withdraw itself from its national Anglican province for similar reasons. Such institutional constraints are inherent in episcopal polity and ecclesiology and have indeed made schisms in episcopal traditions relatively rare.[21] At the very least, aggrieved schismatic groups need to bring a sympathetic bishop along with them, which is a difficult requirement given that a bishop's status and authority depend upon the episcopal structures of the parent denomination.

It is at this point that the significance of developments at the international level of the Anglican Communion to the local situation in Pittsburgh comes more clearly into view. Because some bishops in the Global South were sympathetic to the criticisms of TEC expressed by Bishop Duncan and his followers, these external observers were prepared to offer the ACNA Diocese of Pittsburgh "episcopal oversight" once it withdrew from the structures of the national church. This "realignment" of authority allowed the diocese to claim that it remained within the Anglican Church worldwide, and once the Anglican Church in North America was formed, such external recognition allowed it to assert that it remained a member of the Anglican Communion. The recognition by the primate of the Province of the Southern Cone was thus an important resource—from the transnational level of the Communion—underwriting the efforts at the local level in Pittsburgh to resist the authority of TEC.[22]

The Global South in Pittsburgh

In the lead-up to the schism in 2008, the Diocese of Pittsburgh was particularly active in forging links and formal partnerships with Anglican leaders in the Global South. Many of the Anglican and Episcopalian clergy we spoke with in the region emphasized the significance of such connections. Reverend Daniel of St. Bylsma's (TEC) described the emergence of these transnational relations:

> The conservative bloc, whatever you want to call it . . . found themselves in a decided minority in the Episcopal Church, a voice crying in the wilderness. It is [only] then that they discovered the Anglican Communion. Even Paul Zahl, the former dean of Trinity [School for Ministry], said that "no one was interested in what Africans thought until 2004." That is a quote from Paul Zahl.[23] Okay? So they all of a sudden discovered the Africans, not all of them . . . but the majority of the provinces in Africa that had similarly conservative views. It would give them some clout to be able to say that we are not just a voice crying in the wilderness, [that they] really represent the majority of Anglicanism. Okay? And so the relationship between not just Pittsburgh but also Fort Worth and the African churches was what I call a marriage of convenience because they were able to piggyback on the African people.

Reverend Brooks at St. Orpik's (TEC) also brought up the diocese's connection to Africa and the symbolic value it offered to the ACNA camp. Advocates for realignment often emphasized such partnerships to argue that the majority of the Anglican world was on their side:

> From the day I walked into Pittsburgh diocese, there was a much more distinct awareness of global Anglicans, as there was often some bishop from Kenya or a bishop from South Asia or somewhere around at the [diocesan] convention, clergy colleagues taking mission trips to Rwanda—those kinds of things happening all the time. And so there's a pretty strong rationale among the realigned groups that, although [the] formal instrumental bodies of the Anglican Communion wouldn't [recognize the ACNA], actually the realigned group is nearer to the heart of global Anglicanism than . . . the Episcopal Church [is]. . . . I think here in Pittsburgh . . . people felt much closer to the Church of Uganda than they

did to the Episcopal Church in its national expression. So that I think that's kind of the interesting component of [the situation in the diocese].

Achieving external recognition from leaders outside the national church provided the realignment movement with moral support, and enabled them to portray themselves as part of the majority view of the wider Anglican Communion, rather than as a minority perspective within TEC. Thus, although tension between the Diocese of Pittsburgh and TEC had been developing for decades,[24] it was not until external support from the Global South was available that the leaders in Pittsburgh could seriously contemplate a formal break with their national province.

Constructing Unifying Symbols

In this regard, the impact of the "presenting symbols" of the conflict in the Anglican Communion (chapter 1) at the local level of the church comes more fully into view. For a meaningful partnership to take shape between the ACNA Anglicans in Pittsburgh and leaders from the Global South, some kind of unifying core principles or symbols were required. This was the function of statements issued by Archbishop Duncan and his followers about "defending the Bible," "upholding Anglican orthodoxy," and opposing homosexuality. Each of these positions was employed as a unifying rallying point, not only to mobilize local opposition to the policies of TEC, but at least as much to establish and cement support from sympathetic Anglican leaders in the Global South.[25]

While such core slogans serve as effective tools for mobilizing support, they also involve significant limitations and challenges. As Michael Lindsay has astutely emphasized, such unifying symbols are necessarily *elastic*.[26] That is, they must remain relatively vague and flexible. For example, calls for conservative Anglicans to "stand up for the Bible" or to "defend Jesus" against the "heretical" statements of the presiding bishop serve as powerful rallying points. How one ought to interpret the Bible, or what doctrinal claims in particular ought to be made about Jesus, must be left unspecified in order to draw in as many supporters as possible. Religious convictions, in other words, are stated clearly and firmly, while at the same time the rhetoric employed is strategically rendered sufficiently flexible to enable forging alliances with a large constituency.[27]

There are limits to such elasticity, however, and this is evident when the focus of attention shifts from the transnational to the local. We noted earlier how a number of the clergy who decided to remain within TEC described themselves as "conservative Evangelicals." Clearly, individual clergy in Pittsburgh interpreted that label differently, even as they all claimed it as a term of self-description. The same diversity is true of many other elastic slogans and presenting symbols employed within the different camps in Pittsburgh, including homosexuality, orthodoxy, and the Bible.

Regardless of the prominence of the two symbols personifying the "moral other" in Pittsburgh, and despite frequent deployment of the unifying concepts of homosexuality, orthodoxy, and biblical authority, these devices were not sufficient to ensure a unified front in opposition to the policies and structures of the national church. Following the vote to leave TEC at the Pittsburgh Diocesan Convention on 4 October 2008, twenty-seven of sixty-four parishes (42 percent) announced that they wanted to remain members of the national church.[28] Thus the margin of the vote in Pittsburgh, although decisive, revealed that local churches were much more resistant to leaving TEC than Bishop Duncan and many external observers had anticipated. Underneath the polemics, the local context in Pittsburgh was much more complex than many church leaders and media commentators recognized.[29] It is instructive, therefore, to look more closely at how the dispute was viewed at the local level.

Homosexuality and Other "Unifying Symbols"

On the issue of homosexuality, we encountered a significant diversity of views among members of *both* sides of the divide in Pittsburgh. Reverend Staal, a priest at the realigned church of St. Jordan's, expressed some ambivalent feelings about the process of leaving TEC. When we asked him why he was unable to support realignment wholeheartedly (even as he continued to serve in a realigned parish), he replied:

> The big issue here [at St. Jordan's] is homosexuality. People always say that that's not the issue and it's the Gospel, it's the authority of scripture. . . . The problem is we never divided when those things were very real and very present in the Episcopal Church. We only divided after Gene Robinson got consecrated, which, to me, looks like we're dividing over the fact that he's gay. And that seems to present all kinds of problems in

terms of how you are seen as a church, the kinds of people you'll attract, [and] the kinds of people you'll repel.

Reverend Staal explained to us why, despite his Evangelical identity, he was uncomfortable condemning committed same-sex relationships: "I had a number of conversations with friends from seminary who feel like this battle [over homosexuality] in the Anglican Communion is kind of our parents' battle. It's kind of a 'baby boomer' kind of thing." In his mind, making homosexuality the dividing line of the church is a poor witness to the wider society: "We grew up watching *Will & Grace* and all these crazy things. I mean, we've all known a lot of gay people and none of them have . . . [*pause*] they're not vampires!"[30]

Such a tone expresses concern about the way in which LGBTQ Episcopalians were being framed as a "moral other" by opponents of TEC. This was a rather common concern among the younger church members we interviewed in Pittsburgh. Sara, a woman under twenty-one years of age and a member of St. Gonchar's (ACNA), was careful to emphasize that she thought that members of TEC disregarded the divine authority of scripture. When we asked about the issue of homosexuality, however, she said, "I confess that I have a friend who is gay. . . . I don't agree with him, but I love him. And he's a Christian, and I know he's struggled with it, and the fact of the matter is I have come to a place where I have to admit that I don't understand it." Although not prepared to say that homosexuality is unproblematic, she also would not agree that it is any more sinful than a lot of other activities and practices that most people engage in. Moreover, she told us that she thought it was a tragic mistake for her church to split over this issue.

In an analysis of national survey data in the United States, the sociologist Mark Chaves observes a pattern among conservative Christians that resonates with these observations. He notes that although religious adherents are changing their views more slowly on the issue of homosexuality than Americans who do not attend religious services, there is a steady trend of liberalization on the issue among churchgoers, particularly among younger Christians.[31] He explains a similar trend in attitudes toward other religions with reference to what Robert Putnam and David Campbell call the "Aunt Susan principle."[32] This is the idea that the rise in toleration of religious pluralism is due to the fact that an increasing number of people have family members of a different religion (through interreligious marriage, and so forth), and so they are less willing to reject people whose religion is different from their own. Our interviews in Pittsburgh suggest that the same dynamic may be at work in younger people's attitudes toward homosexuality; many of them have gay or lesbian friends or family members, and have familiar gay reference points from popular culture (for instance, Reverend Staal's mention of *Will & Grace*). This does not necessarily lead these conservative Christians to full acceptance of homosexuality, or to advocate changing official church teaching on the issue, but they are increasingly unwilling to condemn their friends and family members, and they do not agree that their church should split over the issue.[33] This conclusion is supported by a 2015 survey conducted by the Pew Research Center, which found that 67 percent of (non-Episcopalian) Anglicans in the United States think that homosexuality should be accepted by society.[34]

This is not to suggest that we did not encounter strong opposition to the acceptance of homosexuality among Anglicans and Episcopalians in Pittsburgh. Reverend Marc at St. Jordan's (ACNA) told us that homosexuality is "something that the Bible quite clearly forbids and prohibits." Indeed, Chris also spoke with individuals remaining in TEC who opposed same-sex relationships. Norm, a parishioner of St. Bylsma's (TEC), told him that he strongly disagreed with the acceptance of practicing homosexuals, saying, "It's forbidden by the Bible." In his view, TEC "has gone to hell when they favor homosexuals"; "they . . . are actively promoting things that do not fit within the realm of Christianity, you might even say." What is clear, however, is that there was a diversity of views regarding homosexuality on *both* sides of the conflict in Pittsburgh, and thus attention to this presenting issue alone does not adequately explain the dispute in the local diocese.

This finding underlines the fact that the elasticity of the unifying symbols employed by church leaders is such that these concepts do not ensure agreement with the intended agenda. For all the power of the polemics supported by church leaders at the transnational, national, and even local levels, other considerations continue to inform the decisions of individual church members.

Personal and Contextual Factors

Personal and contextual factors shape the decisions of individual church members as much as the leading rhetorical symbols deployed in a conflict do; this is clear in the case of Norm, just quoted above. Norm accepts the primary criticisms leveled against TEC by its Anglican critics: he is opposed to accepting homosexuality and thinks TEC ignores the Bible and core Christian principles. Moreover, when Chris visited Norm in his home, he was met at the door with a pile of printouts from prominent online conservative Evangelical blogs: "Have you read these ones yet? You have to keep informed!" Norm clearly pays close attention to the developments at the transnational level of the Communion, and his views align closely with some of the dominant unifying symbols employed by critics of TEC. Nevertheless, when the split happened in Pittsburgh, Norm decided to remain in TEC when his congregation voted overwhelmingly to stay in the national church.

When Chris asked him why he remained in an Episcopal congregation, despite feeling out of step with TEC, Norm replied simply, "It's my church." He had no intention of leaving *his* parish for another congregation. Moreover, he told Chris that he continued to feel welcome and accepted at St. Bylsma's, saying, "I think [Reverend Daniel] likes me. I think he really does. I'm not afraid to say what I think. . . . They know what I think about homosexuality." Viewed solely through the lens of the presenting symbols of the conflict in the Anglican Communion (or the notion of the "culture wars"), Norm's behavior is difficult to explain; however, his attitude is consistent with the attachment many churchgoers form with their local congregation and with a church building.[35] Despite holding different theological views from those of many in his congregation, he still feels at home there. As Andrew Village observes, two key variables that support a "sense of belonging" in congregations is the length of time someone has attended the church and their age.[36] Norm, who is elderly and has attended St. Bylsma's for almost thirty years, exemplifies this finding. Norm's comfort with his congregation outweighs his disagreement with the clergy in the parish, or any official statements by the national leaders of TEC.

Our discussion with Debbie, a lay member of St. Gonchar's (ACNA), offers another illuminating view into how the polemics of the dispute at the transnational, national, diocesan, and congregational levels intersect with individual concerns and priorities. When Chris asked why she thought her church had to leave TEC, she answered in a voice full of conviction, "We couldn't stay in a sinful church! We had to take a stand! It was a choice between Christ and false belief." Her remarks here closely mirror the statements directed against TEC at the global and national levels, and she employed the unifying symbols encouraged by the ACNA leadership of her diocese. When asked what she thought about those who voted otherwise and had left her congregation to remain in TEC, however, her tone of voice and facial expression changed dramatically: "I never imagined so many would leave! When they [the church leadership] saw what was happening, they should have stopped. It was too much! This wasn't right!" The tension between these two positions—*we had to leave; we shouldn't have left*—is striking. Debbie was convinced by her congregational leaders' framing of the dispute, but she was also ultimately dissatisfied by the results of the schism with TEC congregations in Pittsburgh. The local consequences of being too firm and "inelastic" with regard to the unifying symbols under contestation were unacceptable to her.

> My thinking was that . . . there would only be a few parishes that would not be leaving with the diocese: maybe a 90/10 split at most. But it turned out to be a 60/40 split! I was horrified, absolutely horrified! I'm still horrified because of the carnage that the split brought about, with no one caring about the broken churches. No one actually cared, as far as I can tell, [that] orthodox people [were] being split from orthodox people. . . . When the bishop saw that, he should have said, "Whoa: we can't do this until we're all in agreement or consensus." But as far as I can tell, it's still very ugly.

Noteworthy here is the way in which Debbie adopts the polemical claim of critics of TEC that the national church is heretical and "unorthodox," but at the local level is unwilling to accept that many Episcopalians in TEC congregations are any less "orthodox" than she is. The rhetoric of the conflict, so powerful in the national and transnational spheres, breaks down at the level of the local congregation, where the split has caused "carnage."

Nor was Debbie happy with the alliances that the realigned diocese of Pittsburgh had made. "And the fact that we have aligned with five or six organizations that don't believe in the ordination of women," she said passionately, "I think is just horrible! It sets back women's ministry, as far as one can tell, into the Dark Ages."[37] When Chris caught up with her three years later, her attitude had not changed.

> I still have those reservations, you know. There was an awful lot of "collateral"—what I think the bishop said was—"collateral damage." And whether that could have been avoided [*sighs*], who knows? But there are . . . small congregations who have split. There also have been small congregations who had not been able to maintain their building and have walked away from it.

Accounts such as these were common during our interviews with members of ACNA and TEC congregations in Pittsburgh. Martha at St. Gonchar's

(ACNA) spoke of how discouraged and empty she felt in the context of polemics over the division of her diocese. Previously, she had believed that her church focused on what truly mattered to her: "God was the ultimate; that is why we were there." As the congregation became immersed in conflict with TEC, however, she felt that this priority had been lost: "I'm not sure that we are there at this point." Some members of the clergy, like Reverend Lemieux at St. Bylsma's (TEC) suggested that the damage was still felt in the TEC diocese as well. We were told that five years after the divide, "a great deal of anxiety" often resurfaced when decisions had to be made at the diocesan level. Explaining that there continue to be fears that old wounds will reopen, or that the polemics of the past will reignite, Reverend Lemieux looked up and said, "We throw around the term 'PTSD' [posttraumatic stress disorder] a lot."[38]

These accounts illustrate a number of significant points. First, the conflicts and tensions found at the transnational and national levels of the Anglican Communion had a significant impact on the local congregations in Pittsburgh. Second, the dominant unifying symbols and polemics employed by leaders in the transnational conflict were also prominent in the local churches. At the same time, however, many members of the churches in Pittsburgh expressed discomfort over the immediate consequences of a rigid interpretation of the unifying symbols of the conflict. If standing up for "orthodoxy" meant dividing the church, this was unacceptable to people like Debbie. Thus specific unifying symbols do not necessarily tell everything there is to tell about a person's faith commitment, nor do they necessarily imply a clear political or ecclesial stance toward one's opponents. Such polemical symbols are indeed, as Lindsay suggests, "elastic." Finally, we observed a number of personal and pragmatic issues that help explain why individuals in the end do not fall in line with the dominant rhetoric representing their "side" of the conflict. In Norm's case, for example, these were very local considerations (how long he had attended his church), and they outweighed the significance and power of the presenting symbols and polemical slogans of the moment.

While most individuals we spoke with explained their decisions in terms of their principles, some admitted that they decided for or against TEC for strictly personal reasons. Joe, for example, a member of St. Malkin's (TEC), told us that he had voted to leave TEC but had remained in his parish because his wife had voted the other way. He stayed with his congregation simply in order to continue to attend church with his family.

It was not uncommon to hear stories about individuals presumed to have made their decision for pragmatic reasons, typically those who had positioned themselves on the other side of the conflict. For example, Tanner, a parishioner at St. Sydney's, suggested that some conservative clergy who stayed within TEC were approaching retirement age, and thus fear for their pensions explained their reluctance to leave the national church. He was also prepared to admit that there were "cynical reasons" for his own congregation's reluctance to leave TEC: "Had we gone ahead with realignment . . . the departures of the segment who did not agree [but] who have been such a strength—financially and in terms of manpower—[would have meant] that we could not have continued. Basically, it would have been a decision to close [St. Sydney's]." We frequently encountered people who emphasized such financial considerations as key motivating factors for clergy who opted to remain in TEC. Reverend Joan of St. Talbot's (ACNA) argued that "these are men with families, and the Episcopal Church and the pension fund had tremendous benefits and to leave that or sacrifice that—and probably even pressured by their spouses—[was unthinkable]. If they wouldn't have that to deal with, they probably would have realigned." Father Gino, on the TEC side of the divide, proposed a similar theory to explain why some of his clerical associates had opted for realignment: "Some [realigned] because they had families to support, and they didn't have a whole lot of options. They were serving in parishes that were keen on realignment, even if they weren't."

A similar point, though more charitably put, was offered by Debbie at St. Gonchar's (ACNA). She suggested that conservative priests who stayed in TEC did so only out of a sense of duty, when they realized that their parishioners wouldn't agree to leave: "They knew where their people were, and felt that they needed to be faithful [to them and to their vocation]."

Although we can only speculate on how significant these factors might have been in the split in Pittsburgh, the fact that many of our informants frequently pointed to such pragmatic factors is illuminating. Even after being caught up in a highly polemical battle, the default explanation for the choices made by their opponents had more to do with local, personal, and often material considerations than with ideological commitment.

The Influence of the Leadership

If the "unifying symbols" employed by church leaders to motivate their followers were not always effective, what does this say about the clergy's capacity to influence their congregations? In their study of conflict over homosexuality in the Evangelical Lutheran Church in the United States, Wendy Cadge and her colleagues argue that the role of denominational leadership was crucial in diminishing polemical conflict. They conclude that "differences of opinion did not lead to direct conflict or controversy among members. Rather, clergy and the denominational study materials framed the discussions" in ways that either helped or hindered the debate.[39] This finding suggests that the role of leaders and the ways in which they frame an issue can be decisive for how a church conflict plays out. To what extent was this true in Pittsburgh?

It is notoriously difficult, and some would say impossible, to disentangle informants' accounts of why things happen from the causal factors themselves. At minimum, accounts cannot be taken straightforwardly as indicating causal factors.[40] In any case, the accounts of clergy and laypeople in Pittsburgh bear mixed witness—and assign blame differently—when asked about the role of church leadership in the dispute and its outcome. As we discussed earlier, the diocesan bishop, Robert Duncan, became a rallying symbol, and he is often given credit or blame, depending on a respondent's sympathies. The role of congregational leadership, and in particular of the parish priest, is less clear. Laypeople gave contradictory accounts of the role of parish priests: some felt that they had played a decisive role, while others felt that the role of laypeople had been pivotal. Clergy often thought that their own role was very significant in shaping the direction of their church. Reverend Andrea offered her own gloss on why the clergy were such influential leaders in the debate over realignment: "This is a very interesting lesson to me in terms of the power of leadership. If you teach for ten or twenty or thirty years that something is bad, and you don't produce the examples that would counter that story . . . then people will tend to believe your point of view. So while I could produce any number of churches I know who are perfectly faithful churches—Bible-believing Episcopal churches—that wasn't part of the story." In other words, the way a pastor frames a situation has a lot to do with how laypeople perceive it. Reverend Andrea linked the influence of leadership to the clergy's capacity to shape the narrative that is used to symbolize an existing situation. Reverend Eric (TEC) offered a less positive version of the same point: "I have actually heard one person say, 'You damn clergy have got us into this; you damn clergy had better get us out [of it]!'" There are good reasons for not simply taking these accounts at face value, because we also heard a lot about the pressures clergy faced from their own congregations—enough to know that it was not quite so straightforward.

Reverend Sergei at St. Gonchar's (ACNA), for example, illustrates how some clergy experienced internal pressure from their congregations to take a stand against TEC. He told us that, prior to the realignment, the practice of offering prayers for the leaders of the church (including the presiding bishop) became a real source of tension. "I was getting flak from both extremes," he said. People would say to him, "I can't believe we're still praying for *her* [Jefferts Schori]. We don't accept her authority." But if an intercessor omitted her from the prayers, other people would come to him and say, "I cannot believe we didn't pray for our presiding bishop!" Reverend Sergei smirked when he told us how he resolved the issue: "with 'studied ambiguity,' I think is the word, I thought we would pray for *the* presiding bishop, not *our* presiding bishop. We pray for her as the leader of the church whether we agree with her or not."

This highlights the extent to which some clergy found themselves at intersecting points of tension, as parishioners expressed passionate feelings about even subtle gestures, which they took to symbolize the congregation's relationship to the national church.[41] Moreover, laypeople could apply additional pressure by leaving (or threatening to leave) the congregation. It is significant that the more influential clergy in the ACNA camp came from large and growing churches. Reverend Sergei admitted that one concern confronting parish priests like himself was that some members were leaving their congregations out of frustration with TEC or the Anglican Communion and joining large nondenominational churches. "You started seeing this breaking apart," he said, "a kind of fragmenting going on, and I think it was in that context that the idea . . . of realignment first came up." Likewise, St. Jordan's lost members to other large non-Anglican churches in the period leading up to realignment in 2008. For this reason, as Reverend Marc told us, there was some fear that if the congregation did not take a clear stand against the direction of TEC, a similar new wave of departures would occur: "We had our share of concerns about that." This acknowledgment highlights how leaders of local churches reacted to how their parishioners were responding to developments at more distant levels of their denomination. In such circumstances, the identity of the congregation was being defined by external labels and by battles originating at the national or transnational level. Their discontent, in other words, had little to do with the preaching of their pastor or the quality of the Sunday liturgy.

The Requirement to Choose

In the face of such mixed evidence regarding the influence of clerical leadership during the dispute in Pittsburgh, one thing stands out: individual congregations, clergy, and laypeople were forced to decide for or against remaining in the Episcopal Church. Whatever their views on their parish priest, their local bishop, the presiding bishop, the issue of homosexuality, how to read the Bible, or the parameters of orthodoxy, they were told to cast their vote on whether to remain in TEC or realign with the ACNA. The tensions in the diocese, in other words, were framed in a very specific way, which allowed just two options.

We concluded, therefore, that a primary reason for the schism in Pittsburgh is the simple fact that churches were told that they had to choose sides. After a long history of tension and grievance with TEC, key leaders in Pittsburgh made the decision to initiate momentum toward realignment, and they asked members of the diocese to choose a side. Until that point, many clergy and laypeople had largely agreed on most issues of the day (the limitations of TEC, the opinions of the presiding bishop, the authority of scripture, the need for more evangelism, and so forth).[42] After local churches were forced to choose between TEC or realignment, serious internal fissures broke wide open, accompanied by varied subjective motivations.

Reverend Brooks of St. Orpik's (TEC) shared some observations with us that support this conclusion. While he noted that a few parishes had a strong "evangelical," and others a more "progressive," character, Reverend Brooks suggested that most congregations were more like his own, a church with a "strong neighborhood church identity." "People come to [St. Orpik's] because their cousins go here," he told us. "We have lots of Democrats and lots of Republicans. . . . Here we have a lot of differences, and sometimes the differences are between parents and children and between cousins and so on." Such a congregation was generally content with the status quo, although many members did share the criticisms of TEC voiced by Bishop Duncan and other supporters of realignment. Reverend Brooks continued, "If you were trying to . . . put all the conservative parishes [in the diocese] on one side and all the liberal parishes on the other . . . you just wouldn't be able to know where to put [St. Orpik's]." He told us that the only reason why the question of remaining or realigning would ever have arisen in his congregation was that the bishop instructed them to vote. In the end, "most everybody felt that . . . it was going to be easier for the more conservative half of our congregation to live within the Episcopal Church than it would have been for the progressive half of the congregation to have lived [within the ACNA church], had we gone with realignment." Thus, according to Reverend Brooks, although his congregation encompassed diverse and competing political and theological views, it was not torn apart by "culture wars" or theological differences. When the demand came to choose sides, the parish decided which path would cause less destruction to its own congregational life, and voted accordingly.

In some churches (St. Bylsma's, St. Gonchar's), members were like-minded enough to avoid significant controversy when the vote was taken. In others (like St. Orpik's), differences were transcended and a decision was made on pragmatic grounds rather than firm ideological ones. In still others (St. Malkin's, St. Sydney's), the differences within the community could not be surmounted, and the congregation split. Many of our informants suggested, however, that most members of the diocese would not have made a firm commitment in either direction had a decision not been forced upon them.

We have already noted that one parishioner, Joe, voted in favor of realignment, while his wife voted against, but that he stayed with the congregation in order to continue going to church with his family. For others, the church "family" could not be so preserved. Fred admitted that he continued to mourn what had happened to his wider church "family." "I'm starting to calm down now," he said, but "I started holding a lot of bitterness towards those who left. Because what they did, to me, in fracturing my family . . . I was bitter at them for breaking something that was not broken here!" As at St. Orpik's, so also for the people of St. Malkin's. They made a firm decision about realignment only because one was demanded of them. Only a minority of people wanted to make such a judgment, and fewer still wished to suffer the consequences of a firm decision. As Reverend Staal (ACNA) lamented, "I felt like there are huge forces moving around me. The church is getting ripped apart, and I've got to decide and just sort of go along."

The line dividing members of the continuing TEC Diocese of Pittsburgh from the realigned Anglican Diocese of Pittsburgh thus appear to be rather artificial, contingent on a constellation of forces that could have resulted in many parishes' ending up on either side of the divide. The division fails to fit neatly with the way in which divisions in the Anglican Communion are often described. Thus, once a call to choose interrupted the status quo, the diocese and its parishes fragmented in ways that few had predicted. Perhaps the conflict in the Anglican Communion presents an alternative to Lindsay's notion of "elastic" unifying concepts. We propose here a different metaphor that highlights not how symbols can unify but how they divide; in Pittsburgh, the demand to choose sides hammered a cold masonry chisel against a hard rock; the diocese cracked and split, but not in the way that anyone had expected.

The Local in a Global Context

This image of a chisel striking stone captures the reality of contemporary church conflict, particularly in a transnational organization like the Anglican Communion. As this chapter demonstrates, the conflict in the Diocese of Pittsburgh was shaped by the simultaneous interweaving of local, national, and transnational forces, symbols, and concerns. Sometimes the "presenting symbols" of the polemical battles in the wider Communion were employed to further very local agendas; on other occasions, local pastors were confronted by parishioners disturbed by events in distant Anglican provinces, which they had read about on the internet. Meanwhile, the decisions of some individuals as to how to respond to the polemical dispute surrounding them had more to do with personal concerns than with anything remotely ideological.

Thus, even as leaders in Pittsburgh sought to mobilize supporters with reference to polemical symbols that personified their opponents as monstrous egotists and betrayers of Christian faith, the divisions that resulted did not appear along entirely predictable fault lines. Some "Evangelical conservatives" opted to remain in TEC; some who opposed schism over the issue of homosexuality found themselves members of the ACNA, outside the national church. Others simply elected to follow their family members, while some merely refused to leave the comfortable pew they had sat in for decades, no matter what their personal views or what side their congregation took in the dispute.

What the conflict in Pittsburgh reveals is the way in which the local and transnational have become intertwined in the life of the church. Neither parishioners nor clergy could ignore the tensions and divisions that had arisen between their diocese and the national church, or the pronouncements of Anglican leaders in the Global South. They might try to resist the pressure to choose a side; they might resent the labels used to describe what kind of Anglican or Episcopalian they were; they might even decide to continue attending the same parish they always had, no matter what the outcome of their congregation's vote. But what they could not escape was the reality that their local disagreements and tensions had become enmeshed with conflicts and polemical battles emanating from other regions of the Communion.

In this way, Anglicans and Episcopalians experienced a shift in their experience of church. They discovered that their congregation was increasingly taking the form of what one might call a "global parish." Given the overlapping strands of local and global concerns that ran through their diocese, little in their experience of church remained simply or straightforwardly local. As the theorist of globalization Mark Juergensmeyer puts it, "Today it seems that almost everyone is everywhere."[43] One might live in Pittsburgh, but the concerns of the bishops of the Global South can be very much on the local church's agenda. Alternatively, one might be a "conservative Evangelical" in ACNA but be concerned about the fair treatment of LGBTQ Anglicans in Uganda. The polemical battles in the Anglican Communion may suggest a straightforward ideological struggle between two clear opponents, but how the conflict plays out in a local context is far more complicated than such narrative framing suggests.

Having shown that the local conflict in Pittsburgh, rather than representing a culture war between "liberals" and "conservatives," is better compared to the unpredictable outcome of a cold masonry chisel striking stone, let us now turn to the question of whether conflict is an inherently bad thing for a church. For while the Pittsburgh case illustrates that conflict can bitterly divide people, it can also sometimes hold people together.

5 | NATIONAL STRICTURES, GLOBAL STRUCTURES, AND THE TIES THAT BIND

During the late spring of 2016, a sense of intrigue was in the air, and church media were debating the consequences of the gathering of Primates in January. A particular focus of the discussion was the communiqué released at the end of that gathering, which called for restrictions on TEC's involvement in Communion-level affairs, though it was not accepted in many parts of the church, including the Anglican Consultative Council.[1] Adding to the tension was the fact that the Scottish Episcopal Church had recently passed the first reading of changes to its marriage canon, while the outcome of Canada's General Synod debates over same-sex marriage was yet to unfold. When we caught up with Reverend Shultz, a leader in the American Episcopal Church, in a local coffee shop, he took a surprisingly optimistic tone when talking about TEC's recent history—and its future, despite the lingering international pressures.

Sipping his hot drink, the TEC leader discussed the current climate in the church in a relaxed manner. "The bad times we have had to go through have helped make people in the Episcopal Church aware of the Anglican Communion—many for the first time," he said. "That's a good thing!" Although by no means making light of recent disputes, Reverend Shultz displayed a striking level of ease about the outcome of the conflict that his church had been through over the last fifteen years. "It has made us get to know each other," he said. He explained that a new level of honesty and transparency was evident within TEC, even if it was the result of some painful experiences. He continued at length in this vein. "I'd even go so far as to say that I'm grateful to Rowan [Williams], who gave us the covenant—with all of its faults—because it got us talking across the Communion. I'm even grateful to ACNA, since they made us really talk about what it means to be an Anglican." Schultz spoke enthusiastically of some new conversations and potential partnerships that were emerging between TEC and African provinces, although he acknowledged that these remained tentative and required patience and tact so as to avoid a potentially polemical backlash from opponents of such developments. Nevertheless, from Reverend Schulz's vantage point, relationships at the international level of the Communion appeared, for once, to have taken a turn for the better. Despite the recent polemical turmoil, with the end of the global church nowhere in sight, he suggested that the recent conflicts had actually had a positive effect on the church.

While it may be tempting to dismiss such a perspective as the product of wishful thinking or serious denial, in this chapter we argue that there are grounds for taking this position seriously. Moreover, drawing on sociological research on the productive potential of conflict, we show that conflict and difference can sometimes bind a diverse community together. An important essay by the early twentieth-century German sociologist Georg Simmel provides a useful starting point for thinking about the relationship between unity and conflict, and how these are interconnected with what Simmel calls "forms of sociation"—though others might prefer to call them "social structure" or "church order."[2] In *Conflict and the Web of Group Affiliations*, Simmel remarks that it is a common mistake to see social conflict as a purely negative social force. On the contrary, he argues, while conflict can indeed be destructive and push people apart, it may also hold groups together, or even provide the impetus and opportunity for a group's growth and development. Conflict is only purely negative when conflicting actors attempt to obliterate one another, or succeed in the nearly impossible task of breaking off all ties with the other.

All social groups, Simmel argues, are born from a mix of both centripetal propensities—forces that pull people together—and centrifugal tendencies—forces that push them apart and distinguish them from others. This means that social life inevitably entails some measure of disharmony, but this dialectic produces creative tensions that animate collective life and give groups the ability to change, grow, and adapt to new circumstances. While we often imagine harmonious groups that know neither tension nor friction, such groups exist only in our imaginations—or in our hopes and aspirations. If such a group did exist in reality, Simmel argues, it would be a lifeless assembly, incapable of growth, development, or, one might add, self-understanding. In other words, to imagine the history of the Christian Church without conflict would be to imagine the faith without its creeds and councils, and without the theological works of Augustine and Athanasius, of Luther, Calvin, and Cranmer, of Barth, Bonhoeffer, and Rahner. Arguably, without conflict and sharp differences of viewpoint, Christianity would also be a tradition lacking much of the New Testament, which developed out of, and records, very serious arguments between leaders in the early church.[3] The growth and development of the Christian Church has unfolded through internal disagreement, conflict with competitors, and responses to threats (both real and perceived), as much as through harmonious relationships.

How religious communities deal with their inevitable internal differences is an essential component of the various shapes into which Christian groups form themselves.[4] Simmel makes a distinction between different kinds of religious groups, a distinction he shares—somewhat differently conceived—with his contemporaries Max Weber and Ernst Troeltsch.[5] Simmel sees a fundamental difference between the "church" and the "sect." These are different social forms of religious life not only because of how they relate to "the world" but, equally, how they manage their own internal differences. Weber distinguished church and sect like this: one is born into a church, whereas even a child born to members of a sect must convert (or be "born again") in order to belong. Simmel argues that a sect maintains itself by building strong, rigid, defensive walls between the faithful and the external world. Internal conformity of belief and practice is encouraged because it heightens this powerful distinction between the sect within and the sinful world without. Of course, there is typically a great deal of diversity of belief and practice among members of a sect; publicly, however, the party line must be strictly adhered to. The sectarian mindset will emphasize at every turn the importance of keeping to the level plane, as far as possible from the "slippery slope," which leads inevitably to the abandonment of all that distinguishes the community of the faithful from the world. Even if the markers seem arbitrary or unfair, they demand respect and deference.

While sects retreat into an enclave, churches deal with internal diversity and the boundary with the external world by trying to create and maintain a monopoly within a given territory. While the sect builds strong walls, the boundaries of the church are elastic and somewhat porous, and it is from this that they derive their strength. It is not that difference between the internal community and the external world does not matter to a church; a church is no more likely to recognize the legitimacy of those who stray beyond its broad tent than is the sect. Thus, according to the formulation of the Church of Rome, *extra ecclesiam nulla salus*: there is no salvation outside the church. However, since the church's boundaries are less distinct and more fluid than those of a sect, churches are more willing to encompass "sinners" as well as "saints." Some variation on "orthodoxy" is more likely to be tolerated in a church, as long as it does not openly dispute the church's official teachings or deny its monopoly on salvation. Crucially, churches typically depend on an alliance with civil powers in order to maintain their monopoly and provide it with a center of gravity, a situation that obtains to this day in Orthodox countries like Russia and Greece.[6] This order of things used to be much more common, of course, including the legal monopoly of the Church of England until it began to come undone in the early nineteenth century.

Sociologists of religion have long followed David Martin's argument that church/sect typologies need to be supplemented by an additional type of Christian organizational form, one that characterizes the majority of religious organizations in contemporary pluralistic societies.[7] "Denominations" are religious groups that share many of the characteristics of a church, but membership is voluntary, and denominations are not in a position (nor do they generally express a desire) to exert a monopoly in their pluralistic context. Most provinces of the Anglican Communion are best described as denominations in these terms,[8] although some provinces, dioceses, and parishes undoubtedly lean in a more "churchly" and some in a much more "sectarian" direction.[9] It is easy to see these tendencies in the virtues that are prized by different kinds of Anglicans. Themes like "unity in diversity," "comprehensiveness," "the via media," or the church as a "big tent" are more likely to characterize churches than sects; and indeed many of these values were developed in the context of the English establishment, when the Church of England was a "church" in the sociological sense of the term and enjoyed a monopoly status enforced by the power of the Crown. Other themes evoke what sociologists understand as sects. These emphasize the need for the purity of the church, its need to remain uncontaminated by the corrupt values and beliefs of the "modern world," which are seen as unchristian, even anti-Christian. Those committed to the Christian community on the model of the sect generally hope to reform the church from within, restoring it to authentic Christianity—if, that is, they do not instead break away in order to keep themselves safe from those they perceive as wolves in sheep's clothing.

Church and sect provide different means of dealing with diversity and the conflict that difference can bring. But Simmel argues that conflict, whether in a church or in another social institution, is inevitable, and thus is not inherently a bad thing. Rather, he argues, somewhat counterintuitively, that conflict within a group can be a sign of health; difference itself need not be centrifugal and can even be a source of unity, even if it generates friction from time to time. Where people are free to take dissenting views, disagreements tend to proliferate. Societies that are deeply and dangerously fractured, by contrast, tend to repress conflict if the stakes are serious enough. Conflict that, once unleashed, will inevitably lead to bloodshed or war is often kept under a lid until it finally boils over; people in totalitarian states make every effort to keep their dissenting views to themselves, and will even act "as if" they support the regime.[10] The later twentieth century certainly saw both situations following the collapse of authoritarian states, but one can observe similar conflict avoidance in other social groups, including religious communities.

Conflict may not just be a sign that people feel free to dissent and disagree but may in some instances reflect a deeper agreement or solidarity between the groups in conflict. Thus, Simmel argues, two persons may be deeply opposed to each other in a property dispute litigated in court. But their fight may also demonstrate their agreement over property rights themselves, and mark a shared commitment to the legitimacy of the court to adjudicate their competing claims. This observation has the interesting implication that there may be considerable unity, or at least agreement, even where it is neither recognized nor felt in the midst of conflict and disagreement.

Simmel further suggests that difference, disagreement, and even overt conflict can provide a source of unity for a group, so long as the differences and divisions, disagreements and fractures running through the group are crisscrossing and thus always potentially at cross-purposes with one another. Modern individualism is misunderstood if we take it to mean that each person is an island; rather, as Simmel observes, all have multiple affiliations, interests, concerns, and commitments, and it is the constellation of our relations that make us individuals. Thus we may have particular identities (and corresponding interests) as members of a profession, religious community, social class, ethnicity, gender, political organization, and so on, or we may be a follower of a sports team, a fan of a particular musician, or committed to a particular charity, to name but a few of the many possibilities. The individual is born of the fact that she will share all of her identifications with few others, but each of her identifications (and corresponding interests) will be shared with many others. Because people have these crisscrossing networks of identities and interests, when a conflict of interest breaks out, it is unlikely to divide the society as a whole into warring parts. Rather, such disagreement may well become a source of energy, innovation—even stability. So difference may be a source of both solidarity and conflict, but it is unlikely to result in all-out civil war, for example—unless, of course, *there are not enough sources of difference*. Seen from this point of view, too little diversity of identity and difference can result in a precarious state of affairs. A setting in which groups are deeply opposed to one another, with little crossover between them, can be the seed of situations much more dangerous. To the extent that one identity or concern dominates, creating a clear sense of "us and them," conditions become ripe for secession, revolution, civil war, or even, extreme cases, genocide.

In what follows, we demonstrate that conflict and disagreement have shaped Anglican forms of organization, particularly in the time since the power of the Crown could no longer be relied upon to guarantee the church's coherence globally. At the same time, the leadership of the Anglican Communion has become less homogenous, and some of the older working assumptions about how the church should operate are no longer universally shared. Nevertheless, we argue, Anglicanism is connected by a manifold set of relationships that Bishop Mathew describes, using a metaphor of which Simmel would certainly approve, as a "spilt bowl of spaghetti." We use some of Simmel's ideas on church and sect to look at differences between more churchly and more sect-like organizations within provinces and how they manage difference. We argue that there are different models of more church-oriented provinces, particularly in the more democratic culture of TEC and the "indirect" culture and organization of the Church of England. These differences are seldom acknowledged but represent a significant source of tension within the Communion, both within and between provinces.

Conflict and the Social Forms of the Anglican Communion

Simmel's theory of conflict and unity in religion and social life is useful for looking at the growth of Anglicanism, as well as at its present structures and dynamics. The Anglican Communion was born largely by accident rather than by conscious design, and it has grown and adjusted to changing global and local circumstances, which has resulted in a complex set of institutional arrangements and informal relations. The expanding British Empire took chaplains to the farthest corners of the world, and missionaries sometimes even ventured well beyond the boundaries of the empire (though the empire sometimes followed). Even in missions, there was little by way of coordinated planning: arguably, the defining characteristic of Anglican missions in the nineteenth century was the competition between groups with rather different understandings of what it meant to be Anglican, and different relations to the empire.[11] The high-church missions, exemplified by the Society for the Propagation of the Gospel (SPG), wanted much more independence from temporal rule than the Church Missionary Society's (CMS's) Evangelical missionaries did; Evangelicals were much more inclined to promote a Christian society within a Christian state, both at home and abroad.[12]

The Crown and Parliament were important scaffolding for the stability of the Church of England, but this marks a difference between the Church of England and other Anglican churches, even within the British Isles. The Church of England was the established church in England; in Scotland, Episcopalians were a minority, their Jacobite sympathies often seen as a threat, and they were subject to legal prosecution and even imprisonment for much of the eighteenth century.[13] For this reason, the church had to develop governance structures that did not rely upon the state for its support. Later, as Scottish national identities took hold, Episcopalians had to work hard to disavow their reputation as the "English Kirk."[14] The Church of Ireland and the Church in Wales were seen by many Irish and Welsh in their respective nations as *English* establishments; both were consequently disestablished under political pressure in 1869 and 1920, respectively.[15] The American Revolution, of course, brought its own difficulties for Anglicans in territories that seceded from Great Britain, and the American Protestant Episcopal Church needed, as a matter of some urgency, to develop a religious form independent of establishment by the state;[16] many of its innovations to this end (like the election of bishops rather than their appointment by the Crown) have subsequently been adopted across the Communion. In short, Communion has from the start been something of a jumble of different kinds of churches in different kinds of relations with society and the state apparatus. Today, all member churches (with the qualified and limited exception of England) taking the form of a denomination are unable (even if they had the desire) to exercise a religious monopoly within the geographic boundaries of their provinces.

Relations between provinces have also developed in a distinctly ad hoc fashion, born as much of responses to tension and conflict as of deliberate design.[17] Many of the senior church leaders we interviewed suggested that the recent conflict over homosexuality has brought Anglicans world-wide into much more significant relationship with one another than before. A Canadian, Bishop Simon, describes the international fellowship of the Anglican Communion as something that many Anglicans in his province have only discovered or connected with as a result of recent disputes. This has led many to come to the conclusion that "we are actually interrelated in a new global way." His neighbor to the south, Bishop Cecil (TEC), also felt that the Communion had only become real for many of the faithful in TEC because of the sharp disagreements between and within provinces, echoing some of Reverend Shultz's suggestions with which we began this chapter. In contrast to Bishop Simon and Reverend Shultz, however, Bishop Cecil seemed much more ambivalent about the experience of global interrelations:

> I think it's important to remember that in some real sense—I don't mean this, you know, in a flippant way—but the Anglican Communion has, . . . in one sense, come into being over this issue. That is to say, I don't think there's an Episcopalian prior to 2003 who could have given you more than a one-sentence definition of what the Communion was. It was just not on people's radar screens. I think it came into being as something to be valued or resisted after [the election of Gene Robinson], and when the conservatives in the Episcopal Church realized that they could no longer, as they have done for centuries, get their way legislatively, they turned to the Anglican Communion, and the more conservative parts of it, to try to achieve what they could not achieve here. And so the Anglican Communion rarely plays a part in the lives of everyday Christians here but now, everyone knows about it. . . . Everyone has an opinion about it.

Bishop Cecil argues that conservative Episcopalians looked abroad for allies in their fight against what they saw as the liberal hegemony in TEC (a claim that resonates with Miranda Hassett's findings), and that this meant that the Anglican Communion only then "came into being" for many Episcopalians who weren't really aware of it before. The bishop added, however, that dis-covering the Communion does not necessarily mean liking it. He went on to suggest, in fact, that TEC's commitment to the inclusion of LGBTQ persons could mean that TEC might have to "go its own way" if the newly discovered Communion took a strong stand against their inclusion. A bishop cannot simply abandon gay and lesbian Episcopalians because church leaders in other parts of the world find them unacceptable, he argued, echoing sentiments we heard over and over again, particularly, but by no means exclusively, from leaders in the American church.

If one takes a cursory look at the history of global Anglicanism in the past two centuries, much of its international infrastructure has developed to address the various crises, tensions, strains, and conflicts that have erupted. The first Lambeth meeting of bishops in 1867 had been proposed a number of years earlier by Canadian bishops, and would have included only the churches of England and British colonies, not the Scottish or American churches.[18] Much of the impetus for the meeting was the fact that in many of the colonies, the churches were becoming (where they had not already become) effectively disestablished (a challenge that had already been addressed by the Episcopal churches of Scotland and the United States). The authority of archbishops and bishops to make decisions and enforce them without recourse to English law had become increasingly problematic. The difficulties were brought to the fore when Robert Gray, archbishop of Cape Town, tried to remove Bishop William Colenso from office, citing his authority as the metropolitan, as evidenced by his letters patent.[19] The Privy Council refused to recognize the authority of letters patent outside England (though they did hear Colenso's appeal against his deposition, which suggested to the episcopate that their days of being able to rely on English law to uphold their authority and enforce church order abroad were numbered).[20]

When what was to become the decennial Lambeth Conference did first meet, it did include the Scottish and American churches, and it was explicitly set up as a *conference*—not as a synod or council with enforceable decision-making powers. This reflected a significant disagreement among leaders at the time; two quite different worries coming from two quite different quarters of the church held sway. Some senior bishops had concerns about the legality of a synod not called by the monarch, and feared that such a synod would compromise royal supremacy. Several Evangelical bishops also objected to anything that might resemble a synod or council out of fears that such a body could undermine the status of the Thirty-Nine Articles, or set up a rival authority to that of scripture.[21] The point of the conference was thus limited to being an occasion for bishops to *confer*, and although they passed resolutions, there was no question of their being binding on the provinces.

Two subsequent "Instruments of Communion," the Anglican Consultative Council (1971–) and the Primates' Meeting (1978–), have also sought to promote interprovincial cooperation and fellowship. These emerged largely in response to interprovincial tensions, particularly disagreements over the ordination of female priests and bishops (as we discussed in chapter 1). For some church leaders, these developments were unacceptable in and of themselves; others were more concerned that female clergy could threaten interchangeability of ministry between one province and another, as different provinces took different positions, or moved at different paces, in relation to the ordained ministry of women in the church. Both of these institutions, along with the office of the archbishop of Canterbury and the Lambeth Conference, have attempted to provide the bonds that kept the Communion cinched together and global centrifugal forces contained. And yet, as many observers have noted, the structures as they have developed seem quite inadequate.

Exaggerating somewhat for effect, Bishop Timothy highlighted the apparent inadequacy of the Instruments of Communion:

> You've probably worked out already that the nature of the structure of the Anglican Communion is that it is impossible—you simply can't run an organization in the same way the Anglican Communion runs. You just can't do it. But we do it. It's part of our glory.
>
> And so why is it impossible? Well, because you can't have autonomy within Communion. So what we have is thirty-seven provinces [*sic*] which are autonomous but which are in Communion and the structures which hold that together—the four Instruments of Communion—are flimsy. Flimsy!

Part of the reason for this flimsiness is that the structures and rules that connect provinces to one another do not reach very far into the provinces themselves, which maintain their own autonomous decision-making processes and structures of authority. Any significant interprovincially agreed policy, in order to take effect locally, would require changes to each and every province's own canons.

> And so you're in the situation where [in my province, as in a number of others] there is simply nothing in our rule book, in our polity, which would prevent us [from electing] a partnered gay person as a bishop. The only thing which would prevent us is our understanding of the consequences of that for the Anglican Communion as a whole. So the structures can't possibly cope with the stresses which they're being put under—but even if the structures were really strong, they still probably couldn't cope with it. But clearly this kind of issue pushes the coherence of the Communion to its very limits.

Georg Simmel would suggest that, given the autonomy of the different provinces, each with a different context for mission, each with its own local form and its own constitution and canons, we should expect disagreement to be a normal state of affairs, and for serious tension to arise from time to time within the global church. It is undoubtedly true that the current institutional arrangements for managing disagreement do not seem to be functioning particularly well, but as Bishop Timothy suggests, it is entirely possible that stronger Communion-level institutions might not help the church cope any better. We raise the question below whether, on the contrary, stronger, centralized decision-making power might intensify tensions, creating a fracture line along which the Communion could be effectively fragmented. While attempts were made during the course of our research to formulate and ratify an "Anglican covenant," those efforts broke down over concerns about provincial autonomy, on the one hand, and the loss of support from some GAFCON leaders who felt that such a covenant would be too weak to constrain the actions of provinces with which they disagreed, on the other (see chapter 6).

The Challenge and Opportunity of a Diverse Communion with a Shared Identity

The changing demographics of global Anglicanism have undoubtedly made for a more diverse Communion, but within that diversity there remains both a very strong commitment to an Anglican-Episcopal identity and new opportunities for unity within diversity. When we spoke to him following the Lambeth Conference in 2008, Bishop Timothy noted this growing diversity within the global church's leadership, as evidenced by the bishops attending the conference:

> We've just put the photograph of 680 bishops from Lambeth [2008] to be framed. Well, if you go back, say, twenty years and look at that picture, you're looking substantially at a group of white, middle-aged, middle-class, First World men, many of them Oxbridge educated. . . . You're looking at a group of people who come out of the same culture and environment, that are academically trained and think in very linear terms and who have a shared worldview. Who are probably living in some measure in a colonial or postcolonial mindset, which means that the

Anglican Communion is Anglocentric. And that just isn't the case at all [anymore]. You're dealing with a very heterodox, polyglot Communion where the center is not in England.

One could say that such an increase of diversity has heightened the challenges of cohesion within the church, but this is not Bishop Timothy's point. Rather, he argues that much of the unity previously experienced was actually homogeneity in terms of background and in the universal use of the Book of Common Prayer for the liturgy, which he thinks of as unity of form rather than of substance. He explains,

> In the "good old days," in the days when everybody used the Book of Common Prayer, which of course is another piece that we've lost . . . if you know the Book of Common Prayer, the morning prayer—if you walked into any church in any part of the world, [you knew the liturgy]. . . . That, actually, in terms of worship, there was this extraordinary unity which we've now lost. So therefore the unity, cohesion, and uniformity across Anglicanism was rooted in things which were second order. They were probably form rather than substance. The form was so solid that the substance just looked after itself.
>
> Now we've lost many of the things of form which give unity. The presence of bishops wearing purple shirts with crosses around their necks, curiously enough, is one. And Rowan Williams jokes about the Mothers' Union as being the fifth Instrument of Unity in the Anglican Communion, probably the most effective one, and there's a degree of truth to that.[22] But we've lost bits of visible uniformity, and so we're left struggling with other issues which are really hard to handle which have surfaced.

Even if many of the formal sources of unity and the social homogeneity of the episcopate have gone, there nevertheless does seem to be something that holds the Communion together in spite of its flimsy structures and sometimes strongly divergent views. This is what Bishop Timothy was referring to as part of the "glory" of Anglicanism.

When we asked Canon Adrian if he thought that the Communion itself was falling apart in light of what appeared to be, at the time, the imminent death of the proposals for an Anglican covenant, he responded, "Well, I don't think so, really—it's enormous and it's complex, but there is an immense enthusiasm from a wide range of people who want to hold this community together. I mean, it's a voluntary Communion; therefore, if people don't want to be part of it, they just go away, but there is something there." Making a gesture with his hands as if his fingers were connected by an elastic web, as in a cat's cradle,[23] he explained, "There's some invisible bands that keep bringing it back together again."

> Why did . . . [*pause*] . . . so [*longer pause*] . . . Stephen Bates, who writes for the *Guardian*, has talked endlessly about the complete disintegration of the Anglican Communion, and yet something still holds us together. Mouneer Anis, the bishop of Egypt and presiding bishop of Jerusalem and the Middle East, he's given up on the Anglican Communion and yet he was at a meeting talking about Christian-Muslim relations on behalf of the Anglican Communion, working with Anglican Communion people. What is it that still keeps us coming back, then? Bob Duncan [former primate of ACNA] wants to leave . . . the Episcopal Church . . . but he still wants to be in the Anglican Communion. That is something really deep-seated about this, which is really . . . kind of hard to understand as normally being given a title such as "bonds of affection."

Even where church leaders have seceded from their province (as the ACNA Anglicans have done), or very publicly quit the Anglican Consultative Council (on whose steering committee the presiding bishop of Jerusalem and the Middle East previously sat), or even when they have set up a rival interprovincial organization (as the leaders of GAFCON did), they all continue to claim to be part of the "Worldwide Anglican Communion." Congregations that have left the Episcopal Church or the Anglican Church of Canada can, in fact, often be most readily identified by the prominence they give to signage in front of their churches announcing their membership in the "Worldwide Anglican Communion." This is the case even if they are currently recognized as such by only a very limited number of provinces and are not officially recognized by any of the Instruments of the Anglican Communion (and so technically are not part of the Anglican Communion at all). It may be that these signs are simply seen as good advertising, providing the church with a marker of status, but it is just as likely that they indicate a real, often rediscovered, commitment to the Anglican tradition. We noticed this in our visits to different Anglican churches in the course of our research. At one Canadian Evangelical Anglican church now part of ACNA, familiar to us for a number of years, one finds manifold signs of the church (re)discovering—and becoming much less ambivalent about—its Anglican heritage. Between leaving its previous church building (owned by the diocese) and setting up shop in much less fitting rental accommodations, one of the most immediately visible signs was that the clergy had started wearing clerical collars. In this and many similar Evangelical churches, these collars would previously have been viewed with suspicion by many of the parishioners, who would have expected their church leaders to wear dress shirts and chinos (neckties optional, and probably only expected at funerals). Services have likewise become more clearly and self-consciously liturgical; their reappropriation of Anglican heritage may be selective, but it is undoubtedly sincere, and it has apparently been enhanced in the wake of recent conflicts in the Communion.

Identity, Difference, and the Noodles of Communion

Looking out over the Thames as he stirred his coffee, Bishop Mathew, an Evangelical, seemed surprisingly sanguine about the future of global Anglicanism. The reason for his hopefulness, he explained, is that he is convinced that the Anglican Communion's real strength lies not in the Instruments of Unity but in the many thousands of other, often less official links that connect the faithful all around the globe. Using a metaphor that fits perfectly with Simmel's analysis of unity and conflict, Bishop Mathew explained that, in his view,

> the church has [long] been something like a spilt bowl of spaghetti; it was a bit chaotic and had crisscrossing relationships in every direction. The covenant is really trying to constrain and organize that chaos, whereas there is real strength in the looseness and in the crisscrossing spaghetti-like relationships. . . . This is the real strength of the Anglican Communion, as an international organization that consists of loosely structured relationships and is not, like other international organizations, structured by money and power (at least in the same way and to the same extent, or at least when it works).

These "crisscrossing" informal relationships unite the Communion in a more flexible but also more powerful way than the official Instruments of Communion do, and so, for Bishop Mathew, are much to be preferred to the neatly arranged straight lines that are proposed by some leaders, including advocates of the Anglican covenant. It is the strength of this jumble of informal, overlapping, and crisscrossing relationships that provides hope for the future of the Communion, at least in the long run. "I don't foresee a cataclysmic fallout," Bishop Mathew continued,

> even with GAFCON. I've been thinking to myself about this the last few days, and I'll say it to you. I keep thinking: "So what?" The Evangelicals have always had their conferences, so have the Anglo-Catholics, and so forth. So now we've also got GAFCON. We've got people trying to organize the strands of that spilt spaghetti, taking some of the noodles out and arranging them in neat lines. Who knows, maybe it's just a matter of time before someone comes and stirs it all back in again.

Bishop Mathew's culinary metaphor is useful for thinking about the ad hoc mess of intertwined relationships that make up the global Anglican Church. Even if some end up "out" of the Communion, who is to say that they won't be stirred back in again? The metaphor highlights the relational ties that connect and bind beyond the structures developed explicitly for that purpose, and it does effectively convey the futility of attempts to organize the various strands into straight lines, or to take measures to define clearly who is "in" and who is "out" of the Communion.

The idea that the church has, or ought to have, clear boundaries is itself not universally accepted in many provinces of the Anglican Communion, though this matter is probably most complicated in England as a consequence of establishment. Speaking with us at the time of the GAFCON meeting in Jerusalem, Bishop Mark explained:

> The people meeting at GAFCON are trying to define [what] the shape of doctrine should be, who's in and who's out, and that's something that the C of E has never really done. The edges have always been fuzzy—the C of E has never been very dogmatic about this. . . . The church has always had relatively fluid boundaries with respect to society. And that's partly [due to the legal status of the church by law established], but it's also partly based on a theology that recognizes that God is bigger than the church and operates outside the church. Um, and this now comes into a world where people are much more keen to know, "are you a Christian or not, are you a Muslim or not, are you a Republican or not"

. . . all of those sort of things. Living with uncertain boundaries is not easy for some people.

What Bishop Mark described echoes Simmel's understanding of a "church" rather than a "sect." The Church of England has long recognized the legitimacy of other churches and religious communities in the same territory (which for sociologists of religion is the defining characteristic of a "denomination"), and has lost many of the privileges of establishment.[24] Nevertheless, these churchly values were clearly formed during the period when the church and nation were, at least legally and as an implicit working assumption, consonant. Others, particularly those who think of the church in more sectarian terms, are convinced that the church's open and fluid boundaries, which refuse to separate the sheep from the goats, constitute one of its most serious fundamental flaws. Surely, they remark, the answer to the question "Are you Christian or not?" is not merely incidental to a Christian church.

Unity in Diversity, Uniformity, and the Structures That Make Them Possible

Different approaches to the form of the Christian community imply different organizational requirements, particularly in terms of how power is centralized or distributed. This is the argument that Bishop Peter put to us, identifying what he sees as two different approaches in the Anglican Communion:

> I was in Nigeria last year, and I was talking to [one of the senior church leaders there], and, in a sense, we were just reflecting that Nigeria as a province has a much, much greater uniformity among the dioceses than you would ever get in England, and possibly in Scotland, brought about, I suppose, by Bishop Crowther[25] in the last century, that gave very distinctive shape to the church in Nigeria. So there's a greater uniformity among the dioceses.
>
> For me, there are two Anglican Communions at present. There's the Anglican Communion that looks to a significant uniformity among the dioceses of a province, a wider area, archetypally Nigeria, and a Communion that looks to find a way of containing diversity—the Church of England would be an example of that, but the canonical structures of the church are traditionally geared to the containing of diversity

and the avoiding of conflict, but the avoiding of conflict can have significant diversity. So you have two different models: one where you have uniformity and the other where you have the containment of diversity as being the key. And so they're open questions, really.

Some provinces opt for unity in diversity (generally speaking, a "church" model), while other provinces (but also some congregations and a few dioceses) think about unity as uniformity, at least in their public presentations (a "sect" model). While these are provincial modes of organization, they undoubtedly shape the way leaders from different types of provinces think about the relations that make up the global Communion. As he elaborated on his understanding of the different types of provinces in the Communion, Bishop Peter argued that the model of the church as uniform is built upon, and probably requires, much more hierarchical power relations. He explained that such churches have "an expectation of uniformity" that sets the ideal, and primates have much more power to enforce that uniformity within the province:

> I think everyone knows that when Akinola [then the primate of Nigeria] is at a meeting, he'll say, "Nigeria thinks . . . ," and he'll tell them. If the presiding bishop of the States is at a meeting, he cannot as easily say, "The American Episcopal Church thinks . . . ," because there is diversity [within TEC]. The archbishop of Canterbury cannot say, "England thinks . . ." The primate of Scotland cannot say, "Scotland thinks . . . ," because [those churches] welcome the fact that there is significant diversity [within the province]. But I think you'll get those primates that will deem themselves [entitled] to speak for the province. And within the province, bishops will see themselves under a measure of obligation to voice the views of their archbishop. [But,] you see, if Rowan Williams [former archbishop of Canterbury] speaks on a particular thing, he would not necessarily expect the bishop of Rochester [at the time, Michael Nazir-Ali, who boycotted Lambeth in 2008] to follow suit because his archbishop has said it—same in Scotland and the same in the [United] States.

The constitutional authority of archbishops and primates differs quite significantly from province to province, and in provinces where they are given more power, this does seem to result in more *publicly* uniform views compared with what one encounters in private conversation, or in a confidential interview, as we often discovered.[26] Even in Nigeria, Uganda, and Kenya, often seen as among the more "uniform" provinces (as Bishop Peter argues), one finds leaders holding a surprisingly wide range of views on the controversies around sexuality. Few bishops in these nations take a public position in favor of the legitimacy of same-sex relations for Christians (though we spoke to church leaders in these countries who privately expressed their qualified endorsement of such a position); it is not at all uncommon, however, to find bishops in these regions who do not wish to break fellowship with provinces that bless gay and lesbian members and their relationships, and who quietly hold this view against the official stance of their GAFCON-affiliated primate.

Simmel argues that there is an inherent limit to the size of a sect; at a certain point, it becomes impossible to maintain uniformity without schism. Some of the provinces that aspire to uniformity in belief and practice (sect-like denominations, in our terms), however, are among the numerically largest in the Communion. When Simmel wrote about limits to the size of sects, he had in mind religious groups with a relatively nonhierarchical formal structure, as is typical of true sects.[27] We contend that sect-like aspirations for uniformity can be realized at the level of the province only where there is strong, centralized control. In a number of Anglican provinces, including those with the most sect-like inclinations, the authority (or legitimate power) of primates relative to the rest of the bishops is considerable. For primates, this can include the power to appoint and depose bishops; it is therefore not surprising that they can exert disproportionate influence on the publicly expressed "uniform" views of the churches in their province. Bishop Simon described a scene he witnessed at Lambeth in 2008 to illustrate the difference between provinces: "I saw at Lambeth a bishop from one province come up to the microphone, and the primate of that province just with a finger waved him away from the microphone. That simply wouldn't happen in Canada. If one of the Canadian bishops had moved up, and our primate sort of motioned that they should sit down, there would be a different finger raised." The suggestion that a Canadian bishop would "give the finger" to the primate of the Anglican Church of Canada is not to say that Archbishop Fred Hiltz enjoys anything but the full respect of the bishops in that province. But the anecdote does make clear that a Canadian bishop would not be silenced like this, nor would the primate of Canada attempt to silence that bishop. Much the same is true in England, the United States, Australia, and, a fortiori, Scotland, where the bishops operate as a college and the power of the primate is no greater than that of any other bishop, though the primate takes on more responsibilities in representing the province abroad. The differences in primatial authority across provinces (and in a few cases within provinces) have been a source of considerable misunderstanding,[28] and are themselves a source of friction among those who have sought to bring the recent crisis to some sort of resolution.

Differences in the organization of power among provinces are not limited to the primate's relationship to the bishops; there are also vast differences in the power of bishops in relation to their clergy. These power differentials can result in misunderstandings, and sometimes in bafflement. Bishop James told us about a conversation he had with two other bishops, one from Africa and one from North America.

> We were talking about making appointments of new pastorates and so on, and at one point [the African bishop] stopped us and said, "Do you mean that neither of you actually appoint priests to a congregation?" And we said, "That's right. The choice is made by their vestry, or whatever." And he said, "Well, how can you work as bishops if you don't have power to appoint people?"
>
> This is a completely different way, illustrating the different culture. Things just do work differently. So you've got this definitely hierarchical culture—which is just different. I mean, we've had experience of this in the past—it's not where we are at the moment—but it's where many nations are still in other continents.

While Bishop James alludes to cultural differences, culture is made concrete and durable in the constitution, canons, and accepted practices and procedures of the province (often structured in relation to secular law).[29] Thus one of our respondents, having expressed his surprise at the limited power of bishops in TEC (United States) relative to his own authority in the Anglican Church of Australia, where most bishops have veto power in the synod, went on to compare his own role in leadership with how he is seen by church leaders elsewhere. "You talk to African bishops . . . or bishops from Melanesia, and they think that bishops like me are weaklings. . . . They can't believe we are being encumbered by the kind of democratic and consensus building and taking account of attitudes of people, respectful of a minority position. They don't kind of get that." In some churches, those democratic processes (which are not necessarily the same thing, we note below, as respect for a minority position) are considered absolutely essential, both in the legal framework and in those provinces' self-understanding. Episcopalians in the United States, in particular, are firmly committed to their democratic traditions, expressing exasperation that leaders in the Church of England will regularly refer to the "appointment" of bishops in TEC, when they are elected by the synod in their dioceses. American Episcopalians have expressed serious concerns about international church discussions and decisions being made by bishops alone (such as at Lambeth or the Primates' Meeting), when within TEC significant policy cannot be enacted by the House of Bishops without being authenticated by the House of Deputies (thus including representatives of both clergy and laity in decision making). Little wonder, then, that American Episcopalians view the international conversations at Primates' Meetings and Lambeth Conferences as "incomplete at best" (Bishop Cecil).

Different Models for Containing Diversity: The United States vs. England

Such differences begin to bring under the spotlight significant variation between provinces, even between those that "contain difference" on the more "churchly" model but do so in different ways. For purposes of thinking about different approaches for containing diversity within Simmel's "church" model, it is useful to compare how the Church of England and the Episcopal Church (U.S.) deal with the reality of gay clergy and bishops, and how they have approached the question of blessing same-sex unions in the church. The differences between these provinces undoubtedly reflect both cultural norms and the different positions of these churches in their own contexts. Their differently structured approaches to "containing difference" have themselves sometimes become an additional source of tension, irrespective of the substantive issues in question. We might refer to the American version of the churchly model as transparent and democratic, and the English model as "indirect," following an observation by Richard Sennett, an American sociologist and longtime resident of Britain. Early in his first extended stay in London, Sennett noticed that "discussions were couched in terms of 'possibly' and 'perhaps' and 'I would have thought.' . . . The Brits proved themselves skilled masters in the use of the subjunctive mood." He argues that the subjunctive mood lends itself to diplomacy, because it "is an antidote to polarized positions. The subjunctive mood counters Bernard Williams's fear of the fetish of assertiveness by opening up instead an indeterminate mutual space, the space in which strangers dwell with one another, whether these strangers be immigrants and natives thrown together in a city of gays and straights living in the same street. The social engine is oiled when people do not behave too emphatically."[30] Bishop Simon, a Canadian diocesan bishop, expressed his frustration with how both English and American churches have dealt with the question of same-sex marriage (or the blessing of same-sex unions), and in so doing provided an interesting description of those two models of the church, putting a less positive spin than we have here on the differing styles:

> The English Church I would critique as being hypocritical and fractured. There are things that we do not do or allow in [this diocese] that are just regular occurrences in many dioceses in England, and yet we get blamed for stuff that we're not doing. [At an international meeting, someone I know] was asked how many same-sex marriages [we] did. [This person] said, "Well, that's not allowed. We don't do same-sex marriages in the Canadian Church." "Well, so how many have you presided at and been to?" And [this person] said, "Well, I haven't been to any."
>
> And yet there are same-sex blessings happening in the Diocese of London and many other places all the time. . . . There are people committed in active gay relationships living in English rectories. . . . It really annoys me—that sense of superiority that the English have about situations that happen all the time. And I think what they sometimes resent is that the Americans haven't just . . . allowed it to happen quietly. They want to be transparent about it. The Americans want everything transparent. And I think there's a nice, medium place. And the English policy is "Don't ask, don't tell, and just pretend it's not happening," and as long as it's not frightening the horses . . .

While it is not hard to see some stereotyping of national cultures in this narrative, there is no question that it broadly reflects different provincial practices for the management of diverse beliefs and practices within broad church provinces. These stem not only from national cultures but also from the place of the church in different contexts, particularly for the Church of England as the "church by law established."[31]

Dean Oliver was happy to confirm the general picture painted by Bishop Simon of the place of gay clergy in his diocese and in other Church of England dioceses:

> I mean, this diocese would collapse if it weren't for the gay clergy. I would reckon that probably as many as a third of the clergy . . . is gay.

[Interviewer: Because it's kind of a haven for a gay clergy?]

Well, it's a . . . so is . . . any inner city diocese—(a) because living in a city gives you a relative anonymity . . . and (b) because it's very hard to get—particularly in deprived areas—to get a nice, white, middle-class parish priest with two and a half children and a dog and a packet of corn flakes to go and work there, not least because they worry about the standard of the schooling for their children. But the gay clergy will go there. So, for example, the East End of London . . . has been uniformly populated with gay clergy for generations.

Many gay, and subsequently lesbian, priests long had to hide from their parishioners, caught between their beliefs about a God who accepted them and an institutional church that did not. In other congregations, this side of the priest's life has simply been avoided in the parish.[32] Even in parishes where "Father's friend," is the semiofficial moniker for the priest's same-sex partner, the nature of the relationship usually remained unspoken. In other contexts, this implicit "don't ask, don't tell" policy within the parish community is breaking down, perhaps in part because of broader acceptance of same-sex relationships in the church and society, but also because the question of homosexuality has become an increasingly, and perhaps inescapably, public one in and for the church.[33] Dean Oliver stressed that there was more openness than before in many of his parishes, and he even argued that some parishes express a preference for a gay priest in the vicarage:

> You know, there are parishes in the diocese who will openly say to us, "We want a gay priest." And when you say to them, "Why?" they say, "They've got more time, they are more flexible." . . . I mean, a lot of the Roman Catholic arguments, actually. . . . And "they are flexible, they're terribly dedicated to what they're doing. We couldn't give a hang what goes on in their bedroom. But we know, you know, they have a sense of style, and a real sense of vocation because, actually, you wouldn't be a gay priest if you didn't have a sense of vocation because one isn't going to bang your head against a brick wall all your life for no reward and no recognition, unless . . . you are driven by a sense of vocation."

The appointment of gay bishops gets more attention than that of priests, partly because of their authority in the diocese and their hoped-for capacity to act as a unifying force, as in the election of Gene Robinson in New Hampshire and the appointment of Jeffrey John in the Diocese of Oxford. Nobody could have been under the illusion that Dean John would have been the first gay bishop in the Church of England.[34] It seems to have been John's openness about his personal life—his partnership with another man in a celibate relationship— and his public advocacy for the church blessing of same-sex unions that was the source of the controversy, or at least the reason it could be used effectively by a group that wanted to make an issue of it (see chapter 2).

In September 2016, thirteen years after the controversy over Jeffrey John's nomination, another minor controversy erupted over the personal life of Nicholas Chamberlain, the recently appointed suffragan bishop of Grantham in the Diocese of Lincoln. Following an implied threat from a Sunday news-paper, Chamberlain decided to come out publicly about his sexual orientation and relationship status: the bishop was in a celibate, committed long-term relationship with another man, with whom he had been living for some time. In one sense, there was no story. Everyone involved in the appointment the previous year, including the archbishop of Canterbury, had been aware of Bishop Chamberlain's sexual orientation and relationship status, which were within the parameters of the House of Bishops' pastoral guidance on same-sex marriage. Despite the headlines, Bishop Chamberlain was not the first bishop known to be gay and in a celibate relationship with another man.[35]

Somewhat more interesting than the nonstory were the responses to it. Some of these were predictable, but they were nevertheless instructive. For example, GAFCON Global and GAFCON UK released a joint state-ment saying that the "secrecy" of Bishop Chamberlain's relationship in the appointment process was "a serious cause for concern for biblically orthodox Anglicans around the world" and that the appointment had been "a major error."[36] Mirroring GAFCON's response, the Lesbian and Gay Christian Movement welcomed the news but expressed regret "that Bishop Nick's rela-tionship, about which he speaks in such touching terms in the interview, was not acknowledged at the time of his appointment." The LGCM rightly noted that the Downing Street announcement of a straight person's nomination typi-cally includes information not only about the candidate's job qualifications but about his or her spouse, children and grandchildren, and even hobbies. No doubt the LGCM was well aware that had the announcement referred to Bishop Chamberlain's male partner, the appointment might have ended the same way that Jeffrey John's did. This may be precisely what the general secretary of GAFCON was upset about: the "secrecy" of the appointment prevented conservative critics from repeating their earlier successes.

The theme of secrecy dominates the LGCM press release, even in the concluding suggestions for prayer:

So tonight, please pray . . .
> . . . for Bishop Nick and those he loves, for the people of Lincoln diocese, those with whom and amongst whom he leads and serves . . .
> . . . for those who have an opportunity, now, to stand alongside him . . .
> . . . for those holding secrets and those trying to let them go . . .
> . . . for others who may be feeling fearful of their "secrets," especially the young and those whose safety is at risk . . .
> . . . for Jeffrey John and for Gene Robinson, who have trodden some parts of this path before . . .
> . . . for all those shining light into places of secrecy, that they might be granted wisdom and compassion . . .
> . . . for the presence of the Spirit within and between and amongst us, leading us into all truth, and to the truth that sets us free.[37]

This "secrecy" (or "confidentiality") of the episcopal appointment process in the Church of England is probably possible only as a function of establishment, though this is even more clearly the case where the vacancy of a diocesan rather than a suffragan see is being filled and where confidentiality is required by the Crown Nominations Commission.[38]

In the Episcopal Church, by contrast, while four candidates are nominated for consideration by the diocese, they are voted on locally in the diocese and one candidate is selected, sometimes after several rounds of voting. The elected candidate must then be approved by a majority of national leaders in order to be installed as bishop. It would be nearly impossible to run that kind of gauntlet while keeping key sensitive issues about one's private life in the shadows, nor would it be feasible to stay silent on topics that are important to different church constituencies. Candidates' views on gay marriage, and their understanding of the authority and interpretation of scripture, are thus likely to be interrogated if they are not already part of the public record. Episcopal elections and their national approval then become stakes in disagreements over the current and future policy of the church. While the Episcopalian model is undoubtedly more democratic than the English, the American record is not as strong on the question of protecting minority traditions (such as those who cannot accept the ordination of women). Indeed, Tocqueville's concerns about the "tyranny of the majority" were echoed in some of our interviews with American traditionalist Anglo-Catholics, in particular.[39] They tended to describe joining with the groups that became ACNA less as a decision to leave TEC than as an experience of being pushed out of TEC (Bishop Gregory) because their views had become unpopular in all but a few U.S. dioceses.

The contrast between the two churchly models in England and America holds not just for the question of ordination but also for the contentious question of blessing same-sex unions and marriage. In the name of "gracious restraint," the church held back for nearly a decade after the ordination of Gene Robinson as bishop of New Hampshire before developing and authorizing a liturgy for the blessing of same-sex unions (published in 2012). Three years later, the church changed its marriage canons to allow for the marriage of persons of the same sex. The new primate of the Episcopal Church quickly found himself on the hot seat when he was invited, with the other primates of the Anglican Communion and the primate of the Anglican Church in North America, to a meeting in Canterbury. The proceedings themselves were closed and the discussion confidential (after the English fashion), but at the end, the archbishop of Canterbury announced that since the Episcopal Church, in changing its marriage canons, had made a decision significantly at odds with "the majority" of provinces, the church would be barred from certain kinds of participation in the life of the Communion, and its members would be barred from representing the Communion in meetings with other churches and faith traditions.[40]

By contrast, although same-sex couples can be married in England, the law prohibits them from being married in the Church of England. This is not to say that there are no ceremonies to bless and celebrate the relationships of gay and lesbian couples in English parish churches or, indeed, cathedrals, as Bishop Simon suggested. There is considerable flexibility in canon law that allows various services to be held as a "pastoral" matter, which does not bear directly on doctrine—as some claim solemnizing marriages would do. Although they may look very much like them, these services are not same-sex "marriages," nor are they called services of "blessing" for couples of the same sex.[41] Nevertheless, some parishes quietly charge the standard fee for a marriage ceremony, passing on the appropriate portion to the Diocesan Board of Finance. This means that such services cannot have escaped the notice of the diocese and its bishop, who cannot mistake what these ceremonies entail. The general concern seems to be that they be "pastoral," that they not be called "marriage," and that not too much publicity attend them. Too much attention in the press (always hungry for a controversial story with good visuals) is seen as a deliberate snub of church teachings, though sometimes publicity is clearly sought—and given.[42] Little wonder, then, that some Episcopalians and Canadian Anglicans, like Bishop Simon, see the English church as "hypocritical and fractured."

There is no question that disagreement can be destructive or distracting to the mission of the church, but conflict is not necessarily unhelpful in and of itself. As Simmel has shown us, conflict and disagreement provide much of the dynamism and energy of social life, and are often the means by which organizations adapt to new circumstances. Diversity, he argues, can be a source of strength and unity; it nevertheless needs to be managed. Different parts of the Communion (we have focused here mostly on provinces) have developed different strategies for dealing with the diversity of beliefs and practices within the church, and for managing its place in, and relationship with, "the world." Simmel developed a useful, though not fully adequate, distinction between the church and the sect. We observed that while all the provinces of the Anglican Communion are "denominations" in their own contexts, some take a more "sectarian" approach to managing difference and diversity (as uniformity), and others a more "churchly" approach (containing diversity). Even within this more "churchly" option, we found distinctive approaches to managing difference, as exemplified by the approaches of the Episcopal Church and the Church of England.

Different ways of being a community of Anglican Christians in different contexts bring with them their own sources of tension. Tensions play out in different ways internally in different models, but they also set the expectations and understandings of how disagreement should work in the Communion. Many of those expectations come from the experience of living and working in a province that has a particular, though often not fully explicit, set of assumptions about how things work and how they ought to work. Part of the challenge for the Communion is that it has yet to find a way of managing the difference between provinces, each having its own means of managing internal diversity.

Some of those who have been pushing hard for a pan-Anglican uniformity of belief and practice, particularly the leaders of GAFCON, have approached the question from what Simmel would call a theology that aspires to form the church in the shape of a sect: they wish to establish firm, clear boundaries between the church and the world, and high levels of agreement in belief and practice, with the threat of expulsion for those who stray. But, as Simmel never tired of observing, certain social forms are possible only in relatively small groups: a true sect is really only possible in the long run in a small, localized community. While some of the provinces are able to lean in a more sect-like direction, much of their public uniformity depends on a strong centralization of power that it is difficult to imagine being replicated in the worldwide Communion. Simmel would no doubt contend that the Anglican Communion, with its tens of millions of members and adherents, is just too large to adopt that kind of sectarian approach.

In any case, the hardest substances are often the most fragile, prone to shattering when placed under strain. If the strong, rigid boundaries of the sect are unable to hold the Communion together, Anglicanism has many "churchly" concepts and traditions that could be drawn upon to maintain elastic, flexible, and fuzzy boundaries. Churches, however, in Simmel's sense, have had to rely on the power of the state in order to maintain their comprehensiveness and coherence. This is clearly no longer an option for Anglicans the world over; even in England, one wonders how long the church will maintain its privileged position, which is nevertheless a very long way from being a monopoly.[43] New ways of managing diversity and disagreement need to be explored and developed. In the chapters that follow, we turn to those attempts and the pitfalls that beset them.

6 | AUTHORITY, PRACTICE, AND ECCLESIAL IDENTITY

"I haven't heard you once actually say that you support us!—
that you accept us and that you will fight for us!" Such was the
lament of a young woman addressing the primate of Canada,
Fred Hiltz. The archbishop had been invited to meet with
LGBTQ Anglicans in the Diocese of Toronto in the wake of
the statement released by the primates at their gathering in
Canterbury in January 2016. The meeting of primates had
imposed measures against the Episcopal Church in the United
States for permitting the marriage of same-sex couples.[1] With
the Canadian General Synod set to debate the same issue a few
months later, many LGBTQ members were anxious to learn
what the head of their province thought about the situation.
As this young woman's complaint suggests, not all of the two
hundred people in attendance went home satisfied.

The primate began by offering an account of the gathering
in Canterbury and emphasized that he was "open to listening"
to the concerns and experiences of LGBTQ members of the
church. Most of his talk focused, as he put it, on "explaining where we are" on debates over the acceptance of same-sex
marriage, both at the international level of the Communion
and within the Canadian church. Although appreciative and
respectful toward Archbishop Hiltz, those who followed up
with questions soon began to voice their frustration. One
woman lamented that her teenage children "won't admit they
are Christian to their friends, because if they do, 'They'll think

we're homophobes!'" A man in his fifties shook with anger as he said, "The church is the most toxic place in my life. It's always a cloud over my head! This at a time when the rest of society has shifted and become more accepting!"

It was after an hour of such discussion that the young woman quoted above approached the microphone to ask whether her primate was willing to fight for her, as her mother stood beside her crying in anger and frustration. It was the last question of the evening. Archbishop Hiltz told the young woman that his personal views on homosexuality were "well known" but emphasized that his role as primate meant that his own position could not be decisive: "My office brings with it a responsibility to the whole church."[2]

This conversation between the primate of Canada and LGBTQ Anglicans in the Diocese of Toronto can be described using terms that we drew out of our fieldwork in the previous chapter. Archbishop Hiltz was clearly seeking to explain the "messiness" of the situation in the church, as he sought to clarify what the "spilt bowl of spaghetti" that is the Anglican Communion looks like from his vantage point. It was clear to us, however, as we listened and spoke with individuals afterward, that many were unsatisfied by such explanations. They had little patience for the complexity and diversity of their church; they wanted action, something to break the inertia of the situation. The majority wanted only to know whether their primate, as the young woman put it, "will fight for us."

This tension, between what many in the crowd desired from their church and what the primate was able to deliver, is another example of how the conflict in the Communion confronts church leaders with the need to balance (at least) two competing agendas. On the one hand, there are calls for greater normative clarity on the presenting issues of the moment; on the other hand, leaders face demands for wider inclusion in the processes that establish communal norms. Which of these two impulses one prioritizes shapes what one expects from church leaders. Some expect their leaders to offer a defense of clear normative principles or judgments; others want leadership that emphasizes unity and the inclusion of diverse voices and interests.

Archbishop Hiltz was emphasizing the second of these at that open session in Toronto, acknowledging the concerns of LGBTQ Anglicans but also those of opponents of same-sex marriage; and he was also trying to honor the pleas of some First Nations (indigenous) Anglican leaders in his province for more time "to study the issue."[3] Many in the audience, however, were demanding that the primate take a stand for them and their own normative position.

If the previous chapter highlighted ways in which conflict can sometimes contribute to holding a community together, the analysis in this chapter demonstrates how some of the traditional centripetal forces in the global church exhibit signs of weakening. Just as Archbishop Hiltz finds his role of serving "the unity of the church" under challenge, many other leaders and institutions in the Communion have been discovering that their efforts to deploy long-established practices to respond to tensions in the global church have, to date, had mixed results. Though by no means completely ineffective, such measures do not have the same centripetal force they once did.

In the face of this situation, many Anglicans have concluded that the choice open to them is between establishing more rigid, centralized authority or facing inevitable fragmentation and growing apart. Others propose alternative strategies, from instituting formal dialogue processes to calling upon their fellow church members to rejuvenate what they understand to be the traditional attitudes, manners, and habits that underlie the so-called bonds of affection.

This chapter analyzes such strategies, focusing in particular on the call for a common code of canon law for all provinces, the proposed Anglican covenant, and the "continuing *indaba*" process. We explore why proposals for achieving greater centralization in the global church have thus far been unsuccessful. We also look at the limitations of various dialogue processes in the life of the church, even as we argue that such initiatives have been the most successful mechanism attempted to date by Communion leadership. Finally, our analysis highlights tendencies that threaten to undermine the assumption that traditional "bonds of affection" are sufficient to hold together the churches of the Communion. Some have taken it for granted that Anglicans are becoming too different from one another to enable common backgrounds, liturgical practices, or basic "manners" to support a unified global church. These pressures encourage the rhetorical framing of individual leaders and regions in subtle but powerful ways and fuel the sort of polemical oppositions that leaders like Archbishop Hiltz have found themselves having to confront: "Are you with us or against us?" For leaders trying to hold together people of differing views, the intensification of such demands makes their task even more difficult.

Centralization or Relational Bonds?

The polemical intensity confronting the leaders of the Communion complicates the challenge of balancing the calls for greater normative clarity in church teachings and practices, on the one hand, with demands for greater access to decision-making processes within the global church, on the other. The leaders with whom we spoke across the Communion expressed this in different ways, though they were not always consistent as they did so, perhaps reflecting the real contradictions of trying to hold the two imperatives together. For example, according to Bishop John, "everything is a faith and order issue. There is a continuum between faith and order, but some issues are more towards the order end of that continuum." Such remarks do little to clarify the relationship Bishop John imagines between the particularities of church teaching (faith) and how the church ought to be organized (order), although he initially appeared to leave room for some diversity of opinion. On this point, Bishop John suggested that some disputes in the church can be mediated if there is "provision for those of us who feel that in conscience we cannot accept that. That becomes an order issue: how the life of the church is ordered." Here he implied that differences of belief can be incorporated by the church so long as a sufficiently flexible church order is permitted. He referred to the ordination of women as an example of such an issue. However, according to Bishop John, homosexuality is a matter of clear biblical teaching and thus requires correct normative belief. For this reason, he implied, belief trumps flexible church order in this case. At this point in our conversation, the bishop suddenly switched the terminology he'd been using, claiming that homosexuality represents a "first order" issue of belief and as such permits no compromise in the teaching or practice of the Communion. In his view, this implies the need for firmer authoritative control over the ordering of the global church: "Although we'll say that it's the standard of teaching in the church, people are allowed to dismiss it without any disciplinary action against them and that's what's caused the huge tension."

For those like Bishop Timothy, by contrast, what are often called the "bonds of affection" between Anglicans are what promise to hold the Communion together—not some required adherence to specific moral beliefs. He emphasized that "the depth of commonality among these churches which have almost nothing in common is really astonishing." "If you measured the future of the Anglican Communion," he continued, "not in terms of its structural resilience but in terms of the depth of relationships and the manifest desire to cohere, then you'd have to say that it does have a future." Clearly, the way Bishop Timothy thinks about tensions in the church has more to do with nurturing interpersonal relationships than it does with upholding what Bishop John calls "first order" doctrinal commitments.[4]

Our conversation with Bishop David revealed yet another perspective on the structures of the Communion. Although he emphasized a more immediate role for institutional bodies than did Bishop Timothy (and thus was more concerned with what Bishop John called proper "order"), in the end his position was much closer to Bishop Timothy's view than to Bishop John's. "I'm supporting the covenant and the Instruments of Communion to try to hold the Communion together," he told us, "but if that fails, then plan B, I think, has to go back to relationships, because relationships will continue in the complex ways that relationships and families do, whatever happens." In other words, although Bishop David hoped that the global church would be able to establish a clear and firm church order, he was prepared to accept that everything does not depend on the success of this goal. There is, in his view, a "plan B," which amounts to a trust that existing relationships are sufficiently robust to see the Communion through its present rough patch.

This emphasis on the importance of relationships, which many described as forging bonds of affection between different member churches of the Communion, was a recurrent theme in many of our interviews, to which we return below. Yet we also regularly encountered others who had little patience for the notion that relationships are an adequate and appropriate basis for ecclesial communion. Thus Bishop Christopher, like Bishop John, had no confidence in the unifying potential of relationships: "the previous kind of 'bonds of affection' approach doesn't work anymore in the world in which we live, and we need a more robust structure and procedures for making decisions where there is disagreement."

Like the tension between calls for greater normative clarity and for more widespread inclusion in decision making, the remarks of these four episcopal leaders highlight a related axis of disagreement in the Communion. At one pole are those who advocate greater formal institutional centralization, and at the other are those who emphasize the potential of relationship and dialogue and see these as the source of unity. Bishop Mark introduced metaphors of his own to describe this basic difference: "There are a couple of conceptual frameworks at work in the church right now. The first is pretty mechanistic and the other is organic." He suggested that "the way the Church of England operates is relational and organic," by dint of which it moves and changes slowly and gradually. By contrast, Bishop Mark argued, "Puritanism is mechanistic. There is one set of scriptures that one has to apply . . . almost algorithmic." In his view, "the conflict between them [these two understandings of the church] is particularly stark and dramatic."

With such a diverse range of attitudes among its leadership, it is little wonder that the Anglican Communion has been unable to achieve any semblance of consensus over how to respond to controversial issues like homosexuality. In what follows, we look at the more prominent initiatives and mechanisms that leaders of the Communion have employed to respond to such tensions. We examine two proposals for greater centralization: a recommendation for a universal code of canon law, and the mooted Anglican covenant. We then turn to various dialogue processes that have been initiated in the Communion. The discussion demonstrates that attempts to introduce greater centralization have thus far generated substantial resistance, effectively rendering such proposals unworkable. While the dialogue strategy has met with more widespread appreciation, there are also signs that significant numbers of people either feel shut out by the guiding assumptions of the process, or feel frustrated by its failure to yield firm decisions.

An Appeal for Universal Canon Law

One proposal for fostering more robust disciplinary authority within the Anglican Communion recommends that a common code of canon law be adopted by all member churches.[5] This was suggested by Norman Doe, professor of law at Cardiff University, to a meeting of the primates in March 2001.[6] Doe's position has the merit of drawing on a shared preexisting institutional mechanism, the concept of canon law, which he argues could be employed to establish a universal code of regulations adopted by all member churches. Such a step, he claims, would repair a gap in the normative foundation of Anglican unity. Although his proposal was largely rejected for failing to address the question of expanded participation in decision making, it is instructive to note the grounds upon which he builds his case.[7]

Doe distinguishes between two orders governing the life of churches: a "juridical order" of canon laws that have been formally adopted by a specific institutional body of the church, and a "moral order" of values and principles for which there are no binding legal frameworks. While the moral order is expressed through principles that often remain general and vague, the juridical order is characterized by its precision. In other words, Doe argues that in order to be effective, the church must operationalize its values and principles with the force of legal structures. The problem confronting the Anglican Communion, he continues, is that, at the global level, the Instruments of

Unity at present can exercise only moral persuasion, because they lack juridical procedures to draw upon when conflict erupts between member churches. "It is the exercise of autonomy," he argues, "the freedom afforded by the local juridical order, and the unenforceability of the moral order, that causes conflict."[8]

Doe compares the existing status of juridical canon law in the Anglican tradition, in which each member church establishes its own system independently, with the status of canons in the Roman Catholic Church, in which a universal code of canon law governs the internal affairs of all Catholic churches throughout the world. He suggests that, by contrast, the different Anglican churches are more like independent nation-states than like members of a common federation, and thus they can overcome disagreement only by negotiation and through the signing of treaties on specific issues.

Doe argues, therefore, that the Anglican Communion should adopt a global system of canon law in order to establish a shared understanding of juridical order. He suggests that the foundation for such a system is already in place, in that all Anglican churches already share the concept of canon law, and in that there are considerable similarities between many of these particular systems. Doe argues that adoption of a common code of canon law will translate the values of the moral order into the realm of the juridical. The result would be that the "global communion . . . become[s] a juridical reality for each particular church."[9] He proposes a procedure for implementing this vision: the primates of the Communion would collectively acknowledge the implied existence of an unwritten fundamental Anglican canon law (*ius commune*) and then take such a statement back to their own churches so that work might begin on the final codifying of a shared body of juridical law.

This proposal is noteworthy for a number of reasons. First, if one is primarily concerned with ensuring that the Communion has an authoritative body with the capacity to impose discipline, then the benefits of achieving such a common juridical code are clear. Moreover, Doe's idea seeks to expand the scope of an already existing centripetal force within the life of the Anglican tradition—the concept of canon law—in order to respond to tensions at the global level of the church. Nevertheless, there are compelling structural reasons to conclude that it is unlikely that this proposal has any potential to serve as a useful unifying force.

In the first instance, none of the Instruments of Unity have been acknowledged to possess anything remotely resembling the authority to impose standardized rules, particularly in relation to the role Doe suggests for the

Primates' Meeting.[10] There is thus little clarity about which church bodies (if any) would be granted the necessary legitimacy by member churches to impose a universal code of canon law; neither does Doe suggest which of them would be granted the powers of judge and jury. It is also noteworthy that Doe's proposal is constructed within a Westphalian paradigm of the church, in which a province is conceived as comparable to an independent nation-state. He thus implies that the fault lines of conflict lie chiefly *between* individual provinces rather than also *within* them. Yet the fact that canon law structures within provinces like England, Canada, and the United States have not prevented the intensification of conflict *within* those regions calls into question his claim that the centripetal power of juridical structures is sufficient for stabilizing competing conceptions of the "moral order" of global Anglicanism.

It is in the nature of such centralizing proposals, therefore, that one generally finds them attractive only if one is confident that the power of judge and jury will remain close to one's own constituency. On this point, it is instructive to recall how the concern among Evangelicals in the Church of England to guard against a perceived threat of popelike church authority was at least partially responsible for the first Lambeth Conference's care in limiting its powers to consultation rather than legislation.[11] A similar but more recent concern emerged among Evangelical Episcopalians in the United States, which led them to resist the growing centralization of TEC's General Convention and its canons. They feared that such centralization would force them to comply with policies with which they disagreed (for example, the ordination of partnered homosexuals).

It is not surprising, therefore, that several sociological studies conclude that attempts to centralize power in religious communities are often the trigger for a schism.[12] Any move toward enhanced centralization will prompt resistance—or even withdrawal from the Communion altogether—among those worried that they will lose power. Doe's proposal largely ignores such issues, at the same time that it implies a loss of autonomous authority for provincial and diocesan synods.[13]

Doe's proposal for a universal Anglican code of canon law has found little traction. A second initiative by Communion leadership, discussed briefly above, generated far more interest and attention: the notion of an Anglican "covenant." As the next section demonstrates, however, this second proposal for repairing relations in the Communion has met with concern and criticism very similar to that raised against Doe's suggestion.

The Proposed Anglican Covenant

Conceived as a procedure to both symbolize and formalize the relational commitments of member churches to one another, the covenant was presented by its supporters as a way to resolve the divisions in the Communion in a manner that avoided legalism and radical change to existing structures of authority, while also respecting the local autonomy of member churches.[14] In this way, the proposal sought to work with existing traditions and centripetal tendencies in the church, and to avoid intensifying already considerable centrifugal pressures. The fact that the proposal had to be redrafted four times before being officially presented for approval, however, highlights the sensitivity of the issues it addressed. Both the Episcopal Church and a number of GAFCON provinces, and even a majority of the dioceses of the Church of England itself, eventually rejected the proposal, which further illustrates the difficulties of fashioning an institutional mechanism that could satisfy the diverse constituencies in the Communion. Ultimately, many thought that the various drafts did not go far enough in the direction they wanted.

Most of our informants made reference to the covenant in the course of our conversations with them. Although a few expressed outright support of the process, many shared a fair degree of skepticism or concern. Bishop Martha, for example, recalled that at an international meeting of Communion leaders, one participant offered a sermon on the Easter story, which focused on the stone being rolled away from the empty tomb, where the disciples were looking for the body of the resurrected Jesus. The preacher suggested that the Communion "had been creating a lot of stones" for itself, and referenced the covenant in particular as an example of this. In other words, he was suggesting that the global church was erecting barriers to the work of the Holy Spirit by introducing mechanisms like the covenant.

Other leaders avoided specific criticism while remaining lukewarm toward the idea. Without offering a direct opinion, for example, Bishop Justice simply noted, "the Anglican covenant came into effect in an endeavor to enhance the cooperation in the Communion; however, this does not seem to have worked." Even those who, like Bishop Jordan, expressed support for it, tended to admit that the proposal was unlikely to succeed: "You probably wouldn't be surprised that I support the covenant. It may well be close to dead in the water, I suspect, and, yeah, look . . . [*pause*] probably . . . [*pause*] in a way . . . [*pause*] I mean, in a sense, I am sort of hardwired to be really positive and think the Communion's a good idea." A lukewarm endorsement, to say the least.

The idea to establish an Anglican covenant was first proposed by the *Windsor Report*, a document issued by the Lambeth Commission on Communion for the Anglican Communion in 2004. The commission had been established by the archbishop of Canterbury at the time, Rowan Williams, in response to the tensions in the global church following the consecration of Gene Robinson. The hope behind the covenant initiative was to establish agreement between the different member churches of the Communion, as an alternative to a centralized code of canon law. A covenant, the *Windsor Report* stated, would "make explicit and forceful the loyalty and bonds of affection which govern the relationships between the churches of the Communion." Yet even the report's own draft version of the covenant already hinted at the key tension around which subsequent debate would revolve. While it reaffirmed the autonomy of individual member churches, it also suggested that each of these churches would need to "place the interests and needs of the community of member churches before [their] own" when dealing with "essential matters of common concern." In other words, the intention was to place "limits on the exercise of autonomy."[15] The document does not specify what such "essential matters" are, but it suggests that the Instruments of Unity will make such a determination (article 23). Should disputes arise over the proper interpretation of the covenant, the *Windsor Report*'s version of the proposal gives the archbishop of Canterbury the power of adjudication (article 27).

In response to the vague nature of these details, many wondered what the proposal ultimately implied about the local autonomy of provinces and diocesan synods. Bishop Timothy suggested that reactions to the proposal had much to do with how one interpreted its institutional implications: "You can have a debate about whether it's a 'soft' covenant, which says, 'This is the state of the ethos around which we gather,' or whether you have a 'hard' covenant in which it's possible to throw people out."

The proposal continued to receive a wide range of commentary and criticism.[16] A series of revisions ensued, led by the "Covenant Design Group" (established by the archbishop of Canterbury in 2006): the Nassau draft (2007), the St. Andrew's draft (2008), and the Ridley-Cambridge draft (2009). The last draft was itself amended before being sent to the churches for approval.[17]

The Nassau draft toned down the emphasis in the *Windsor Report* version on being "forceful," but it called for member churches to exercise their autonomy with "regard for the common good of the Communion" when handling "essential matters of common concern" (article 6.1). While the document upheld the original mention of a need to "heed the counsel of our Instruments of Communion" (article 6.4), this draft specified that matters of serious dispute should be submitted to the Primates' Meeting (article 6.5), which was to offer guidance and direction.

That few church leaders were satisfied with the document produced in Nassau is clear in the subsequent revisions. The St. Andrew's draft, produced a year later, contained stronger statements on provincial autonomy. It also downgraded the Nassau emphasis on the Primates' Meeting as the arbiter of disputes, leaving this responsibility more generally with all of the Instruments of Unity. These instruments, rather than "giving guidance and direction" (Nassau), might "request" that member churches "adopt a particular course of action," while having "no legislative, executive or judicial authority in our Provinces" (article 3.2.5.d).

The opening section of the Ridley-Cambridge revision was less proscriptive still in terms of specifying a process for mediating disputes. It stated that those who commit themselves to the covenant agree to "receive the work" of the Instruments of Communion "with a readiness to undertake reflection upon their counsels, and to endeavour to accommodate their recommendations" (article 3.2.1). Section 4 of the document, however, refers to a joint standing committee, which, after consulting with the Anglican Consultative Council and the Primates' Meeting, may judge a specific action to be "incompatible with the Covenant" and declare that an offending church is now in impaired communion with other member churches (article 4.2.5).[18]

Two things about this revision process are particularly noteworthy. The first is that there was little dispute over, or attention to, the overtly theological content of the different drafts: the affirmation of the Trinity, statements on the importance of holy scripture, baptism and the Eucharist, and the historical episcopate.[19] Instead, the energy and controversy surrounding the numerous drafts all revolved around questions of transprovincial authority: Who has the authority to mediate conflict in the Communion? Who has the ultimate capacity to adjudicate between competing interpretations of the boundaries of acceptable disagreement? Who has authority to declare that communion has been impaired? Answers to such questions in the covenant drafts became increasingly vague; consequently, the final version failed to satisfy either those seeking greater centralized authority in the Communion or opponents of greater centralization. The form of transnational authority implied by the covenant proposals remained unclear to both constituencies.

The values underlying the procedures and policies in the various versions never really became the focus of debate during the drafting processes, so that those evaluating the different policy recommendations made their judgments on the basis of differing values and theological priorities. Thus, while the opening sections of the different drafts address those seeking a renewed emphasis on the doctrinal beliefs and spiritual values of the tradition, these same statements did not directly shape the sections dealing with questions of how to adjudicate disagreement between member churches.

The core issue undergirding the limitations of the final draft, however, is the contradictory way in which it handles the question of local autonomy. The final draft emphasizes that individual churches will remain autonomous and will not be coerced into signing the covenant: "Each Church, with its bishops in synod, orders and regulates its own affairs and its local responsibility for mission through its own system of government and law" (article 3.1.2). Moreover, the document takes pains to clarify that participation in the covenant "does not represent submission to any external ecclesiastical jurisdiction" (4.1.3). These statements clearly intend to reassure those who are concerned about the potential imposition of external authority over their local church: "Nothing in this Covenant of itself shall be deemed to alter any provision of the Constitution and Canons of any Church of the Communion, or to limit its autonomy of governance" (4.1.3). The language of "voluntary" commitment and independent decision, however, elides an obvious issue: should a church decide that it is not prepared to sign the covenant, then it will effectively find itself outside the structures of the Communion. Thus, while the freedom of member churches to choose their own path is initially emphasized, behind this reassurance lurk the consequences of not making the proper choice: suspension from participation in the Instruments of Unity "until the completion of the process" (4.2.5). In other words, making the wrong "autonomous" choice effectively leads to being excluded. To complicate matters further, none of the drafts addressed the fact that many provinces would have to amend their canons and constitutions for it even to be possible for a single representative (the primate) to sign the covenant on behalf of their church. This reality would seem to contradict the statement earlier in the draft that nothing in the covenant usurps the autonomy of any province or requires amendment of its constitution or canons (article 4.1.3). To conform to any covenant agreement, many Anglican provinces would have to submit to granting new powers to their primate to make binding commitments on their behalf.

Many supporters of the idea of the covenant admitted that the final document was imperfect, but they argued that it was nonetheless a useful way to engage with the tensions in the Communion.[20] Some did so because they understood it to imply at least a certain degree of centralized control over the exercise of autonomy by individual churches. For example, N. T. Wright (formerly bishop of Durham), when commenting on the St. Andrew's draft, suggested that the covenant would "provide a line in the sand" prohibiting "the kinds of things" that TEC has done.[21] Andrew Goddard (at the time at Wycliffe Hall, Oxford) compared section 4 to the grievance and disciplinary policies that characterize employment contracts in the workplace. Although he argued that the covenant did not represent a significant move toward centralization, Goddard also suggested that the proposal would not be accepted or function properly unless the Instruments of Unity, which were to play a central role in mediating covenantal relationships, were reformed and granted greater power.[22]

As the proposed covenant began to be considered for internal approval by the Communion's member churches, the sitting archbishop of Canterbury, Rowan Williams, issued a general appeal for its acceptance. Williams urged all Anglicans to support the proposal, emphasizing that the process did not involve "some sort of centralising" authority with the "right to punish people for stepping out of line."[23] He compared the covenant to the way family members must be accountable to one another. On the controversial fourth section of the proposal, he argued that it did not imply a "disciplinary system. It's about a process of discernment and discussion. Nobody has the power to do anything but *recommend* courses of action." In this way, the archbishop emphasized the relational and voluntary nature of the covenant and the idea that it would improve dialogue by acknowledging that "we are all obliged to one another."

Such a defense was common among those who supported the covenant process. For Victor Atta-Baffoe (a member of the Covenant Design Group), the proposal captured the sense of a kinship-based understanding of community, one that embraced the idea that "I exist to belong to a family."[24] The English theologian Paul Avis echoed this view by suggesting that the covenant was intended to be an "embodiment of mutual commitment," to "flesh out in practical terms what interdependence might mean."[25] According to these interpretations, the proposal did not represent a significant shift in Anglican theology or polity but was more a relational gesture that remained within the traditional institutional structures of the Communion. In similar fashion, Norman Doe described it as simply being "a restatement of classical Anglicanism . . . not a revolutionary document."[26]

The minimizing of any implied centralized authority, however, is precisely why most of the leaders associated with the GAFCON movement rejected the proposal. In November 2010, following a meeting in Oxford chaired by Archbishop Gregory Venables (Southern Cone), the GAFCON leadership issued a statement criticizing the "old structures" of the Communion. More specifically, they declared that the Anglican covenant was "fatally flawed" and that they would not support it.[27] GAFCON presented its "Jerusalem Declaration" as an alternative solution to the Communion's problems, thus rejecting the proposal on the basis of a call for greater doctrinal clarity and enhanced centralized authority. The archbishop of Kenya, Eliud Wabukala, reiterated this view in his chairman's address at a meeting in April 2012. GAFCON did not support the covenant, he explained, because it sought to resolve "a merely institutional problem." The failings of the Communion, he suggested, were not "managerial and organizational" but "spiritual." What was required, Wabukala continued, was greater obedience to biblical truth.[28] Other voices joined with GAFCON in rejecting the covenant for similar reasons, including the Diocese of Sydney.[29]

By contrast, others who opposed the covenant generally understood it as a radical departure from traditional Anglicanism, and as implying greater centralization. Mark D. Chapman (Oxford University and member of Affirming Catholicism), for example, saw the proposal as ignoring the fact that many provinces are governed by synods, not primates, rendering unworkable the notion of having one representative from each province commit to the covenant agreement. Moreover, he argued that the supposed emphasis on "voluntary commitment" in the document actually implied "what amounts to an understanding of international catholic order and structure," which he described as "untenable."[30] The theologian Marilyn McCord Adams (at the time a faculty member at the University of North Carolina, Chapel Hill) offered an even sharper critique. She argued, contradicting the archbishop of Canterbury's position, that the covenant was a "radical change from the *status quo ante*." It presented, she said, a "woolly ecclesiology" that ignored the history of the development of the Anglican Communion.[31]

As debates raged among theologians, the fate of the proposed covenant was sealed by the end of the summer of 2012. By this time, a number of churches (Mexico, Myanmar, the West Indies, Southeast Asia, and Papua New Guinea) had voted to adopt it; other provinces had rejected it, and several had declared that they were unable to adopt it (the Episcopal Church in the Philippines, the Episcopal Church of Scotland, and the Anglican Church in Aotearoa, New Zealand and Polynesia).[32] In July 2012, the General Convention of TEC declined to take a position on the matter. Finally, it became clear that the proposal lacked majority support even among the dioceses of the Church of England, which was required for the "mother church" of the Communion to adopt the covenant (of forty-four dioceses, twenty-three had voted against).[33]

After a decade of intensive institutional debate and dispute on this issue, the Anglican Communion found itself no closer to resolving the tensions and divisions that the controversy surrounding the consecration of Gene Robinson had brought into view. For some, this became a matter of considerable anxiety. After the failure of the proposed covenant, what were those who had described it as "the only realistic option on the table" to conclude?[34] Did it mean the end of the Anglican Communion, at least as an institution able to conduct itself as a broad and inclusive global organization?

Some conservatives greeted the apparent defeat of the covenant process with enthusiasm. They argued that the only remaining option for the future was GAFCON's "Jerusalem Declaration." When the Church of England failed to adopt the covenant, Bishop Nazir-Ali (retired, Rochester, UK) described that declaration as "the only game in town."[35] But the covenant was not the only game left to play, nor were strategies for increasing centralized authority the only answer to the tensions in the Communion. One of the more widespread and effective possibilities that remained was the promotion of formal dialogue.

The Call for Dialogue

In contrast to those who advocate stronger legal or institutional mechanisms for binding the Communion together, others contend that through dialogue, diverse groups and agendas can come to better understand one another, and thus learn mutual acceptance, even in the face of disagreement. Bishop Terrance expressed this spirit when he suggested to us, "I think we have to stick to our traditional Anglican way of doing things, which is to sit down and talk, and to engage in dialogue. . . . Because we exist on relationship rather than rules and regulations. . . . So, unless we have a good relationship, we can't do anything."

This is precisely what the planners of the 2008 Lambeth Conference sought to achieve by introducing an "*indaba* process" into the proceedings.[36]

When Rowan Williams, then archbishop of Canterbury, described his goals for the gathering, he introduced this concept by announcing that the meeting would revolve around a series of small-group discussions: "We have given these the African name of *indaba* groups, groups where in traditional African culture, people get together to sort out the problems that affect them all, where everyone has a voice and where there is an attempt to find a common mind or a common story that everyone is able to tell when they go away from it."[37] The conference was thus organized around sixteen study groups, each composed of forty bishops. Many participants described their experience of these conversations as "powerful," since the practice allowed them to get to know one another, and to listen and begin to understand how the issues of the day were affecting Anglicans from different parts of the globe. Bishop Peter John Lee (South Africa) expressed his appreciation of the process, commenting, "Open-endedness creates real freedom."[38] Bishop Geralyn Wolf (United States) described her *indaba* experience as helping to overcome the divide separating her from Anglicans from very different contexts. "Engaging in an honest and open debate that leads to discernment without premature interpretation and frequent distortion from outside 'commentators' is a challenge for the Church today," she wrote.[39]

It is this challenge that the planners of the Lambeth Conference sought to meet. After the conference, the Anglican Communion Office continued to promote this agenda through a "continuing *indaba*" process.[40] The organizers hoped that through dialogue, the differences and divisions troubling the Communion would become better understood, and that when bishops came to know each other personally, they would be less inclined to demonize those with whom they disagree. Such a prescription for what ails the Communion implies that conflict and disagreement are chiefly the result of differing personal backgrounds and cultural contexts, and that bridging these gaps through dialogue would be the most promising antidote.

Many of the bishops we spoke with who had participated in *indaba* groups reported appreciating the experience. "I keep in touch with the members of my *indaba* group—that is my way of trying to respond to all of this," Bishop Martha told us. "Every month I write to them to keep the conversation going." Bishop Paul reported that he and his colleagues left Lambeth 2008 "with a spring in our step" after their *indaba* experience, while noting the limitations inherent in the model. "This is a good way of working—to enable us to maintain the unity of the Communion with increased harmony," he said. "It's better that we do it that way; I mean, if one wants an outcome with decisive things said, well, sorry to disappoint you on that one." Bishop William, though more reserved in his remarks, suggested that "the *indaba* method . . . has been positive for those involved. It has bridged differences."

Critics of the *indaba* approach argued that it failed to achieve consensus and was incapable of imposing discipline on churches or individuals violating the limits of orthodox doctrine and practice.[41] Such detractors faulted the process for not achieving something that its supporters did not intend it to accomplish, so some would undoubtedly reply that such arguments miss the point. But for those not content with the trajectory of the Communion, the failure of the "listening process" to produce concrete decisions merely left the status quo in place. In many cases, it was simply too much to ask of them that they sit with those they saw as willfully undermining the faith and the church to which they had committed their lives. This was the view of Bishop Christopher, who attended the first GAFCON meeting instead of Lambeth 2008. "I deal with Buddhists quite easily," he told us, "because Buddhist beliefs don't threaten the character of the Christian organization to which I belong." But engaging in dialogue with some of his fellow Anglicans felt like "threaten[ing] the integrity" of his church.

Along similar lines, Stephen Noll (formerly of Trinity Episcopal School for Ministry in Pennsylvania and subsequently the vice chancellor of Uganda Christian University) argued that "the result of Rowan Williams's '*indaba*-ing' is that the liberals wink and move on with their agenda."[42] Others contend that the dialogue strategy, by implying that contextual differences are the primary cause of conflict, holds that there is no universal truth of Christianity, and that the Gospel message is malleable and can be shaped to suit a particular agenda. Eliud Wabukala (then archbishop of Kenya and chair of GAFCON) criticized those who urged the church "to continue this dialogue endlessly in order to wear down resistance"; he advocated instead a return to "the plain sense of scripture."[43] Such skeptics see the tendency of the *indaba* process to embrace a wide variety of opinions as simply reinforcing the dominant norms of a pluralist culture. Their approach, by contrast, is to invoke a specific moral vision and theological norm. These critics are unwilling to compromise their personal convictions for the sake of holding together a wider range of views.

Francis Bridger and Andrew Goddard have evaluated the strengths and weaknesses of the ways in which the *indaba* process has been subsequently employed in debates within the Church of England. They acknowledge that dialogue does build relationships between differing individuals, but they are also highly critical of *indaba*'s limitations. In particular, Bridger and Goddard emphasize that the process only permits the sharing of personal views, instead of encouraging participants to "grapple together" with controversial biblical texts. Moreover, they argue that power dynamics within the groups generally go unacknowledged (particularly when mixing bishops and laypeople, or LGBTQ individuals and opponents of same-sex marriage and gay bishops). Finally, they lament the "thinness of explicit biblical and theological input."[44]

These criticisms aside, some success stories have come out of the various dialogue processes. The Consultation of Anglican Bishops in Dialogue, for example, brings together bishops from the United States, Canada, and various African countries. Initiated by the Anglican Church of Canada in 2009, eight such gatherings have taken place to date.[45] At the meeting in Accra, Ghana, in May 2016, twenty-three bishops from Ghana, Swaziland, Tanzania, Kenya, South Africa, Burundi, Zambia, Canada, England, and the United States signed a statement titled "A Testimony of Unity in Diversity."[46] "Our purpose is neither to resolve nor to ignore differences," the document explains, "but to deepen relationships and therefore to nurture mutual understanding. We continue in our desire to be globally diverse and to keep searching for the ties that bind." The statement emphasizes the bonds formed through such a process: "Our conversations are intended neither to condemn nor to condone, neither to agree nor to disagree, but to love. Without face to face encounters it is easy to apply labels, to stop listening, and no longer to see one another as brothers and sisters in the body of Christ."

When we spoke with an African bishop who participated in this meeting, he suggested that the dialogue has helped break down the distrust between participants from the Global South and Global North. "The whole postcolonial thing is still very significant," he said, "but among the younger bishops, they are sort of post-postcolonial. It is less reactive, a more nuanced defense of African autonomy and identity." Another church leader involved in the dialogues shared his optimism about the potential of the process. "The people who have been very strong about not wanting to commune with the other are on the extreme, and are becoming increasingly isolated," he told us. "And the people who have tried to meet, and who have engaged in conversation—they seem to be bridging that gap." In his enthusiasm he went so far as to suggest that "the rift that everybody feared would break up the Communion, I think, if I may be so bold as to say, may be behind us now" (this was in the summer of 2012).

The Church of England's dialogues in July 2016 have not met with quite such success. That is perhaps not surprising, given the much larger scale of the conversation. The agenda for a synod in York outlined a process of open-ended structured discussion on sexuality titled "Shared Conversations."[47] The event followed a two-year process of similar regional conversations that involved more than thirteen hundred members of the church.[48] In a highly publicized move, a group of thirty-two conservative members of the synod released a statement expressing their "lack of confidence" in the talks; ten of them refused to participate at all.[49] Ian Paul, one of the signatories, claimed that many of the speakers who began the plenary sessions "advocated that we could learn to live together, so there was a strong sense of the process leaning into a 'live and let live' approach, without exploring the possibility that this question [homosexuality] might not be one of the adiaphora."[50] He added,

> The fundamental problem here was the underlying approach—that there are no right answers, and no given positions, and so what is needed is a juxtaposition of different views so that mutual respect can emerge. This might be just right for a position of political conflict, where there is no "objective" position which can act as a reference point. But how can this be right in a context where the Church itself already has a committed position, one that has the weight of history behind it, and a position which, in theory, all the clergy and the bishops have themselves signed up to believing, supporting and teaching.[51]

Echoing the tone of the remarks of other signatories, Reverend Paul warned, "if those managing the process do not demonstrate a much better understanding of and engagement with those who actually believe in what the bishops currently teach then there will be trouble ahead."[52]

These criticisms resemble remarks we encountered among critics of the continuing *indaba* process. Bishop Henry, for example, argued that "this theology is about inclusion, but when those in power act, they act with authority and do things as they see fit. So there's a contradiction here." In contrast to this concern with the overt imposition of power, Bishop Timothy complained of a more general attitude he perceived among organizers of the dialogue process, which he characterized as "liberal self-righteousness." In his view, "some of the management of the [2008] Lambeth Conference was profoundly illiberal and that was because it was being run by liberals." In this way, the bishop echoed a common criticism of the liberal concept of "tolerance." Although liberal thinkers often claim that they tolerate the legitimacy of all views, some prove to be very intolerant of those who do not share their enthusiasm for tolerance.[53]

Such concerns highlight the fact that the ideals of dialogue and *indaba* are not simply neutral processes but are value-laden. For example, defenders of dialogue commonly emphasize the significance of local context in shaping theological opinions and interpretations of biblical texts.[54] For a theologian like Stephen Sykes, however, the idea that key elements of the Christian faith can be treated as "topics for debate and discussion" seems outrageous, since, in his opinion, it reduces what he thinks are essential truths of religious belief to the status of mere opinion.[55] This explains why some Anglicans are highly critical of *indaba* and other listening processes in the Communion, for they do not share the assumptions underlying them. In their view, what is meant to include actually excludes them.

This is ironic, since it is the explicit intention of the dialogue strategy to encompass the diverse concerns and opinions found within the Communion. Yet such criticism of the dialogue process is neither surprising nor unique to Anglicans. A number of scholars argue that such interactions often do not begin on a level playing field, and that those who initiate and establish the conditions and parameters of a conversation do much to control the possible outcomes.[56] This criticism does not come only from conservative quarters. Returning to the question-and-answer session between LGBTQ Anglicans in Toronto and the primate of Canada, some of those in attendance voiced concerns about the format of the meeting. "It's not only the language used, but the position from which someone speaks," suggested one man, adding, "the primate kept saying, 'Thank you for your patience,' when it wasn't offered freely. That's disingenuous." Another criticized the structure of the evening: "The primate kept talking for almost an hour, which became a kind of wall that prevented [him from] listening."

Such turbulent dynamics are often inherent in a dialogue process. While the format and structure of dialogue can always be improved to minimize ways in which people feel excluded or silenced, no process can ever fully include all potential participants in exactly the same way. This can be due to the guiding assumptions behind the way a dialogue is organized, or because of more basic practical limitations. The first of these issues was highlighted by the conservative critics of England's "Shared Conversations," who argued that the process presumed that it is legitimate for the church to debate the question of same-sex relationships. Some conservatives are unwilling to grant the legitimacy of that initial premise.

Bishop Michael offered us an example of the second kind of logistical issue that can complicate dialogues: almost all of the *indaba* conversations at

Lambeth 2008 were conducted exclusively in English. He explained that this represents a barrier for nonnative English speakers, "and when you add onto that a whole raft of culturally demanding expectations and the whole cultural package, this becomes a very difficult conversation to have." Anglican bishops for whom English is a second or third language, in other words, might well feel at a disadvantage in an *indaba* group with a majority of native English speakers.

Yet another logistical challenge confronting organizers of a dialogue process is the simple fact that participants often begin from very different starting points, which may generate frustration at the very outset. During the 2016 General Synod of the Anglican Church of Canada, for example, members were divided into small "neighborhood groups" to discuss the most controversial issue on the agenda: same-sex marriage. The goal was to encourage open and honest dialogue, in the hope that mutual understanding and respect would be generated across differences. Although some of the groups were successful, other participants reported feeling silenced, marginalized, or mistreated. Some LGBTQ members expressed frustration and fatigue over what felt to them like a very old conversation. As one man put it to us, "It's like a broken record. I've been having this same conversation for over thirty years now! When can we finally move on?" The synod included another constituency—indigenous people—many of whom were confronted with this issue for the first time. Some of these individuals did not understand English and could only follow the debate through simultaneous translation. One woman spoke dismissively of the indigenous members of her neighborhood group: "They haven't even read the report on sexuality prepared by the church beforehand!"[57] Such tensions eased somewhat when it was pointed out that these materials were only printed in English. Nevertheless, recognizing that different members were beginning from different starting points did little to diminish the frustration felt by some. Those who had been debating the legitimacy of same-sex orientation for decades and those encountering the subject for the first time often found that this gap was difficult to bridge.

These factors limit the capacity of dialogue to unify the diverse interests and opinions within the Anglican Communion, but by no means do they fatally undermine the strategy. It is noteworthy, for example, that only 2 percent of members refused to participate in the "Shared Conversations" at the Church of England's General Synod (10 of 483). While that number is not insignificant, the fact that the vast majority were willing to talk to one another suggests that the main objective was achieved. Yet the question remains: how might the English church work to include the roughly 2 to 3 percent of its membership who cannot (yet?) find a way to participate in a process that claims it wants to include them? Moreover, compared with the small minority in the church of England who refused to participate in dialogue, the GAFCON critics of the "continuing *indaba*" process represent a significant demographic within the Communion, so the possibility of a change of heart among that constituency seems elusive, at least in the short term.

In the face of this challenge, Adrianus Sunarko's insight into the dynamics of interreligious dialogue is instructive. Sunarko argues that if the dialogue process is to succeed, it must be complemented by a sense of cooperation geared toward building community. In other words, dialogue for its own sake, or with the aim of mere mutual tolerance, is not enough to foster better relationships. Moreover, such a process "should not be oriented to purely religious matters, but needs to be directed also 'outward' for the sake of public interest."[58] This insight is borne out in the relative success of Canada's Consultation of Anglican Bishops, for it is clear that the participants in that process have understood their involvement as relating to much more than theoretical debates internal to the Anglican tradition. As the Kenyan theologian Esther Mombo notes, the consultation's dialogue process

> comes to us against the backdrop of a world in turmoil with negative implications on all in society but especially on women and children. We think of the conflicts in the Sudan, Egypt, Democratic Republic of Congo, and Central Republic of Congo; the atrocities committed in Northern Nigeria and Somalia, to name just a few places in Africa. . . . In all these places the presence of the church is noticeable and for those who are Anglican leaders with a testimony of reconciliation [we] are expected to practice [it]. The divisions in the Anglican Communion, rooted in biblical and theological differences[,] are within the context of the realities mentioned above.[59]

This perspective suggests that many of those attending the consultation process are not motivated simply by a desire to "listen" or to "get along" but are seeking allies and partners who will help them respond to concrete and immediate challenges facing their churches. Successful dialogue processes make practical concerns and motivations immediate and transparent.

Most of the church leaders with whom we spoke strongly supported dialogue programs. There is considerable evidence that dialogue has been the most successful strategy pursued by the Communion's leadership in recent decades and has helped hold the global church together. But we also encountered church leaders who have chosen to opt out of these dialogues. Some are frustrated by the lack of decisive action; others are unwilling to grant the possibility that opinions different from their own are valid; still others fear that the process is manipulated by the agendas of those who lead the dialogue.

If the dialogue strategy is to remain an effective mechanism for unifying different constituencies in the global church—if, that is, those who reject the premise are to be brought into the process—it may be necessary to modify what is presented as the central topic or issue. It may also be helpful to provide more concrete and practical reasons for entering into a dialogue, for participants to be joined together by a common sense of purpose. With this in mind, Bishop William pointed to the importance of an Anglican development network for giving Anglicans engaged in these conversations a larger sense of purpose, which keeps the church's disagreements in perspective: "We've got to have those debates—we can't ignore them—but I think the more we focus on the Anglican Alliance, and our international responsibilities to those in the greatest need, the poorest of the poor, the least, the last, and the lost, which is what Jesus says, of course. [Unclear] I think some of the doctrinal, ecclesial, and dogmatic issues will fall into better place, and into better perspective. Because in the face of life and death, differences over schism, matters of doctrine, can pale into insignificance."

The limitations of the proposals discussed above for restoring unity in the Anglican Communion have led some to be pessimistic about its future. Other Anglicans suggest that the Communion has yet another resource at its disposal: the more intangible "bonds of affection" that have built up among Anglicans across the globe over the long history of the church. These historical connections, some suggest, are the true source of the Communion's ongoing unity. If institutional mechanisms and formal dialogue appear inadequate to the task of holding the global church together, perhaps relational affect and historical goodwill may be sufficient. As we shall see, while this hope may not be entirely unfounded, the bonds of affection have also begun to show signs of strain.

The Bonds of Affection: Common Backgrounds, Practices, or Manners?

Over the course of our interviews with church leaders, we heard many references to the significance of the relational "bonds" between Anglicans. Bishop

Paul praised Lambeth 2008 for reinforcing feelings of connection among the gathered bishops. Rather than rely upon parliamentary procedures or some other mechanism, he told us, "we respected the reality of the human condition, . . . we worked within its flawed condition, and . . . we sought not to do anything that will cause lasting damage or offense to any one individual bishop who may have been at Lambeth. And by maintaining the bonds of affection the way we did, we've genuinely done a good thing. People have gone away feeling that, and therefore, I dare to think, living out the prayer of Jesus in John 17 ['that they may all be one' (17:21)]." Bishop Timothy also made reference to Lambeth 2008 to suggest that personal relationships represent the greatest potential to hold the Communion together:

> One of the great learnings of Lambeth was that the much-talked-about bonds of affection really do exist. And even though the bits of structure that hold together the Anglican Communion look pitifully frail and inadequate for the task which they're now having to do, the depths of commonality among these churches which have almost nothing in common are really astonishing. I looked at bishops whose names I never heard of, and I could look at them and say, "I know pretty well what you do." And that really did surprise me, and the atmosphere of the conference was warm and easy. And so if you measured the future of the Anglican Communion not in terms of its structural resilience but in terms of the depth of relationships and the manifest desire to cohere, then you'd have to say that it does have a future.

Yet given that about 230 bishops did not attend the 2008 Lambeth Conference (compared to 650 who did),[60] it remains an open question whether such "bonds of affection" will be sufficient to repair relationships that have been strained or broken over the past twenty-five years. Moreover, the verdict is still out as to whether such bonds merely need to be "strengthened" in order to be effective, or must first be "restored," or whether their very "survival" is currently in jeopardy.[61]

Related to that open question is the precise nature and meaning of the rather vague notion of the "bonds of affection." Do these bonds chiefly depend upon the relationships among bishops—who are replaced at regular intervals—or are they somehow structurally nurtured and supported? What secures and sustains the bonds that are treasured by members of the Communion? There is little concrete agreement on these particulars. In what follows, we identify three common ways in which these bonds are described: in terms of common formative backgrounds, shared liturgical practices, or common "manners." While all of these traditions in the Anglican Communion remain influential, increasing diversity among Anglicans suggests that no one historical element of the Anglican tradition can be the primary source of the bonds among members of the global church.

For some, such as the American priest Harold Lewis, the answer to these questions about the relational bond between Anglicans is rooted in a shared approach to Christian education and spiritual formation.[62] Yet Lewis cautions that this key formative source of Anglican identity is under threat because, he suggests, new seminarians are increasingly marginal and relatively new Anglicans. Fewer are now drawn from those "nurtured in the bosom of the church." The result of this trend, Lewis concludes, is the loss of a shared understanding of a common ethos of "church life." The emphasis on the need for a common understanding of ministry and the church implies that a shared vision and ethos are necessary if Anglicans are to commit themselves to one another. In other words, Lewis suggests that many Anglican clergy are not sufficiently "Anglican" to form the bonds of affection required to sustain the Communion.[63]

This view is not uncommon among Anglican theologians. While some emphasize the primary formative role of education, others point to liturgy as the key generative experience of Anglican identity that can bind members of the Communion together.[64] Ephraim Radner and Philip Turner argue that the way forward for the Anglican tradition is to reemphasize "a particular sort of ethos that is defined by a distinguishing set of practices rather than by reference to a teaching authority, or the promulgations of an ecumenical council, or by a confession." "The doctrinal content Anglicans share is embedded primarily in liturgical practices," they suggest. "It is here, in the accepted belief and practice of the people, that a satisfactory resolution of these issues will finally be achieved."[65]

While embodied practice and shared *habitus* no doubt do much to forge a common identity,[66] one limitation of such proposals is that they frequently fail to address the fact that no standardized universal practices are currently in force across the Anglican Communion. The days are long past when one could expect to encounter the liturgy of the 1662 Book of Common Prayer in an Anglican church in any corner of the globe. An emphasis on respect for local context and "inculturation," which has been celebrated throughout the Communion since the 1970s (being a core component of its attempt to embrace postcolonial respect for non-Western practices), has encouraged many provinces to adapt their liturgies accordingly. As a result, considerable liturgical variety is found across the churches of the Communion, and, increasingly, even within individual provinces and dioceses.[67]

Furthermore, it is by no means self-evident that shared practice necessarily generates common assent and belief. The legacy of the Book of Common Prayer reveals all too clearly that uniformity of church order does not establish uniformity of belief, pastoral vision, or moral conviction. Slave owner and abolitionist, Tractarian and Evangelical, historical critic and Charismatic have not found a common liturgical text sufficient for "manufacturing the consent" of their fellow Anglicans.

If the bonds of affection that unite Anglicans are not to be found primarily in shared liturgical forms or standardized seminary formation, then where do they come from? Some theologians, rather than emphasize a particular institutional source, focus on the legacy of a shared cultural ethos. Martyn Percy suggests that "good manners is not a bad analogy for ideal Anglican polity." He goes so far as to suggest, in fact, that "the coherence of Anglicanism depends on good manners."[68] The message here is that Anglicans, when they are being "truly Anglican," comport themselves in a polite, restrained, diplomatic, and patient manner. The church can thus be described as a "community of *civilised* disagreement."[69] Paul Avis emphasizes a similar view when he writes, "The character of Christ also provides the template for the ideal of intra-Anglican relations: peaceable, courteous, empathetic and kind; an Anglicanism that remembers its manners and knows how to debate respectfully."[70]

Clearly, there is much to be said for good manners, and those who practice them no doubt enhance the possibility that constructive conversations can be achieved across difference.[71] At the same time, however, there is a danger that the close association between authentic Anglican identity and a particular conception of "manners" is overly narrow, for "manners" are a culturally laden category.[72] A firm handshake is welcomed in England or North America, but it may be awkwardly received in Asia. A loud belch after a meal may be taken as a compliment to the chef in China, but it doesn't go over well at an Oxbridge high table. Such distinctions are even found in liturgical practice. Someone with a cold might elect to practice "intinction" at the Eucharist in Scotland (dipping the bread into the wine instead of drinking from the common cup), whereas such an act is strictly forbidden in the Canadian church (for hygienic reasons). There is thus a real possibility that what is described as "typical Anglican habit"[73] has as much to do with English class culture as it does with how Anglicans have historically practiced their faith, and to which habits they should continue to adhere.[74]

In this regard, it is instructive to recall that at the end of the 1950s, the majority of bishops in the Communion (outside the United States and Canada) were English nationals educated in England. Of the 199 diocesan bishops in the Communion, 43 percent were graduates of either Oxford or Cambridge, and 54 percent trained at English theological colleges. William M. Jacob's description is thus apt: "Lambeth Conferences must have been very upper-middle class, 'high table' occasions."[75] In the twenty-first century, however, Anglican leaders no longer automatically share basic relational "habits" rooted in a common cultural background. Such shifts in the composition of the global church are what led Bishop Mark to suggest that "there are bids of power going on, that are across the Anglican Communion. The bid is to say that we and we alone know what the Anglican Church is." Being in a position to define "good manners" and to determine what counts as a "proper relationship" is itself a kind of power.[76]

We noticed two tendencies in particular among those who criticized the cultural behavior of other Anglicans. Notably, among the churches of the Global North, some leaders seemed inclined to criticize the conduct of their colleagues in the Church of England. We observed that others (particularly in England) could be equally cutting in their remarks about their American colleagues.[77] In both cases, our informants implied that the Communion's troubles were often related to the bad manners of individuals from one of these provinces.

Bishop Thomas, for example, complained that "the English . . . tend to think of themselves as the norm for the episcopacy." In similar fashion, Bishop Timothy suggested that "England" had not "worked out" that the center of the Communion was no longer England. "England," he continued, "still has a strand of colonialism as it relates to the rest of the world." We even heard such criticism applied to the archbishop of Canterbury, Justin Welby, as some local leaders described how they experienced his visits to their provinces.

Others, by contrast, blamed the Communion's troubles on the lack of manners of American members of the church. Bishop Jordan's remarks offer a representative example: "It seems to me from a distance, you know, there are issues of American culture . . . that are more 'winner-take-all' than probably we're used to in [my province]. I think the routing of the Evangelicals in the early twentieth century in the Episcopal Church, you know, set up a bit of a pattern where, hey, the majority is going somewhere. You know, 'What's the problem? Get in line,' you know. And maybe U.S. culture is much more authoritarian than I think [people here] are used to." The way the American church operates, in Bishop Jordan's view, leads minority groups within it to be concerned that "they'll roll the steamroller over us." Americans, in other words, "take no prisoners." Bishop Timothy also said pointedly, "the American church decided to take action, knowing that there were going to be these consequences Communion-wide, and they went ahead!" To his mind, American culture is ill-mannered in the sense that it has a propensity to behave arrogantly and to disregard others.

Comments like these recall the pattern in church conflict that encourages the portrayal of one's opponent as a "moral other" in order to mobilize political support. As the discussion in chapter 4 illustrated, a great deal depends on how a situation is framed. The ways in which leaders describe their opponents, and the nature of the expectations they encourage among their followers, do much to shape a conflict. This issue emerges even in dialogue processes that are intended to include all Anglicans, and even among those who seek to encourage certain relational virtues. In a global church, there are many opportunities for subtle exclusionary assumptions or expectations to arise.

This tendency to single out certain individuals, groups, or regions as the principal cause of the Communion's difficulties represents one of the biggest threats to its unity. It certainly suggests that the celebrated notion that "bonds of affection" will hold the global church together is by no means guaranteed. Should this tendency to point fingers establish itself even more firmly in the rhetoric and behavior of members of the Communion, the tensions and pressures dividing Anglicans from one another will only continue to build. More and more leaders will find themselves—like Archbishop Hiltz at the forum in Toronto—confronted by people who demand that they align themselves with their agenda, or risk being treated as an enemy. The politics of division, and the polemics of dualism, would then triumph.

This chapter has demonstrated why some of the most prominent attempts to resolve the contemporary pressures and tensions in the global church have thus far fallen short. Efforts to introduce greater centralization into the structures of the Communion have proved unsuccessful and are unlikely to be broadly accepted in the future. Although dialogue processes have achieved some success, many Anglicans continue to feel alienated by them. Even the way in which some Anglicans describe the nature of Anglicanism and its ethos risks fueling the dualistic and culturally specific polemics that have emerged in recent Communion disputes. Although there are indeed strong bonds of affection between Anglicans across the globe, there are also signs that the foundations of these historic relationships are under increasing strain.

These observations might be taken as sealing the fate of the Anglican Communion. If neither greater centralization, nor canon law, nor formal dialogue, nor even established manners and long-standing bonds of affection can guarantee consensus or reconciliation, what hope is there for the global church? It is to this question that we turn in the next chapter. For in our conversations with leaders across the globe, although we heard a great deal of frustration, we also encountered substantial hope about the future. Many leaders told us that they not only hoped and prayed for the unity of the church but believed that unity might yet be achieved.

7 | ANGLICAN IDENTITY IN THE TWENTY-FIRST CENTURY

The Australian theologian Bruce Kaye expresses the basic challenge confronting the contemporary Anglican Communion as follows: "The issue in world Anglicanism . . . is what pattern or character of communion is appropriate in this kind of worldwide community." Kaye suggests that existing proposals to resolve conflict at the international level largely beg the questions of what kind of communities actually make up the Anglican Communion on the ground and what sort of global church it should become. He argues that "the form and character of communion in a parish is different from what is possible or appropriate in a diocese or province, and even more in the globally scattered Anglican Communion."[1]

It is on precisely such issues that the global church has found itself stuck for at least the past two decades. Anglicans have been at a loss as to how to translate the complex web of interests, theologies, and missional agendas that span their parishes, dioceses, and provinces into a shared sense of identity, and have been unable to establish an agreed range of procedures to coordinate global corporate decision making.

What often remains unacknowledged in discussions of the Communion's future is that this complicated "mess" is not really unusual or surprising. In fact, it is a common reaction to the challenges experienced more generally in diverse multicultural societies, and in the face of a post-Westphalian sociopolitical context. The Communion's capacity to respond to these challenges, however, has not to date been very effective. As previous chapters have demonstrated, part of the reason for this is a tendency for commentators to beg the question and neglect the complexity of the global church's struggles.

The basic challenge has become the need to find a response to two competing tensions: the call for clearer and more institutionally legitimized normative commitments within a global church, around which to focus both corporate identity and shared mission, and the call for changes to the current organization and leadership structures of the Communion. Bishop Daniel, a senior English bishop, describes the second issue as a "toxic question." "It's easy to play the colonial card and that runs still quite strongly at the moment," he says. "How can the Communion be led by an English bishop who is appointed by a process in which they have no say? That's quite a toxic question and it will become a more toxic question because it has church and state implications in England and the UK." While the antidote to this "toxic question" has remained unclear, frustrated calls continue to proliferate for the establishment of more robust normative principles as anchors for Anglican teaching and practice. Bishop John's conversation with us emphasized this concern. "Homosexuality," he told us, "is . . . the presenting problem of how seriously we take the authority of the Bible and especially of how seriously we are committed to the faith of the apostles." The problem at the heart of the Communion's difficulties, he argued, is that the Communion is not operating according to clear "standards." Citing Lambeth 1998 Resolution 1.10, he suggested that "although we'll all say that it's the standard of teaching in the church, people are allowed to dismiss it without any disciplinary action against them, and that's what's caused the huge tensions." Other leaders dispute this claim, noting in particular that the Lambeth Conference has historically lacked the authority to pass motions that establish the "standard teaching" of its member churches. From this perspective, Bishop John's position is the one that represents a break with Anglican tradition.

Both the question of Anglicanism's normative content and the issue of who gets to participate in making decisions are clearly at the heart of the tensions dividing Anglicans. Yet it is possible to overemphasize the novelty of such challenges. These issues have long been contentious even within individual provinces.[2] Members of a national church often hold differing opinions on the controversial issues of the day (whether the form of the liturgy, contemporary or traditional music, divorce, women's ordination, or same-sex relationships). Moreover, debates over how to include minority groups and aboriginal peoples in the structures of ecclesial decision making are ongoing in many provinces. If such tensions remain difficult to resolve within national churches, how much more complex is the task of achieving consensus on these matters at the transnational level of the church?

To address such concerns, in this chapter we demonstrate in more detail why the contemporary conflicts in the Anglican Communion are not necessarily signs of fragmentation and disintegration. We begin by showing that much depends on how one describes and "frames" the tensions in the Communion. Much of the discussion since 2004 has been shaped by the *Windsor Report*, which emphasized the novelty of the differences in the global church, downplaying evidence to the contrary. The second section of the chapter shows how this way of framing the conflict has led many Anglicans to conceive of solutions in sentimental and idealistic ways. This has included employing references to the "authority of scripture" to try and transfer political influence away from traditional sources of power and influence, idealistic notions of "communion" that foster anti-institutional sentimentality, or merely pragmatic attempts to "manage" or "contain" the conflict that leave few satisfied.

By showing the limitations of these various reactions to the dominant way of framing the situation in the Communion, we demonstrate that the basic issue confronting Anglicans throughout the world is how to conceive of "Anglican identity" and church "unity." Are these things that must be agreed upon in advance, on the basis of formal principles and set procedures? Or are Anglicans content to think of their shared identity and unity as achievements still to be sought and discovered in relationship with their fellow Anglicans? Although no one can predict the future course of the Communion, or whether it will be able to withstand the tensions that threaten to fragment it, the chapter concludes by suggesting that there are compelling reasons to hope for a future for the global church.

The Power of a Label: How Leaders Frame the Conflict

The Anglican Communion's troubles have not developed in a vacuum, nor is it alone in facing its current challenges. Many societies are experiencing new levels of tension about diversity and its impact on existing political structures. These tensions arise in response to shifts both in local demographics and in the accelerated movement of people between different contexts. In Europe and North America, such tensions are driven largely by immigration and changes in the global economy.[3] In South America and Africa, internal migration and increasing urbanization are transforming long-standing social norms and expectations.[4] Heightened awareness of the differences among human cultures, which has accelerated in the wake of globalization and advances in communication technology, leads some theorists to describe our age as one of "hyperpluralism."[5]

Previous chapters have discussed widespread tensions over diversity within the Anglican Communion. In chapter 5, for example, Bishop Peter suggested that Anglicans display two basic attitudes regarding the plurality of views in the global church: "There are two Anglican Communions at present," he said, "two different models: one where you have uniformity and the other where you have the containment of diversity as being the key." Both of these positions share the perception that difference among Anglicans needs to be managed. In the first instance, the goal is to resolve the problem by enforcing a common unifying position; the second seeks to control or reconcile differences that it is assumed will persist within the church.

The felt need to "do something" that somehow "deals with" the level of diversity in the global church is fueled by a sense of urgency, for many Anglicans are convinced that the Communion's recent tensions are impeding rather than nurturing growth and well-being. Bishop James, for example, cautioned that "those who feel hurt are now seeking to inflict hurt" on others, while Bishop David warned of "a crash waiting to happen." Such laments and anxieties are common; Bishop Michael suggested that "at the moment, the conflict is shaping the Communion; the Communion is not shaping the conflict." This may well be how the contemporary situation in the global church feels at an emotional level, but if Simmel's theory of conflict is correct (chapter 5), these concerns do not necessarily describe a unique or even unusual situation; they express a pattern familiar to any large organization going through a period of transition.[6] Moreover, the likelihood that such tensions will emerge and the degree of their intensity are heightened in a transnational body like the Anglican Communion experiencing the forces of globalization.[7]

How one responds to the situation—whether one understands it as cause for anxiety and lament or as a sign of hope and an opportunity for renewal—depends a great deal on how the conflict itself is understood and described. For more than a decade now, many (perhaps even most) Anglicans have, understandably, tended to focus on anxiety rather than hope.

A case in point is the way in which the *Windsor Report*, issued by the Communion leadership in 2004, summarized the situation in the global church. Its warning, which some interpreted as a threat, read: "Should the call to halt and find ways of continuing in our present communion not be heeded, then we shall have to begin to learn to walk apart."[8] Without diminishing the seriousness of the tensions felt by many leaders in the wake of Gene Robinson's consecration, for "walking apart" was clearly a euphemism for schism, notice what is implied in this way of describing the situation. First, the tone suggests that, up until that moment, the churches of the Communion had essentially been "walking together" in an intimate and united manner. Yet the situation could be construed in this way only by papering over some significant details. As we discussed in chapter 2, it was not as if the situation in 2003 resulted from the sudden eruption of a new level of diversity in the Communion. Rather, long-standing differences had simply come more clearly into view.

On the issue of homosexuality, the presenting issue behind the *Windsor Report*, the movement in American and Canadian churches toward accepting same-sex clergy was not some sudden, shockingly new act of "walking apart" from Anglican practices elsewhere. The only truly novel thing about the developments in those provinces was their transparency. Other provinces were aware of what was going on because the decisions of TEC and Canada were made in public, and because the internet quickly spread the news across the globe. Many now acknowledge that quiet acceptance of gay clergy had long been common in other provinces, particularly in the Church of England, but on a "don't ask, don't tell" basis, without public acknowledgment.[9] On this issue, then, some churches had for all intents and purposes been "walking apart" from one another for a very long time, just as they had done on such issues as the ordination of women, lay presidency at the Eucharist, and the interpretation of scripture. Previously, these differences were not presented as threatening real schism. The *Windsor Report* thus exaggerated the novelty of the situation in the Communion, as it largely accepted the way in which critics of the status quo framed the situation.

This is not to deny that some leaders threatened to try and break global relations if the Communion did not discipline TEC and the Anglican Church of Canada. What the report downplays, however, is that other differences over doctrine and practice in the past had been framed in ways that sought to avoid schism. The long history of intense rivalries between Anglo-Catholics and Evangelicals, Tractarians and Puritans, had surely taught members of the Communion something about the challenges of remaining within the same denomination despite significant differences. Moreover, such experiences had trained many in practical coping skills in their interactions with individuals from a rival church party.[10]

When the "presenting symbol" of homosexuality is invoked in Communion-level disputes, these substantial differences among Anglicans are often disregarded, as the conflict becomes framed as a confrontation between two clear opponents. The *Windsor Report* did little to interrupt this pattern; in fact, it only amplified the implication that there were only two positions in the church (conservative "traditionalists" and liberal "revisionists") and ignored the fact that considerable internal differences exist within and among these supposedly unified camps. One could point to recent empirical scholarship from many regions of the Communion that illuminate substantial tensions over internal differences within individual national churches, including such provinces as Rwanda,[11] Congo,[12] and Tanzania.[13]

We can also look at a church that receives surprisingly little attention in Communion-level debates: the Anglican Church of Australia. This national province contains substantial levels of diversity and internal tension.[14] It is home to strong Evangelical and Broad Church parties, and to an ethnically diverse population that includes significant aboriginal communities. Internal differences are exacerbated by the fact that Australian Anglicans have historically considered themselves a national church in the British colony, thus encouraging a self-understanding that we described in chapter 5 in sociological terms as a "church" rather than a "sect" (although the contemporary Diocese of Sydney might better be described as aspiring to the character of a sect).

In his description of the Anglican Church in Australia, David Hilliard quotes an Episcopalian visitor in the 1960s who claimed, "Nowhere in my entire tour of Anglicanism did I encounter questions of churchmanship so divisive, so much a source of distrust, and rancour."[15] Historical tensions between Evangelical dioceses like Sydney and other regions have been so great that Sydney did not accept the 1995 revision of the prayer book, nor have all dioceses adopted the canon authorizing the ordination of women.[16] This effectively results in *internally* impaired communion, in terms of both worship and the recognition of orders.[17] In other words, Australian Anglicans were effectively "walking apart" on some rather significant issues long before the publication of the *Windsor Report*, and these tensions have fueled public polemics over the direction of Anglican thought and practice as intense as those found in the United States.[18]

Until the voluntary poll on the question of same-sex marriage in the autumn of 2017, homosexuality has not served as the "presenting symbol" of these internal conflicts; this may explain why tensions in Australia receive less global attention than those in other provinces.[19] The differences within the province are nevertheless such that Bishop Liam told us, "If we didn't have the current constitution that we have in the Australian church, which binds us together in terms of . . . a legal requirement to meet and listen to each other at least once every three years at General Synod, twice a year at the General Synod standing committee . . . if we didn't have those primary commissions that met across the church divides . . . we would never meet. We would *not* meet." Granted, when the *Windsor Report* employed the term "walk apart," it was as a euphemism for schism rather than a reference to significant diversity and difference among Anglicans in the Communion. Yet set against the long-standing internal realities in the Australian church, the report's framing of the situation in the global church remains curious, for it stands in sharp contrast to the attitude we encountered in our respondents from Australia. The leaders in this internally diverse church argued that they simply had to find ways to coexist with their fellow Anglicans. Seen in this light, it is striking that the rhetoric of the *Windsor Report* presents the possibility of breaking off relations as a live option. Whereas our Australian informants framed division in their province as something they could not afford to seriously contemplate, the *Windsor Report* implies that the Anglican Communion *can* afford to consider schism.

This shift in tone marks a sharp break from the traditional ethos of the global church. Previous chapters have demonstrated that the Anglican Communion has long been a rather informal and decentralized community of autonomous churches. This has been beneficial to Anglican churches by enabling them to incorporate diverse viewpoints from various sectors of society. Many Anglicans have both celebrated and cherished this part of the tradition. They often describe it as the appropriate response to the incarnation of God's presence in particular historical contexts, or as recognition of the ways in which the Holy Spirit calls people to discipleship in the particular cultures and environments in which they find themselves.[20]

Beyond the Church of Australia, Anglicans have consistently demonstrated a determination to prevent their differences from driving them to "walk apart." One might point to the way in which many nineteenth-century bishops found it prudent to permit wide variances in liturgical practice in order to keep the peace between Anglo-Catholics and Evangelicals.[21] Even though previous disagreements touched on the theology of the sacraments, and the doctrines of justification, sanctification, and divine presence, comparisons with the current dispute over homosexuality are often dismissed on the grounds that liturgical practice is only a "secondary" or "pastoral" matter.

We can leave that debate aside, because other examples that go to the heart of Anglican polity present themselves. One of these is Anglicans' willingness to compromise on the role of the episcopacy in order to hold the church together in spite of its differences.

Bishops have consistently remained a core feature of Anglican ecclesiology. The third Lambeth Conference in 1888 adopted Resolution 11, later known as the "Lambeth Quadrilateral," which clarified that one of the four features of Anglican identity was the historic episcopate.[22] While this provision allowed local adaptations to the precise way in which a bishop exercises and administers authority over a diocese,[23] an innovation introduced by the Church of England has gone much further: the notion of "alternative episcopal oversight," better known as the "flying bishop."[24] The Church of England introduced this innovation during the debate over women's ordination, as a way to reassure those who refused to accept the ordination of women. Alternative episcopal oversight allowed clergy who could not tolerate serving under a bishop who ordains women to serve instead under the authority of a bishop from outside their diocese.

This practice illustrates the lengths to which Anglican leaders have been willing to go to prevent schism. The notion of a "flying bishop" violates a central feature of Anglican tradition, the premise that "the diocese, as the community united in its bishop and as the bishop's sphere of ministry, is regarded ecclesiologically as the 'local church.' It is the locus and sphere of the bishop's oversight."[25] Alternative episcopal oversight breaks this strong link between the local bishop and the geographical diocese; moreover, it undermines the bishop as a symbol of unity for the local church. Yet, in order to avoid the threat of serious schism, Anglicans have repeatedly shown a willingness to compromise on this and similar issues out of a sense that "walking apart" was not only undesirable but contrary to their calling to work for the unity of the church.[26]

It is this tradition of ongoing commitment to unity despite intense differences that the *Windsor Report* undermined in its framing of the situation in the global church. The report suggested that this aspect of the Anglican tradition is not only causing the church serious problems but is no longer tolerable. The perceived sense of expanding diversity has undermined confidence in the benefits of shared association. Indeed, the more diversity and difference are recognized and encouraged within the Communion, the more the interests and agendas of its various members appear to diverge. As William Sachs bluntly puts it, "Certain common features, such as English descent, structures of global scope, Catholic forms, cultural malleability, and Reformation heritage pervade this family of churches. Yet Anglicans have no coherent sense of identity and no apparent means to resolve their uncertainty."[27] Yet such accounts of the Communion's current situation often overlook the fact that its tensions are largely the result of a long-standing willingness on the part of the global church to grant significant autonomy to its members—both in regions within dioceses and provinces and in relations between provinces. Local autonomy has long been recognized as an important missiological tool, and in more recent times as essential to enabling a postcolonial release from the "Anglo-Saxon captivity of the church."[28] In other words, the current challenges confronting the church are the result of its own consciously adopted policies.

In emphasizing the novelty of the divisions over homosexuality, the framers of the *Windsor Report* were forced to downplay earlier historical differences in the Communion. Their interpretation of the conflict in the church thus also shaped the options that presented themselves and encouraged certain ways of understanding and depicting their opponents. As Bishop Mark emphasized, "much depends on the metaphors you use." Given the intense and urgent atmosphere in which the *Windsor Report* was composed,[29] the tone of the document is understandable, and perhaps it was unavoidable. But the report has painted the leaders of the Communion into a corner, by encouraging the perception among many Anglicans that they are becoming too different from one another to remain in the same church. This way of framing the issue lies at the heart of the conflicts in the Communion. Many Anglicans now feel that the shared history and traditions that have held the member churches together have lost their power to counteract the pressures that appear to be pulling those churches apart—the disagreement over homosexuality, interpretation of scripture, proper deployment of the Instruments of Unity, and so on.

Given the long-standing ethos in the Communion encouraging openness to diversity, why have so many Anglican leaders begun suggesting that the global church can no longer continue on as before? If the province of Australia does not think it can afford schism, why do other global leaders feel differently?

First, there is the simple fact that the structures of the Communion appear much more distant and abstract to average church members than those of their local diocese or province.[30] While this may once have indeed been the case, our analysis of the internet's impact on church communities (chapter 2), and of the conflict's impact on local congregations (chapter 4), suggests that a tidy separation between the local and the transnational levels of the church cannot be assumed. This raises a second issue pertaining to the framing of the conflict in the Communion. A tendency persists to describe the tensions in the global church as occurring *between* different provinces rather than also *within* each province. The *Windsor Report's* reference to walking apart only reinforced this tendency.

What a number of our informants stressed, however, is that, as Bishop Timothy put it, "this is not an interprovincial conflict; it's an intraprovincial conflict." Bishop Peter explained that this was particularly true of the tensions over women's ordination: "It's internal to most provinces, but the international side is used as a way of characterizing the debate because one can see why the heat is there, but it's internal to provinces as well."

The persistent tendency to describe the tensions in the Communion as arising chiefly *between* provinces is linked to the ongoing pattern of conceiving of provinces as if they were individual nation-states that relate to each other as autonomous agents. This view sharply contradicts the impact of globalization and how it has resulted in a "post-Westphalian" global context.

Until recently, international relations were conceived primarily in terms of interactions between nation-states and were governed by principles like territorial integrity and national sovereignty, as established by the Peace of Westphalia in 1648.[31] Today, however, many developments have complicated this way of thinking of nation-states as self-enclosed and autonomous entities; these include global warming, immigration and mass migration, trade deals and multinational corporations, human rights protections, acts of genocide, terrorism, the drug trade, and mass communication. None of these issues respect territorial borders. For this reason, the political theorist Nancy Fraser argues that, in many international situations, "the problems debated are inherently trans-territorial and can neither be located within Westphalian space nor can be resolved by a Westphalian state."[32]

What is true of the general global context is also true of the churches within it. Disputes within the Anglican Communion have become transnational, yet many leaders, along with the general membership, continue to conceive of their national denomination chiefly in Westphalian terms. Different interests and groupings within each province develop networks and strategic links with like-minded groups in other provinces, disrupting the Westphalian model.[33] What has emerged is a much more complicated web of partnerships, strategic maneuvering, and the mobilization of support for different causes.

Despite these developments, many leaders in the global church continue to describe the churches of the Communion largely in terms of independent nation-states. For example, although alert to the shifting sands within the structures of the Communion, Bishop John imagines ecclesial tensions as existing chiefly between provinces: "What's happening in the Church of England and the Anglican Communion is really what happened in the Commonwealth about twenty years ago. . . . The old Commonwealth acknowledged the queen . . . [and] the chairman . . . was the English prime minister. The new Commonwealth of the last twenty years or so isn't that at all. It's these fledgling democracies that have come of age and say, 'Hang on a minute: We've got more people than England has.'" Many Anglican leaders have followed suit by arguing that the demographic size of their province ought to grant it greater authority in the life of the Communion than smaller provinces enjoy. Some have expressed considerable anger over the "trespassing" across the geographical episcopal boundaries of one province by leaders from another province. This is fueled by the tradition of seeing such national territorial boundaries as sacrosanct.[34]

This was indeed how national churches operated in a Westphalian age. But in the wake of new transnational partnerships between Evangelicals across provincial boundaries, and the emergence of extra-geographical incursions of primates and mission organizations into the jurisdiction of other provinces, it has become more difficult to prevent others from exercising influence within other provinces than it used to be.

In our conversation with Bishop Christopher, he highlighted the way in which the resulting tensions aggravate the split between two different ways of conceiving of the nature and purpose of the church:

> I think there is a tension here, to be frank, in the Anglican Communion. . . . Because of the foundational document, there is an impetus towards catholicity—towards understanding the catholic nature of the church across the world and down through the ages. . . . There is also, because of the formative events of the sixteenth century, a kind of view of the church, which is derived from the paradigm of the nation-state, and I think that in a way the present trouble could be seen as a struggle between these two ideas. On the one hand, you want a highly interdependent Communion where the different national or provincial churches are in a very close relationship with one another; and on the other, you have the view that each church, each national or provincial church, is autonomous in the way a nation-state might be.

Anglican theologians generally describe this as a call to be committed to *both* local context and catholicity.[35] Indeed, Communion documents like the *Windsor Report* encourage members to think of the global church as simultaneously an intimately related unity and a voluntary association of independent churches. Even as the report does so, however, it reveals a concern over a potential contradiction between these ideals. The report thus labors to add nuance to the concept of "autonomy" with statements like the following: "A body is . . . 'autonomous' only in relation to others: autonomy exists in relation with a wider community or system of which the autonomous entity forms part. The word 'autonomous' in this sense actually implies not an isolated individualism, but the idea of being free to determine one's own life within a wider obligation to others. The key idea is autonomy-in-communion, that is, freedom held within interdependence."[36] But this does not clarify which structures or intentional patterns of relations will embody "autonomy-in-communion." Essentially, this language only gestures at an ideal; it does not offer a clear model for the governance structures of the Communion, or any obvious parameters that might guide church leaders, to use the language of contemporary management, in how to "operationalize" this understanding. Thus, without specific alternative models that could shift the way Anglicans conceive of their local church and its relation to the global Communion, the habit of imagining individual provinces in terms of autonomous nation-states remains largely intact.[37] As we shall see, it is precisely the prevalence of this kind of vague and imprecise discourse that has invited hollow posturing in the arena of public opinion in the global church. Meanwhile, the resulting frustrations only intensify the forces pulling against traditional structures and relationships in the Communion.

The Legacy of this Framing of the Conflict

It is clear that this way of framing the diversity and tensions in the Communion has done little to help it confront its problems. In the previous chapter we explained why initiatives introduced by church leadership have thus far done little to quell calls for more radical change in the Communion. Here, we examine the reactions to this way of framing the conflict. Distinct from the proposals discussed in chapter 6, these reactions have not led to specific documents or procedures; they are much less specific, taking the form of abstract ideals and vague models, and we will explore three of them here. The first and perhaps most vocal is an appeal to "biblical authority" in support of altering the existing power structures in the Communion. The second is a form of anti-institutional idealism, which confronts the tensions in the global church with sentimental evocations of the notion of "communion." The third response has been more pragmatic, imagining new structures or models that might manage or contain the tensions in the church. Each of these reactions will be explored in turn.

(1) LEVERAGING POLITICAL INFLUENCE: INVOKING THE AUTHORITY OF HOLY SCRIPTURE

One of the most prominent examples of sentimental rhetoric in the global church is the way in which many leaders speak of the "authority" of holy scripture as the key to restoring unity in the Communion. As with the symbolic phrase "Anglican orthodoxy," discussed in chapter 1, many who invoke the "authority" of the Bible speak as if this authority is immediately transparent. As we observed in chapter 2, however, the invocation of scripture's authority often amounts to a demand that others obey one's interpretation of a biblical text. When the Bible's authority is spoken of in this way, however, it is deployed as if the meaning of the text is obvious to any honest person. Disagreement is thus framed as duplicity.

GAFCON press releases are perhaps the most prominent example of this pattern. The chairman of the first meeting of this network, Peter Akinola (Nigeria), declared that the GAFCON movement was "well-known for our stand on Scripture as the foundation stone of our tradition and reason."[38] He explained that acknowledging the authority of the Bible means accepting the final authority of scripture in all matters of faith and conduct; upholding marriage as between men and women only; approving sexual relations only between a married couple; and professing opposition to homosexuality, rape, and child abuse. "Our beloved Anglican Communion," Archbishop Akinola concluded, "must be rescued from the manipulation of those who have denied the gospel and its power to transform and to save; those who have departed from the scripture and the faith 'once and for all delivered to the saints' from those who are proclaiming a new gospel, which really is no gospel at all." These remarks suggest that different readings of the Bible are inherently wrong. The archbishop does not support this claim with argument or evidence, nor does he clarify or support the statement that the Bible should have final authority on all matters of conduct. His invocation of the clear "authority" of scripture does not linger over the particular details of the text; he merely asserts this view as if it is straightforwardly self-evident. Thus, on the issue of child abuse, the archbishop does not pause to consider Jephthah's sacrifice of his daughter (Judges 11:39), dashing the heads of infants against the rocks in Psalm 137, or God's call for genocidal slaughter of the Amalekites, including children (1 Samuel 15). Further, the archbishop's logic is tautological. He states that homosexuality is unbiblical, but then defines what counts as biblical by its opposition to homosexuality. The declaration, in short, is its own legitimation. Thus when the archbishop describes himself and his companions as those "who have chosen to stand where the Bible stands," he is really saying that where he stands represents the biblical position, and so standing with him is standing with the Bible. What he is in fact defending, therefore, is his own authority to declare what is orthodox and what is "unbiblical."

When we spoke with Bishop John, he employed a term that is often used to bolster this way of speaking about scripture: "the plain teaching of the Bible." Initially, Bishop John sought to demonstrate that he held a very nuanced and considered understanding of this notion:

> Some people say to us (those of us conservatives), "You're just reading the Bible in the flat and it's a literalistic view of the Bible." No. I've been very careful not to use the word "literal," because the Bible is full of poetry, elliptic language, and all sorts of stuff. It talks about the sun rising but it doesn't really mean that we believe in a flat earth. No, it's a kind of poetic way of talking. But as I read that to you, it's very plain what the Bible is saying, and it's consistently true within the Bible that God's ideal is a heterosexual relationship within marriage for a man and a woman, and that's the proper place for sexual encounter.

It is noteworthy that although the bishop claims that the Bible is complex and nuanced, on some issues, he asserts, its meaning is "very plain" and must be taken literally (this even as he insists that he does not have a "literalistic" view of scripture). Because Bishop John insists that "plain" teaching on homosexuality is a "first-order Gospel-related issue about the authority of the Bible," there can be no compromise in the church with alternative readings of the text.[39]

The issue here is not whether one agrees or disagrees with Bishop John's interpretation of the Bible; the issue is the immediacy with which he demands consent to his interpretation. The message, he insists, is "plain," by which he means that it is beyond discussion. He declares not only that it should be but also that it *is* obvious to *any* sincere reader what particular biblical passages affirm about complex issues like the modern concept of homosexuality. Bishop John's way of speaking about the authority of scripture demands that one agree—immediately and without the need for debate—with his own understanding of the text. His tone is romantic and sentimental, for agreement depends on sharing the same assumptions about the concept being evoked.

The point here is not that holy scripture is always already interpreted. That would be a debate over hermeneutics and how the Bible ought to be correctly (and faithfully) interpreted. Most Anglicans (including Bishop John) readily acknowledge this.[40] The point is not so much the relationship between the Bible and the community that gathers around it but the relationship between the biblical text and those who claim to speak on behalf of its "authority." If James Bielo defines "Biblicism" as "prioritizing the relationship between biblical texts and communities of practice" in a manner that encourages prooftexting and selective reading,[41] what we are concerned with here is better described as employing the Bible as a device for political leverage. What stands out in the various declarations and communiqués issued by GAFCON is that they seldom discuss specific biblical texts. Rather than concern themselves with the content of particular passages of scripture, such declarations speak only of the "authority of scripture" in toto. Thus, instead of privileging the text over the community ("Biblicism"), GAFCON leaders privilege their own authority to adjudicate what counts as "Gospel" over the particularities of the text itself. In the case of Archbishop Akinola's address, the one speaking on behalf of scripture is privileged over the community to which he speaks. It is clear that when the representatives of GAFCON invoke biblical authority in this way, they are presenting themselves as an alternative to the structures and ways of relating that have traditionally characterized the Anglican Communion. In effect, the notion of "biblical authority" is employed as political leverage against the long-standing influence of those who have largely controlled the church at the global level: the Church of England and the Episcopal Church in the United States.

In this way, many critics of the status quo in the Communion claim to be defending "the Gospel" without at the same time addressing the specific content (pertaining to either doctrine or practice) of the Bible. Instead, Anglicans are either implied to be with them (and can thus be considered authentically Christian) or against them (and thus fall short of biblical "orthodoxy"). It is noteworthy that this is not *engaging* with scripture but *leveraging* the rhetorical power of the concept of scripture to advance their alternative agenda for the Communion.[42] Anglican leaders who are trying to wrest control from the traditional sources of power in the Communion seek to subvert the legitimacy of those traditional powers by invoking a more basic form of authority—that of holy scripture. Since the Bible predates the Church of England and the structures of the Anglican Communion, the concept of biblical authority promises to offer a more immediate and compelling rhetorical foundation upon which to mount a challenge to the balance of power in the global church.

We are not arguing that Anglicans should not hold strong views about the biblical text—quite the contrary. At the beginning of this section, we argued that at the heart of the conflict in the Anglican Communion is a desire to identify the church's normative context, the shared truth claims and moral commitments around which Anglicans can gather. We also suggested that a second key issue at the heart of the conflict is the question of who gets to establish these truth claims. As the Church of Australia and the practice of "flying bishops" illustrate, Anglicans have generally made room for those with differing readings of the Bible and tradition. The problem inherent in sentimental and idealistic ways of speaking about scripture, then, is not that they are normatively laden. The problem is that these ways of evoking scriptural authority exclude Anglicans who do not immediately agree with the speaker's own position. For this reason, we argue that this kind of reaction to the tensions in the Communion only strengthens, rather than diminishes, the centrifugal forces that risk pulling the global church, and many of its provinces, apart. It is a political stance based on declaration rather than on deliberation or negotiation.

(2) SENTIMENTALITY AND IDEALISM IN THE FACE OF COMPLEXITY: THE IDEA OF "COMMUNION"

Rather than invoke the notion of "biblical authority," some Anglicans respond to the global church's struggles by advancing an understanding of "communion" that seemingly dismisses the need for ecclesial structures altogether. The Brazilian theologian Carlos Calvani, for example, suggests that "the need for institutional and juridical mechanisms clearly indicates that we do not have a 'true communion' and that the discussion has moved off in a political direction."[43] Calvani's argument implies that a church that requires formal procedures and policies is encumbering itself unnecessarily in bureaucratic matters. Such a view suggests that if Anglicans could just meet face to face, their differences would cease to be divisive.

In chapter 3 we showed how many African leaders we spoke with expressed their sense of belonging to an Anglican "family." Although we noted that such statements suggest a significant level of commitment and enthusiasm for that vision, we also observed that much depends on how one envisions the structure of this "family" and the roles assigned to different members within it. The same is true of the concept of "communion."[44]

Sentimental references to the concept of "communion" imply that anything that falls short of seamlessly intimate relationships betrays the church. Like Calvani, many of the leaders we interviewed spoke as if the struggles and limitations of the global church signaled that the Anglican Communion had betrayed their ideal image of "true communion." Bishop Elias put it this way: "I think the word 'Communion' now is very inaccurate and that it requires courage to say we are not really a real communion." The bishop then back-tracked slightly, recalling how, at Lambeth 2008, Rowan Williams had stated, "We are a wounded Communion." But after pondering that phrase, Bishop Elias quickly restated his initial diagnosis: "To be honest with you, it is very difficult to call it communion in the current situation."[45]

We encountered this tone among a number of our informants. They expressed the emotional dimension that many people attach to the concept of "communion"; one is in communion, they suggested, if one feels seamlessly united to others. In an article on church unity, John Yates offers a theological rationale for such an understanding: "Christian unity . . . is not something that we can generate. It is a gift we receive when we turn to faith in Christ and we are embedded in his body, the Church."[46] Yates employs the theological understanding of the sovereignty of God, and an emphasis on the idea that human beings are wholly reliant upon God's grace, to suggest that if something is imperfect or broken, it is not of God. By such logic, when the institutional church fails to live up to its ideal form, it must be rejected.

This vision of a unified community implies the social form of a "sect" rather than a "church" or "denomination" (chapter 5). Modeled on a notion of purity—and in theological terms of "holiness" and "faithfulness"—this conception of what "true communion" entails leaves little room for serious disagreement.[47] Moreover, given the many differences within the various provinces of the Communion, rhetoric that encourages the possibility of a pure and unmediated communion is not only sentimental but disingenuous.

The philosopher Gillian Rose has suggested that although the notion of communism as the ideal community has now collapsed, many people have fallen "more deeply in love with the idea of 'the community.'"[48] By this she means a romantic vision of social life without the annoyances of any of the inner or outer boundaries that require a lot of work to negotiate and adjudicate. Rose notes that such sentimental notions of community discourage reliance upon any mediating concepts or institutions, such as rational debate, law, or authority structures. This description of community captures Calvani's notion of communion, but also Yates's portrait of church unity.

In our conversation with Bishop Mark, he expressed his growing impatience with this vague and sentimental conception of communion. "People are saying," he told us, "'if you don't do want we want, we shall stamp loudly enough until we get our own way.' I'm . . . parodying it a bit, but a lot of it feels a bit like theological tantrums." Perhaps Bishop Mark would appreciate Bishop Jordan's more eschatological description of the Communion, which he offered as an alternative notion of "communion" as something for the church to strive toward: "I think the Anglican Communion is a thing in creation. You know, we thought it was one thing, but then you, sort of, put a bit of pressure on it, and you discover that it's not an Anglican Communion. It is maybe on the road to an Anglican Communion." In either case, the warning to the churches of the Anglican Communion is clear: Sentimental notions of what "true communion" entails, and romantic conceptions of "community" based on sentimental immediacy rather than reliance on mediating institutions, will not help the global church address its current challenges.

If evoking the authority of scripture and a sentimental notion of communion characterize many Anglicans' response to the situation in the Communion, a third response has been to seek a new model that might help contain or manage the tensions in the global church. This pragmatic approach to the conflict is noteworthy for its avoidance of the root of the problem, even as it scrambles to try to fix it.

(3) THE PRAGMATIC RESPONSE: NEW MODELS FOR MANAGING DIVERSITY

The English theologian Paul Avis describes the pragmatic search for new structural processes to stabilize church governance as "trying to pin down what exactly the Anglican Communion of thirty-eight self-governing churches around the world *is*, ecclesiologically speaking. How should we describe and define it theologically?"[49] From this emphasis on a theological understanding of the global church, Avis turns to a number of organizational options currently under consideration, including both "federalism," the model of relationship employed by ("Eastern") Orthodoxy, and some uniquely Anglican concept of "communion." But debates over what model should be adopted are often conducted at some distance from considerations of what the Communion actually *is*. The felt need to find a new procedure or institutional arrangement to manage the present mess thus gets reduced to a pragmatic concern: Will it "work"?

When he was archbishop of Canterbury, Rowan Williams outlined the options available to the global church in a manner similar to Avis's: (1) a "loose federation" of diverse Anglican churches with little coordination or mutual obligations; (2) a family of independent regional churches that would come together over matters of common concern; (3) a firmer and more consistent control of diversity. Williams suggested that "each of these is attractive in some ways to people at both ends of the theological spectrum. Yet each of them represents something rather less than many—perhaps most—Anglicans over the last century at least have hoped for in their Communion."[50] In his view, a loose federation risks being reduced to open competition between rival members. The vision of independent national churches, by contrast, ignores the impact of globalization, while firmer centralized control is vulnerable to "powerfully motivated groups from left or right." As an alternative to these options, the archbishop advanced the idea of the "Anglican covenant," which was eventually rejected by many members of the global church (chapter 6).[51]

In the wake of the failure of the covenant proposal, the leaders we interviewed throughout the Communion referred often to such debates and proposals. Bishop David, for example, seemed at a loss over how to conceive the future shape of the global church, asking rhetorically, "Is it a family? A federation? A communion? Is it magisterial? What is the appropriate model?" Bishop Christopher engaged with these questions more directly, after discussing the long legacy of different visions of the church, particularly those of the catholic and reformed models in the Church of England. "On the one hand," he said,

> you want a highly interdependent Communion where the different national or provincial churches are in a very close relationship with one another, and on the other you have the view that each church, each national or provincial church is autonomous in the way a nation-state might be. What you have, then, in addition, is a kind of federation or association of such autonomous churches. In the end, these two ideas are incompatible because you either end up with a Catholic church, if you

see what I mean, which is very closely related and where the sacramental and other life is shared very closely. On the other, you end up with an association of churches who can live together despite strong disagreement because they don't have anything to do with each other's internal life.

Bishop Christopher's preference for a more centralized model of catholicity is evident in his association of federalism with an autonomy that he thinks will guarantee isolated individualism. Critics of a federal model often voiced this concern. Paul Avis, like Williams, is also sympathetic: "such a model would do scant justice to how the Anglican Communion has seen itself up to now and would fly in the face of the theology of communion (*communion, koinonia*) that has been developed in the Roman Catholic, Orthodox and Anglican traditions."[52] It is also clear that the federalism proposal (in either its weak or its strong form—Williams's first and second options) is problematic in the way it ignores the post-Westphalian structure of the churches of the Communion, for the conflicts and tensions in the Communion emerge not only between provinces but also within them. The federal model largely ignores this reality.

None of our informants advanced the Eastern Orthodox churches as a model for the Anglican Communion,[53] but some referred to the concept of "conciliarism." This is essentially a model of ecclesiastical governance that emphasizes the rule of bishops in council. Just as the Council of Nicaea in 325 C.E. gathered together the bishops of the early church to discuss matters of controversy and to render judgment,[54] some Anglicans have proposed some new form of conciliarism as the way forward for the Communion. Intriguingly, the stance of GAFCON leaders who emphasize Lambeth 1998's Resolution 1.10 resembles the conciliar vision. The claim, for example, that Resolution 1.10 is the "official teaching of the Anglican Communion" treats Lambeth 1998 as if it were a church council with "conciliar" authority. Moreover, the manner in which GAFCON leaders speak of the authority of the Primates' Meeting, over and against provincial general synods or the Anglican Consultative Council, implies that they conceive of primates as having a conciliar function.

Of course, the conference at Nicaea was called by the Roman emperor Constantine, under whose authority it met.[55] Under what sovereign authority would a new conciliar arrangement be implemented? Ephraim Radner alludes to this issue when he acknowledges the rather troubled legacy of conciliarism in the Church of England, under the rule of the Crown and Parliament. "Ironically," he notes, "it was in *America*, and in the United States specifically, that the conciliar character of Anglicanism found a new and vital form." This occurred with the emergence of the General Convention, which included bishops, clergy, and lay representatives. Yet this is precisely the form of church governance that many now blame for a drift toward congregationalism and theological disorder in the Anglican tradition. Radner himself suggests that this model's emergence in the context of a political revolution, "where questions of representation and consent were paramount," goes some way to explain why "theological concerns regarding the Body of Christ and the discernment of Scripture were, at best, secondary" to this process.[56]

This kind of criticism makes clear the extent to which the particular model of church governance that is advanced quickly gets drawn into either idealism or pragmatism. Notice the way in which Avis's entry into the debate proceeds by advocating for the ideal theological form of church, thus sidestepping the organizational challenges within and between existing historical Anglican churches that have resulted in the confusion in the first place. His method, which begins by arguing what form the church *should* take, without regard for the existing forms that Anglican churches at present *do* embody, leaves itself vulnerable to the very theological polemics it intends to avoid.[57] When the uses of scripture and tradition become politicized, even as they advance ecclesiological claims, one "blueprint ecclesiology" simply becomes a weapon with which to bludgeon the rival "blueprint ecclesiology" of one's opponent.[58]

At the same time, the suggestion that the churches of the Communion should be content with some loose form of federation (Williams's first option) is based largely on the existing state of affairs. Such a stance is essentially reactive and instrumental, a coping mechanism that corresponds to the status quo. It can thus be described as pragmatic rather than theological. Rather than wrestle with the question of what the Communion should become (in theological terms, "what it is called to be"), this approach is content to define it according to what it looks like at present. Moreover, basing the future structure of the Communion on the status quo is a recipe for further fragmentation, given the prominence in some quarters of the view that Anglicans have become too different from one another to remain united. Assumptions and misinterpretations of the existing state of affairs rule the day.

The church leaders we interviewed hinted at alternatives to framing the situation as a choice between idealism or instrumental pragmatism. Rather than perceive an intractable contradiction between a federation, on the one hand, and a communion, on the other, Bishop Liam sees a process. The Anglican Communion is already a federation, he suggested, but perhaps it can move to being an actual communion, something that is already implied in Anglicans' self-understanding. "I think we've always understood ourselves as a communion of churches," he said,

> and that has meant access to the Eucharist all over the world, it has meant being in communion with the archbishop of Canterbury, it has meant that bonds of affection tie us sacramentally without having international canon law. What we're discovering now, and in the last two decades, which was something that was always there from the beginning, at least potentially, [is] that our ecclesial reality is federal. We are experiencing ourselves in a kind of federality, rather than the perhaps naïve, superficial view that we were utterly and totally one communion. I personally think that, sociologically and ecclesially, we need to acknowledge that the Anglican Communion is behaving like a federation, while nevertheless striving for deeper degrees of communion.

The federal reality of transnational Anglican polity, Bishop Liam argued, has only really become apparent through the divisive issues of homosexuality and women's ordination. But he suggested that acknowledging this reality should not be seen as a "disaster"; rather, it is an important "recognition of human limitation and human difference." While it is true that the existing state of affairs is a product of "paradigm shifts, some talking past each other, some ethnocentrism, some radical historical divergence in the postcolonial world," nevertheless, in his view, the provinces of the Anglican Communion remain a communion "in hope." Even as they remain diverse and divided, he suggested, they might be understood as unified through their longing for a deeper relationship that awaits them in the future.

Essentially, Bishop Liam began from the concrete messiness of the current state of the Communion (the stance that informs the pragmatic proposals discussed above), while holding on to the possibility that the global church might become much more than its current lived reality (a position that begins to approach the more idealistic vision of theologians like Avis). In this way, his perspective opens up a way to both acknowledge the Communion's current "messiness" and take it seriously, without reducing to its present circumstances our understanding of the global church's possibility and calling.

This chapter has demonstrated that a great many of the Communion's struggles have to do with how church leaders have framed the conflict, sometimes misrepresenting the differences among and within member churches and treating them as radically novel challenges. At the same time, the resources that member churches possess to cope with such diversity have often been overlooked. These failures have encouraged unhelpful reactions to the tensions in the global church, notably the use of the "authority of scripture" to try and leverage political influence away from traditional sources of power and influence; reliance upon idealistic notions of "communion" that foster anti-institutional sentimentality; and merely pragmatic attempts to "manage" or "contain" the conflict that leave few people satisfied. After demonstrating the limitations of each of these responses, we argue that describing the members of the global church as inhabiting a space between mere federalism and full communion provides a better way to frame the current situation. While this perspective acknowledges the Communion's current tensions and fragmented state, it also encourages Anglicans and Episcopalians to understand themselves as called to a broader purpose and end that lie ahead. As a project to live into, rather than a foundational status from which to begin, the concept of the Anglican Communion might yet find a way to weather the storms in which it finds itself.

CONCLUSION

The "End" of the Communion?

As our preparation of this book entered its final stages, the archbishop of Canterbury, Justin Welby, sent a letter to the primates of the Communion, inviting them to a Primates' Meeting to be held in October 2017. In this letter, the archbishop compared the Communion to the boat in which the disciples were traveling when it was caught in a great storm (Mark 4:37–41). "The disciples were seeing the reality of the great spiritual battle in which we are engaged," he wrote, "and our minds are taken to Ephesians 6:12. Our battle is not against flesh and blood, least of all against each other." Having thus framed the tension in the boat as the product of "spiritual" conflict rather than interpersonal dispute, Archbishop Welby concluded, "We are all in the one boat. There is no other boat than the church, because only there do we find the presence of Jesus and only from the boat are we able to witness to the Kingdom of God."[1]

Welby no doubt used the story of Jesus calming the stormy seas to encourage the primates to recommit themselves to the unity of the Communion. His appeal was quickly dismissed by the usual critics online, and rumors soon began to spread that the GAFCON primates might refuse to attend the meeting.[2] This reaction, it seemed to us, showed that the Anglican Communion was no closer to repairing the cracks in the hull, or healing its broken relationships, than it was when we began this project almost ten years earlier. Strong criticism of the Instruments of Unity has continued to proliferate, grandstanding has remained a standard mode of communication, and calls to return to the purity of the past have persisted. The prominence of homosexuality as a "presenting symbol" has proved to be an enduring rallying point for discontented Anglicans across the globe. Moreover, the way in which the internet and blogosphere continue to be employed to criticize the leadership of, and status quo in, the global church illustrates once again how new communication technology represents a challenge to traditional religious authority (chapter 2).

Yet the question remains: Does the fact that Anglicans appear no more unified in 2018 than they were in the aftermath of Lambeth 2008, or even than they were fifteen years ago in the wake of the consecration of Gene Robinson, signal that the Communion is coming to an end? As we discussed in chapter 7, the answer to this question depends on how one frames the situation. One might emphasize that there is little sign of improved relations between GAFCON primates and the provinces of the United States and Canada, even though many of the leaders have changed since 2003. This framing could encourage a description of the Communion as suffering ongoing polarization and fragmentation. Alternatively, one might note that even though GAFCON has been declaring for more than a decade that TEC has abandoned "the Gospel" and that GAFCON alone speaks for the "Anglican orthodox," the Communion has yet to suffer a major schism. Few provinces have realigned themselves with GAFCON in that period. Nor has the GAFCON message matured much beyond the objection to beliefs, practices, and persons in other parts of the Communion with which it disagrees. Framed in this way, the Communion appears no closer to "walking apart" than it did when the *Windsor Report* introduced that phrase in 2004.

Leaving aside these competing ways of framing the conflict in the global church, this book has demonstrated reasons for the stubborn persistence of the Anglican Communion in the face of the many tensions and challenges confronting it. Chapter 1 showed how, despite the intensity of the polemics against homosexuality (and against the status quo in the Communion), protest movements like GAFCON face considerable obstacles to marshaling a feasible alternative to the existing Instruments of Unity. For all the power and mobilizing potential of GAFCON's attacks on homosexuality, and its use of the symbol of "Anglican orthodoxy," under the surface its countermovement is riddled with competing agendas and perspectives. Opponents to the ordination of women are paired with staunch supporters of female priests; advocates for lay presidency at the Eucharist find themselves in the same camp as those who uphold traditional Anglo-Catholic sacramental theology; defenders of strong episcopal authority are partnered with groups that value fluid missional activity over ecclesial structures and institutions. The only thing really holding these divergent groups together is their shared opposition to homosexuality; should they ever actually withdraw from the rest of the Anglican Communion in a formal schism, internal rivalries and conflicts would in all likelihood soon break out between these allies of convenience.

This reality is one of the factors that has thus far prevented serious momentum toward schism. Chapters 3 and 4 demonstrated some of the diversity within the churches of the Global South and within the Anglican Church in North America (ACNA). Although many have persisted in describing the conflict in the Communion in dualistic terms—as North versus South or liberals versus conservatives—these binaries, as we have shown, often dissolve under close scrutiny. There is thus no single fault line along which the church could split decisively; any split is likely to be a ragged tear with many threads nonetheless holding on.

That the interrelations between Anglicans are more diverse and complex than they are often portrayed as being could be taken to mean that the Communion's quest for unity is even more hopeless than many members fear. As we hope to have made clear, however, such diversity can be a source of strength. Different agendas and perspectives, when they crisscross along many axes and prevent large monolithic binaries from developing, can actually weave together a very tight network of relationships. Instead of two polar-opposite camps, a complex assortment of groupings can end up forming a tangled web of interconnections. While there may be a great deal of tension along some of these tangled fibers, a "balance of power" among rivals and a tangled web of relationships provide stability to the system. The evidence we have marshaled to demonstrate the diversity within the Global South, the ACNA, and the "liberal" Global North suggests that the Communion has not yet arrived at its end. No one agenda or party in the global church had managed to forge a movement sufficiently unified and dominant to seize control of the Communion. Nor do the various camps at present seem either self-sufficient or internally coherent enough to simply go their own way. These restraints on formal schism go some way to explain why the Anglican Communion has yet to split, and if it does, why it is unlikely to be a clean tear.

There remain significant positive resources that enable many Anglicans to continue to seek to "walk together." In chapter 3 we related how many in the Global South spoke to us of their ongoing love and commitment to their Anglican "family." Many in the Global North shared their appreciation of the Communion's "bonds of affection," which surpass the technical arrangements of church structures and canons and emerge out of concrete relationships and shared histories. In chapter 6, while acknowledging the limitations of initiatives like the "continuing *indaba*" process, we saw that some of the formal gatherings between church leaders across geographical regions and theological divides are bearing fruit. Particularly when linked to specific missional or social outreach projects, these "gatherings" and "consultations" have generated not only deeper understanding between leaders and provinces but also greater sympathy, solidarity, and mutual recognition of one another as fellow travelers in Christ.

The ongoing push and pull of these centripetal and centrifugal forces in the life of the Anglican Communion leave the global church in a state of ongoing tension and uncertainty. In chapters 6 and 7, we showed how many of the attempts to resolve these difficulties in recent years have fallen short. Sometimes this has been due to the failure of leaders to take into account the ways in which the dynamics of the Communion have been changed by new communication technology, changing demographic patterns, and the emergence of a "post-Westphalian" global context. On other occasions, leaders have either misdiagnosed the conflict in the church or responded to it with sentimentality, vague proposals, or empty signifiers. Such attempts to fix the problem may in fact constitute the greatest continuing source of tension, and could eventually push the global church to a formal schism.

Yet we concluded the final chapter by returning to Bishop Liam's suggestion that, despite their many differences, the provinces of the Anglican Communion can still decide to remain a "Communion in hope." Even as Anglicans remain diverse and divided, Bishop Liam suggested, they still might be unified through their longing for a deeper relationship that awaits them in the future that God has in store for them.

Some might object that this position could become a form of sentimental idealism in its own right. Might Bishop Liam's notion that the Communion is in "process" rest on the same assumptions that inform the "continuing *indaba*" agenda? Critics of the *indaba* ideal argue that it does nothing to disturb the status quo.[3] What may look like a dynamic and dialectical perspective on the world, according to those critics, is only a smoke screen behind which those in power remain in control.[4]

This is not the position we are advancing here. The key element in Bishop Liam's vision of the global church, which resists the pressure to prop up the status quo, is that it points beyond itself. Not content with seeing it as a mere "federation," Bishop Liam advances the fullness of communion as an eschatological achievement that the church is called to pursue and live into. While allowing for the reality that Anglicans begin from different starting points, this position urges all members of the church to pursue a common end.

This stance is based on a faith and hope that the members of the Communion do indeed have a common mission, and that it will be revealed to them in time. In this way, the unity of the global church, rather than resting on a grounding declaration (for example, GAFCON's "Jerusalem Declaration") or on some novel pragmatic proceduralism, is founded on a common commitment to the future discovery of a shared calling and mission as disciples of Jesus of Nazareth.

This notion of communion as a shared quest for future unity recalls the success of the Consultation of Anglican Bishops in Dialogue (chapter 6). Its achievements are tied to its clearly stated goal of helping participants respond to the concrete and immediate challenges facing their churches. This group does not sponsor dialogues for the sake of dialogue but has specific objectives that point beyond the gatherings themselves. In the same way, if the Communion is to be more than a loose and chaotic federation of independent churches, then its members will need to exhibit a commitment to pursue a much more ambitious vision for their future association.

Such a vision shares a resonance with some of the goals of the proposed Anglican covenant, specifically with the principles outlined in the first section of the various drafts (as opposed to the sections focused on disciplining those who fall short of the covenant's expectations—for example, section 4 of the final draft). Indeed, refocusing the conversation on the purpose and end of the Communion, framed in terms of living into a goal and calling, would emphasize those preliminary sections of the covenant discussions that received so little attention in debates over the proposed covenant. Time will tell how much resilience this understanding of the church still has, in the face of the rhetorical power of "biblical authority," on the one hand, and sentimental expectations of perfect and seamless "communion," on the other.

Another merit of framing the Anglican Communion as a process toward unity, rather than an already achieved state of foundation agreement, is that it meets member churches where they are and encourages them to accept that they are on a journey toward future unity. This position implies the need for some form of shared institutional life to help mediate existing "federal" relationships, and interrupt the temptation to attempt to wipe the slate clean, or to introduce new quick-fix instruments or "solutions" to the global church's present structures. As chapter 6 demonstrated, two decades of debate over which of the four Instruments of Unity should be granted new powers of adjudication has come to naught, and there is little reason to think that a sudden breakthrough is forthcoming. If Anglicans can agree that the current state of the Communion's governing bodies is less than ideal, but not hopelessly flawed, they will be able to have a less polemical and divisive conversation about the relative strengths and weaknesses of each of these instruments, and about the extent to which each requires modification in response to the changing needs and mission of the Communion.

Whether the members of the global church are prepared to accept such a tentative stance toward the tensions in the Anglican Communion remains to be seen. As Martyn Percy has acknowledged, "before conflicts can be resolved, they must first of all be *held*."[5] The question confronting Anglicans is whether they are committed to seeking solutions to tension and conflict because they believe that doing so is part of their calling as Christians. In many ways, this is to ask whether Anglicans continue to have any interest in holding on to each other.

Our interviews with leaders throughout the Communion suggest that church leaders from a wide range of positions and perspectives do continue to value the Anglican Communion. For some, it remains very much part of their Christian "family." Others feel compelled to work for the church's unity out of a sense of its historical "catholicity," or on the basis of the biblical call to live as one (John 17:21). The polemical battles of the past two decades have not yet exhausted these resources. What remains to be seen is whether the leaders of the Communion will find ways to reframe the global church's struggle, perhaps in terms of a quest for a shared purpose and end—or whether the voices calling Anglicans to "walk apart," and for an end to the experiment that is the Anglican Communion, will continue to strengthen.

NOTES

INTRODUCTION

1. Solheim, *Diversity or Disunity*, 65. The story was widely reported on 5 August 1998, including independent reports by the BBC (see "UK Confrontation at Lambeth Conference") and the *Independent* (Garner, "How I Felt the Wrath").

2. For discussions of Lambeth 1998, see Tarsitano and Toon, *Dear Primates*; Turner, "'Communion' of Anglicans After Lambeth." For a subdued response to the Lambeth Conference, see the essays in Stevenson, *Fallible Church*. For a critical discussion of the media coverage of the conference, see Sollis, "Bearing False Witness," 19.

3. For such accounts, see Porter, *New Puritans*; White, *Authority and Anglicanism*; Zahl, *Protestant Face of Anglicanism*.

4. Williams, "Foreword," x.

5. For a discussion of how other resolutions have been ignored, see Mitchell, "Lambeth's Forgotten Teaching."

6. See Solheim, *Diversity or Disunity*, and conservative commentator Stephen Noll, "Lambeth Diary 1998."

7. The text of the statement is available at http://www.globalsouthanglican.org/index.php/blog/comments/the_kuala_lumpur_statement_on_human_sexuality_2nd_encounter_in_the_south_10.

8. Hassett, *Anglican Communion in Crisis*, 102–7; Noll, "Lambeth Diary 1998."

9. See, for example, Groves, Holder, and Gooder, "Witness of Scripture."

10. For an account of those organizing the apology, see Solheim, *Diversity or Disunity*, 78–84.

11. "Pastoral Statement to Lesbian and Gay Anglicans."

12. Noll, "Lambeth Diary 1998."

13. The assumption that homosexuality is un-African has been widely discussed and criticized. See Vincent and Howell, "'Unnatural,' 'Un-African,' and 'Ungodly.'"

14. The court majority found that "there is no core doctrine prohibiting the ordination of a noncelibate, homosexual person living in a faithful and committed sexual relationship with a person of the same sex." See Niebuhr, "Episcopal Priest Absolved."

15. Those opposed to such a shift certainly read it as a sign of the times. See Hassett, *Anglican Communion in Crisis*, 50–51.

16. Ibid., 132–38.

17. The Nigerian Church would follow, consecrating its own "missionary bishops" to the United States after the election of an openly gay man as bishop of New Hampshire in 2003 and declaring the illegitimacy of TEC and its bishops.

18. Having bishops is widely understood as an essential part of Anglicanism, as outlined in the Chicago-Lambeth Quadrilateral. See Norris, "Episcopacy."

19. See Larmondin, "New Westminster Synod."

20. See *Bentley v. Anglican Synod of the Diocese of New Westminster* 2010 BCCA 506 (CAN LII) (British Columbia Court of Appeals), https://www.canlii.org/en/bc/bcca/doc/2010/2010bcca506/2010bcca506.html.

21. Goodstein, "Gay Man Is Made a Bishop."

22. See Thompson, "Global Anglican Future Conference."

23. Ibid. See also Brittain and McKinnon, "Homosexuality and the Construction"; and Sadgrove et al., "Constructing the Boundaries."

24. Primates of the Anglican Communion, "Walking Together."

25. Drake, "New Zealand Postpones Decision."

26. McGowan, "Sydney Anglican Diocese Donates."

27. A good brief introduction to the subject is found in Mark Chapman's *Anglicanism*.

28. Some Anglicans prefer to argue for an origin of the Church of England that predates the Reformation, and they point to the sixth century, when Pope Gregory sent Augustine of Canterbury to Britain. Such claimants emphasize the distinctive Celtic influences on the Roman tradition, through figures such as Saint Aidan. See, for example, Grafton, *Lineage from Apostolic Times*; Hardinge, *Church in Celtic Britain*.

29. MacCulloch, "Putting the English Reformation on the Map."

30. Helpful brief histories of each of these provinces can be found in Markham et al., *Wiley-Blackwell Companion to the Anglican Communion*.

31. Somewhat confusingly, a number of the Anglican Communion's provinces are divided into regions that are also called "provinces," each with an archbishop (including the Church of England, which has the Provinces of Canterbury and York; this is also true of the United States, Canada, and Nigeria, among other provinces).

32. For a comprehensive overview of the canons of different provinces, see Doe, *Canon Law in the Anglican Communion*.

33. For discussions of such concerns regarding the Instruments of Unity, see Faulds, "Anglican Communion"; Wilkins, "Back from the Brink"; Cameron, "Tortoise in a Hurry."

34. See Neill, *Anglicanism*, 99–132.

35. For an important and insightful overview and analysis of the Anglo-Catholic movement, see Pickering, *Anglo-Catholicism*.

36. Churchmen's Union, "Objects."

37. See Gore, *Lux Mundi*.

38. We had planned an interview with a leader from the Church of Wales, but it fell through for scheduling reasons.

39. See Brittain, *Plague on Both Their Houses*.

40. Pittsburgh has been one of the local hot spots in the conflict, and this resulted in the diocese's being divided down the middle. It also became the headquarters of the ACNA when its bishop, Robert Duncan, was elected the first archbishop of the new province. This is why we chose it as a case study, though it is undoubtedly something of an outlier.

41. Those with an interest in church politics may well be tempted to guess at the face behind the mask of a particular pseudonym. In our experience, when people make such guesses, they are more likely to be wrong than right, but we do not confirm either way.

42. On the use of snowball sampling (the recruitment of interview subjects on the basis of recommendations and/or assistance from existing study subjects) in qualitative field research, see Handcock and Gile, "Concept of Snowball Sampling."

43. The figures that follow thus do not include our interviews in Pittsburgh.

44. A pseudonym.

45. For discussions of the politics of the terminology used to designate sexual orientation and gender, see Valentine, "Categories Themselves"; Bohan, *Psychology and Sexual Orientation*; Donovan,

"Homosexual, Gay, and Lesbian"; Eliason, "Exploration of Terminology."

46. Even two very closely allied (and soon to be merged) organizations like Changing Attitudes (UK) and the Lesbian and Gay Christian Movement will adopt slightly different terminologies. This was evident in the two organizations' responses to a 2017 statement from the House of Bishops that upheld the two-gender definition of marriage. See Beardsley, "(Church of England) Lock Out"; and Byrne and Pemberton, "Letter to the House of Bishops."

47. See Epprecht, *Heterosexual Africa*. See also chapter 3 of this book.

48. This undoubtedly stems in part from a statement from the House of Bishops titled "Issues in Human Sexuality."

CHAPTER 1

1. Chaves, *Ordaining Women*; Kniss, *Disquiet in the Land*.

2. For detailed analysis of women's ordination in the Anglican Communion, see Rubenstein, "Anglican Crisis of Comparison"; Smith, "Response to the Ordination of Women"; Fletcher, *Beyond the Walled Garden*; McAdoo, *Anglicans and Tradition*; Wetherell, *Women Priests in Australia*.

3. Yinger, *Religion, Society, and the Individual*.

4. Ammerman, *Baptist Battles*.

5. Kitschelt, "Political Opportunity Structures."

6. For denominational-level splits, see Liebman, Sutton, and Wuthnow, "Exploring the Social Sources"; Sutton and Chaves, "Explaining Schism." The structural dimensions of the Anglican Communion conflict are discussed at greater length in chapter 5.

7. For a discussion of "new institutionalism," see DiMaggio and Powell, *New Institutionalism in Organizational Analysis*.

8. Wallace, *They Call Her Pastor*. Wallace was well ahead of the curve in noticing this phenomenon. According to John Allen of the *National Catholic Reporter*, as of 2007 there were thirty-one thousand lay ecclesial ministers working in U.S. parishes, more than the twenty-nine thousand diocesan priests. See Allen, "Lay Ecclesial Ministry."

9. McCarthy and Zald, "Resource Mobilization and Social Movements."

10. Benford and Snow, "Framing Processes and Social Movements."

11. Kniss, *Disquiet in the Land*, 136.

12. For a survey of the history of prayer book revisions in the Church of England, see Jasper, *Development of the Anglican Liturgy*. A more focused case study is provided in Maiden, "English Evangelicals." For discussion of the delicate politics of church music, see Tucker, "Music Wars"; Watson, "Ancient or Modern."

13. Maiden and Webster, "Parliament, the Church of England."

14. Roudometof, *Globalization and Orthodox Christianity*.

15. Hassett, *Anglican Communion in Crisis*.

16. The Conservative–Liberal Democrat coalition government of David Cameron passed legislation making same-sex marriage legal in England and Wales. There was remarkably little opposition (and much support) from within the Conservative Party. The prime minister ultimately was overcome by his inability to control the Eurosceptics within his own party.

17. Note that many dispute the "culture wars" thesis as a whole, denying that Americans are divided into two opposition camps with a growing gap between them. See Davis and Robinson, "Are the Rumors of War Exaggerated?" Among sociologists, James Davison Hunter has been a somewhat lonely voice in this debate, though many journalists have seen value in his thesis. See Hunter, *Culture Wars*. We address the limitations of Hunter's thesis in the American context in chapter 4.

18. Note Andrew Atherstone's caution in "Identities and Parties."

19. For a detailed account of such nuanced differences among Evangelicals in the Church of England, see Vasey-Saunders, *Scandal of Evangelicals*, 115–50.

20. This is an estimate, as we have been unable to find a precise and reliable count for any recent point in time; both the general picture and the trajectory, however, are clear.

21. Ward, *History of Global Anglicanism*, 257–59.

22. Kaye, *Introduction to World Anglicanism*.

23. On 13 June 2012, the primate of the Province of TEC, Katharine Jefferts Schori, presided at the Eucharist at Southwark Cathedral in London, England. Because the Church of England did not permit female bishops at the time, Archbishop Jefferts Schori was not permitted to wear her miter during the ceremony. She carried it instead.

24. On this phenomenon, see Brown and Woodhead, *Church That Was*, 45–46.

25. Bishop Newman in particular, while generally sympathetic to Reform, thinks that this reasoning is based on a misunderstanding of the biblical passages in question.

26. After 1992, 487 priests in the Church of England accepted compensation from the church and left their posts, though sixty-seven of them had returned by 2002. A few priests may have left without accepting financial compensation, and some no doubt opted to retire if they were approaching retirement age. See Jones, *Women and Priesthood*.

27. Jones accepted retrospective self-reports for attitudes of priests in 1992, so there is very probably some harmonizing of present and past views. This would suggest that there may have been slightly more change in the direction of support for women priests than is reported in the study.

28. These figures are not derived from a nationally representative sample, and they should be taken as broadly indicative of attitudes within the different constituencies but not as an accurate picture of the size of different constituencies. Sophie Gilliat-Ray's survey of ordinands at the same time is undoubtedly more accurate in this respect, with 12 percent identifying as Conservative Evangelical, 36 percent Open Evangelical, 19 percent Liberal, 28 percent Affirming Catholic, and 2 percent Forward in Faith. See Gilliat-Ray, "Fate of the Anglican Clergy."

29. And in particular in the spirit of the commitment of the National Evangelical Anglican Congress to remain in the Church of England. See Atherstone, "Keele Congress of 1967."

30. The technical term for an issue about which there can be legitimate disagreement and practice is *adiaphora*. See Thomas, "Doctrine of the Church."

31. These concerns and reservations are discussed at greater length in chapter 4.

32. Cf. Crockett and Voas, "Divergence of Views."

33. Pickering, *Anglo-Catholicism*, 184–206; see also Hilliard, "UnEnglish and Unmanly"; Jones, "Stained Glass Closet."

34. Pickering, *Anglo-Catholicism*, 163–83.

35. GAFCON, "Complete Jerusalem Statement," article no. 2.

36. This is discussed at greater length in chapter 4.

37. Anglican Consultative Council, *Virginia Report*.

38. Long considered a very serious matter and a potential source of church conflict in any episcopal tradition, a cross-border incursion occurs when a bishop acts within the jurisdiction of another bishop or another province altogether.

39. Once upon a time, social scientists used to believe that values determine human conduct, and they built elaborate theories of social life around this conviction. Unfortunately, there is very little evidence that this is the case, as attested by a very significant literature on the "values-action gap," and particularly by the disjuncture between pro-environmental values and

anti-environmental behavior. For the classic statement of this view, see Parsons, *Structure of Social Action*. For a review of some of the attempts (both practical and theoretical) to bridge this gap, see Kollmuss and Agyeman, "Mind the Gap." For an influential restatement of this problem, see Swidler, "Culture in Action."

CHAPTER 2

1. For more on the concept of "time-space compression," see Harvey, *Condition of Postmodernity*, 284–307.

2. Bevans, *Models of Contextual Theology*. See also West, "Do Two Walk Together?"

3. The locus classicus for this problem in philosophy and social theory is of course Hegel's *Phenomenology of Spirit*.

4. Gitari, *Anglican Liturgical Inculturation* and "Claims of Jesus"; Trisk and Pato, "Theological Education and Anglican Identity."

5. McQuillan, "When Does Religion Influence Fertility?"

6. Bruce, "Authority and Fission"; Liebman, Sutton, and Wuthnow, "Exploring the Social Sources."

7. Kaye, *Conflict and the Practice*, 41–64.

8. See Wallerstein, *Modern World-System I*, for a good analysis of this development.

9. Held, "Regulating Globalization?"

10. Robertson, *Globalization*, 97–114; see also Beyer, *Religion and Globalization*.

11. Ritzer, *McDonaldization of Society*.

12. Spickard, "Religion in Global Culture."

13. McKinnon, "Sociological Definitions." See also Smith, "Religion, Religions, Religious"; Masuzawa, *Invention of World Religions*.

14. If the church ever encompassed the majority of the English people, it has not done so for a long time. Identification with any church extends beyond simple

attendance of religious services, but even in 1851 people in the pews of the Church of England accounted for just under 52 percent of the 7,261,032 whose attendance was recorded in England and Wales. See UK Census Office, *Worship in England and Wales*. Thanks to Steve Bruce for his help on this point.

15. There were, of course, attempts to impose episcopacy (and the prayer book) in Scotland in the seventeenth century, but this is only one minor strand of the long and complex history of the Episcopal Church in Scotland. See MacDonald, "James VI and I"; Donald, *Uncounselled King*; Davies and Hardacre, "Restoration of the Scottish Episcopacy."

16. These are admittedly mostly smaller provinces, but far from insignificant, especially when considered collectively. The group includes Mexico, Brazil, Central America, Cuba, and South America (Southern Cone), but also Rwanda, Burundi, the Democratic Republic of the Congo, South Korea, Japan, and the Philippines; other provinces have a mix of areas once part of the British Empire (west Africa) and some were under British imperial rule for a relatively short time (Tanzania).

17. Lambeth Conference, "Lambeth Conference of 1920," Resolution 34.

18. Bishop Robert Gray of Cape Town tried to have Bishop John Colenso of Natal declared a heretic by the synod of the Church in South Africa (in which he was successful in 1863) and ousted from his office (in which he was much less so, Colenso appealing to the English courts and having his appeal upheld). See Jacob, *Making of the Anglican Church*, 144–51. See also Colenso, *St. Paul's Epistle to the Romans*.

19. Global electronic communication is undoubtedly fast, but it is far from perfect.

20. McLuhan, *Understanding Media*, 24–35.

21. See Broersma and Graham, "Social Media as Beat"; and, on blogging

and "micro-blogging" by journalists, Lasorsa, Lewis, and Holton, "Normalizing Twitter."

22. Murray, "Will Not to Know."

23. Brown, "African Christians Will Be Killed."

24. For a starting point on this complicated question, focusing on Nigeria, see Ukiwo, "Politics, Ethno-Religious Conflicts."

25. See chapter 3.

26. This is described in the scholarly literature by Sherry Turkle in *Life on the Screen*.

27. Nardi and Whittaker, "Face-to-Face Communication."

28. Bates, *Church at War*, 222–23.

29. Reference to interview withheld to maintain confidentiality.

30. This is probably a reference to Brittain, *Adorno and Theology*.

31. Weber, "Politics as a Vocation," in *From Max Weber*, 78.

32. Campbell, "Religious Authority and the Blogosphere." See also Campbell and Garner, *Networked Theology*.

33. The other obvious questions entail reception of the blogger's message: how, why, when, and by whom are bloggers' messages taken as authoritative? Authority claims are often conflated with acceptance of authority claims, even by erudite thinkers like Max Weber, the sociologist who wrote more influentially on the question than anyone else. See Parkin, *Max Weber*, 88.

34. Because of the tensions in the Communion, there was no voting on motions at Lambeth 2008. Rather, the conference was structured around *indaba* (a Zulu word) groups, which met and engaged in "purposeful conversation." For further discussion of this model, see chapter 6.

35. See Naughton, "Following the Money"; Hassett, *Anglican Communion in Crisis*.

36. Handley, "ACNA Primate Was Given Ballot Paper."

CHAPTER 3

1. Welby, "Archbishop's Message to GAFCON."

2. GAFCON, "Nairobi Communique and Commitment."

3. Thinking Anglicans, "Will There Be Another Lambeth?"

4. Solarz, "North-South."

5. Center for the Global South, http://www1.american.edu/academic.depts/against/cgs/about.html.

6. One often hears this suggestion put forward by church leaders, publicly and privately. For example, following the passing of Resolution 1.10 at the 1998 Lambeth Conference, the primus of the Episcopal Church of Scotland, Bishop Richard Holloway, accused American conservatives of having influenced the vote by mobilizing the African bishops to support their cause: "These Americans have lost the battle in their own Episcopal Church so they have hired a proxy army," Holloway said. Solheim, "Sexuality Issues Test Bonds." A more measured version of this point is put forward in Ward, *History of Global Anglicanism*, 313.

7. As reported in Ashworth, "Software Suggests Minns Rewrote"; and Episcopal Café, "Who Speaks for Africa?"

8. Goodstein and Banerjee, "Money Looms in Episcopalian Rift."

9. Naughton, "Following the Money."

10. Anderson, "Conservative Christianity," 1597.

11. Quoted in Jenkins, *New Faces of Christianity*, 20. In this context, it should be recalled that Bishop Harris was confronted by considerable hostility from some of the bishops at Lambeth who opposed women's ordination, which included being "hissed" at. See Rubenstein, "Anglican Crisis of Comparison," 346.

12. Murray, *Proclaim the Good News*.

13. Hooton and Wright, *First Twenty-Five Years*.

14. O'Connor, *Three Centuries of Mission*.

15. Willis, "Nature of a Mission Community." In 1965, the SPG and UMCA merged to form the United Society for the Propagation of the Gospel.

16. See, for example, Ogungbile and Akinade, *Creativity and Change*.

17. For illuminating studies of the intersection of African culture, local situations, and Christianity, see Soothill, *Gender, Social Change*; Ranger, *Evangelical Christianity and Democracy*; Englund, *Christianity and Public Culture*.

18. Wild-Wood, "Attending to Translocal Identities," 95.

19. Sanneh, *West African Christianity*, xii.

20. These figures are from Johnson and Ross, *Atlas of Global Christianity*, 75. See also Jacobsen, *World's Christians*, 373.

21. Jacobsen, *World's Christians*, 163, 164.

22. Jenkins, *Next Christendom*, 1.

23. Ibid., 15.

24. Johnson and Ross, *Atlas of Global Christianity*, 75.

25. It is perhaps instructive to compare the statistics with which we are concerned here with the fictions that stand in for even the most basic economic statistics (import, export, agricultural production, unemployment) across much of sub-Saharan Africa. In this regard, Morten Jerven's careful research in *Poor Numbers* makes for instructive reading.

26. Quoted in Christian Today, "Africa Anglicans Criticise Church."

27. Orombi, "What Is Anglicanism?"

28. These 2010 figures are reported in Johnson and Ross, *Atlas of Global Christianity*, 73.

29. Church of England statistics for October 2014 found 980,000 people attending church each week (including 150,000 children). See Church of England, "Statistics for Mission 2014."

30. Muñoz, "North to South."

31. Goodhew, *Growth and Decline*, 7.

32. If we accept that earlier statistics are much more reliable than more recent ones, there were roughly 742,300 Anglicans in Kenya in 1970. Assuming Galgalo's higher estimate of Anglicans at present, this would mean a growth rate of just over 600 percent between 1970 and 2015. This would indeed be somewhat ahead of the total population, which grew by just over 400 percent in the same time period; the lower end of Galgalo's estimate brings this down to Anglican growth of 540 percent in the past forty-five years against the overall population growth of 400 percent. See United Nations, *World Population Prospects*, table A-9, pp. 18–21.

33. Quoted in Mbogo, "Election of Homosexual Bishop."

34. Quoted in Zoll, "World's Episcopalians Watch Vote."

35. Scholarly literature also emphasizes the economic and political factors at the root of ethnoreligious conflict. See Salawu, "Ethno-Religious Conflicts in Nigeria." Salawu's article shows that this conflict has a much longer history and much deeper roots, and it makes no mention of inter-Anglican politics as a cause of violence.

36. According to the most accurate figures for Africa as a whole, 62 percent of the population is under twenty-five years old. See Bongaarts, "Human Population Growth," 2988.

37. Meyer, "Christianity in Africa."

38. Johnson and Ross, *Atlas of Global Christianity*, 112.

39. Ibid.

40. These things are, of course, inter-related, and they are affected by religion in complex ways. In a region where HIV/AIDS has had such a devastating impact, one cannot discount the impact of different rates of mortality in different religious communities as important factors in their relative growth or decline.

41. For a good account of these problems, see Jerven, *Poor Numbers*.

42. Flexible, but not necessarily straightforward or uncontended. See Wild-Wood, "'Free from Shackles.'"

43. The term is Max Weber's. See McKinnon, "Elective Affinities."

44. Paul Gifford refers to this as the product of an "enchanted religious imagination." See his *Christianity, Development, and Modernity*, 14.

45. See Epprecht, *Heterosexual Africa*.

46. On Nigeria, See Obadare, "Sex, Citizenship, and the State." On Ghana, see Essien and Aderinto, "'Cutting the Head.'" On Uganda, see Sadgrove et al., "Morality Plays and Money Matters"; Ward, "Role of the Anglican and Catholic Churches"; Boyd, "Problem with Freedom." On southern Africa, see Vincent and Howell, "'Unnatural,'Un-African,' and 'Ungodly'"; Currier, "Political Homophobia." And on southern-central Africa, see Klinken, "Homosexuality, Politics"; Epprecht, "'Unsaying' of Indigenous Homosexualities."

47. Awondo, Geschiere, and Reid, "Homophobic Africa?"; Epprecht, *Sexuality and Social Justice*; Epprecht, *Heterosexual Africa*.

48. See Bleys, *Geography of Perversion*; Epprecht, *Heterosexual Africa*. Jeffrey Weeks notes that in Britain during the first quarter of the nineteenth century, there were public moral panics about sodomy, especially in the navy, and that in 1806 there were more executions for buggery than for murder. See Weeks, *Sex, Politics, and Society*.

49. Weeks, *Sex, Politics, and Society*, 119–57.

50. Ibid., 122.

51. Greenberg, *Construction of Homosexuality*.

52. Epprecht, "'Unsaying' of Indigenous Homosexualities," 644.

53. Ibid.; Currier, "Political Homophobia."

54. Essien and Aderinto, "'Cutting the Head'"; Obadare, "Sex, Citizenship and the State."

55. McKinnon, Trzebiatowska, and Brittain, "Bourdieu, Capital, and Conflict."

56. Hoad, *African Intimacies*, 61.

57. Ibid., 66.

58. Hassett, *Anglican Communion in Crisis*, 51–70.

59. Western governments followed through on their threats after the bill was signed into law in February 2014. See Agence France-Presse, "Uganda Tells West It Can 'Keep Its Aid.'"

60. Morris, "Commonwealth Nations to Have Aid Cut."

61. Gifford, "Trajectories in African Christianity," 278. See also Bowers, "African Theology"; Mana, *Christians and Churches of Africa*; Martey, *African Theology*.

62. Congar, "Fraud Complaint Filed."

63. Ward, "Role of the Anglican and Catholic Churches."

64. Boyd, "Problem with Freedom," 701.

65. Sadgrove et al., "Morality Plays and Money Matters," 126.

66. Boyd, "Problem with Freedom," 701.

67. The sense of global interconnectedness is undoubtedly more acute for the leadership than for the faithful. See Vanderbeck et al., "Meanings of Communion."

68. Kaye, *Introduction to World Anglicanism*, 250.

69. Tutu, *No Future Without Reconciliation*, 31.

70. Despite the wide range of views we heard, there may be some bias in our sample; several of the key GAFCON leaders we had hoped to speak with declined to be interviewed.

71. On the importance of context for understanding religious metaphors, see McKinnon, "Metaphors in and for the Sociology of Religion."

72. Yinger, *Religion, Society, and the Individual*, 137.

CHAPTER 4

1. Quoted in Johnston, "Church of England Leaders." Similar dismissals of the goings-on at the global level of the Communion were voiced by others across the political and theological divides. For example, Colin Coward, founder of Changing Attitudes, responded to the primates' statement, "I've reached the stage where what they decide will make no difference to my faith, my spirituality or my presence with God in creation. I have no need to give Primates authority or control over my life and my relationship with God." Likewise, in *Living Church* magazine, Neil Dhingra contrasts "the apparent unreality of the Primates' Meeting" with "the reality of communion in the local church." See Coward, "Primates' Meeting"; Dhingra, "Primates and the 'Reality.'"

2. Admittedly, it may be that some parishioners in an established church structure like the Church of England are more insulated from external tensions than those in provinces like the Episcopal Church in the United States.

3. For critical engagement with Hunter's hypothesis, see Hunter and Wolfe, *Is There a Culture War*; Bean, *Politics of Evangelical Identity*, 4–7.

4. James Nieman describes a "congregational study" as the use of multiple research methods to examine a congregation holistically. "Fundamental to this approach," he writes, "is that the centrality and integrity of a congregation are preserved rather than the congregation being reduced to an illustration for a scholarly theory." While the scope of this chapter prohibits as textured and detailed an exploration as a single congregational study, Nieman's basic principle very much shapes its intention and spirit. See Nieman, "Congregational Studies," 133.

5. In order to protect confidentiality, the names of individuals and churches have been changed, and details that would facilitate their identification have been omitted. For further analysis of our findings, see

Brittain, *Plague on Both Their Houses*. For an account by a cleric from Pittsburgh involved in the dispute, see Lewis, *Recent Unpleasantness*.

6. Examples of such statements from Pittsburgh include Duncan, "Anglicanism Come of Age"; Millard, "Making the Case."

7. Hamill, "Pittsburgh Episcopal Diocese Votes."

8. Bates, *Church at War*, 199.

9. A letter to Bishop Duncan from twelve of these clerics, informing him of their decision, was subsequently published in a local paper. See Levin, "Letter Shows Rift."

10. This is often referred to as the "Thomas theorem": "If men [*sic*] define situations as real, they are real in their consequences." See Thomas and Thomas, *Child in America*. This idea has subsequently been picked up by students of social movements, among others. For example, see Snow, "Framing Processes, Ideology"; Benford and Snow, "Framing Processes and Social Movements."

11. Williams, "Politicized Evangelism."

12. The legal theorist Carl Schmitt is (in)famous for arguing that the driving force of politics is the distinction between friend and enemy. See Schmitt, *Concept of the Political*.

13. Williams, "Politicized Evangelism," 145–46.

14. Hoffer, *True Believer*, 86.

15. Duncan, "Anglicanism Come of Age: A Post-Colonial and Global Communion for the Twenty-First Century," 18 June 2008, excerpted in Duncan, "Bishop Duncan Addresses GAFCON."

16. Vasey-Saunders, *Scandal of Evangelicals*, 152–78. The alternative interpretation offered by Vasey-Saunders is developed with reference to René Girard's theory of mimetic rivalry. He argues that English Evangelicals are in fierce competition over authentic "evangelical" identity, and displace the intensity of this rivalry on homosexuality as a "scapegoat." This Girardian analysis of British evangelicalism's

"crisis of undifferentiation" is insightful, although it remains curiously isolated from evangelical movements outside the UK. This leaves a significant gap in the argument, given, as Vasey-Saunders acknowledges, the interconnected ways in which British Evangelicals are linked with counterparts in the United States and, increasingly, the Global South.

17. Ibid., 12–16.

18. Ammerman, "American Evangelicals," 62.

19. Sutton and Chaves, "Explaining Schism."

20. Liebman, Sutton and Wuthnow, "Exploring the Social Sources."

21. This is not to say that schism in episcopal traditions is unheard of. Notable here is the small-scale split within the Episcopal Church (ECUSA) in 1873, when a suffragan bishop and twenty-one clerics and laypeople withdrew to form the Reformed Episcopal Church. See Guelzo, *Union of Evangelical Christendom.*

22. See McKinnon, Trzebiatowska, and Brittain, "Bourdieu, Capital, and Conflict."

23. Paul Zahl is a well-known Evangelical critic of TEC. See his *Protestant Face of Anglicanism.* He was president of the local evangelical seminary in the Pittsburgh diocese, Trinity Episcopal School for Ministry, from 2004 to 2007.

24. See Bonner, "Pittsburgh Paradigm" and *Called Out of Darkness.*

25. For further analysis of the unifying power of shared convictions, see Smith et al., *American Evangelicalism.*

26. See Lindsay, "Politics as the Construction of Relations."

27. For more on this tendency among American evangelicals to use unifying slogans, see Kemp and Macedo, "Christian Right."

28. Hamill, "Pittsburgh Episcopal Diocese Votes." See also the Episcopal Diocese of Pittsburgh website, http://www.episcopalpgh.org/resources /2008-special-convention-documents/.

29. For a nuanced analysis of conflict in an Episcopalian congregation in Virginia, see Mercer, "Conflicting Identities." Mercer draws upon peace studies scholars Marie Dugan and John Paul Lederach to show how various elements, rather than single issues, shape conflict. See Dugan, "Nested Theory of Conflict"; Lederach, *Building Peace.*

30. *Will & Grace* was an American television sitcom broadcast on the NBC network from 1998 until 2006. The program revolved around the platonic friendship between Will Truman (played by Eric McCormack), a gay lawyer, and his best friend and roommate Grace Adler (Debra Messing), a Jewish woman. During its eight seasons, the show won sixteen Emmy Awards. For discussion of the impact of this program on attitudes toward homosexuality, see Battles and Hilton-Morrow, "Gay Characters in Conventional Spaces"; Silverman, "Comedy as Correction"; Quimby, "*Will & Grace.*"

31. Chaves, *American Religion*, 100.

32. Ibid., 25. See also Putnam and Campbell, *American Grace*, 526–27.

33. Social scientific studies consistently suggest that contact with gay and lesbian people plays a significant role in shaping attitudes toward same-sex relationships and acceptance of homosexuality. See Merino, "Contact with Gays and Lesbians"; Vonofakou, Hewstone, and Voci, "Contact with Out-Group Friends."

34. Murphy, "Most U.S. Christian Groups." Since there is a small number of Anglicans in the sample (111), the margin of error is quite large (there is a 95 percent chance that the true value lies between 55.2 percent and 78.8 percent), and so these results must be viewed with caution.

35. Wuthnow also noted this phenomenon in *Restructuring of American Religion.* Norm articulates what Penny Edgell Becker suggests is typical of a "family congregation" during a church conflict, although the size and diversity of St. Bylsma's do not meet the parameters of

her definition of such a congregation. See Becker, *Congregations in Conflict*, 77–100.

36. Village, "Feeling In and Falling Out," 271, 283.

37. The other dioceses that left TEC at that time to form the ACNA with Pittsburgh (Fort Worth, Quincy, and San Joaquin) did not permit the ordination of women.

38. Starke and Dyck predict that those who remain in the original denominational structure after a congregational schism will experience the split as more disruptive than those who depart from the parent church. They note that while those who leave might articulate a sense of liberation, those who remain "described themselves as distraught, abandoned, betrayed, and shell-shocked." See Starke and Dyck, "Upheavals in Congregations," 169.

39. Cadge, Day, and Wildeman, "Bridging the Denomination-Congregation Divide," 253.

40. In the sociology of religion, this problem has been discussed at length with reference to accounts of conversion. See, for example, Beckford, "Accounting for Conversion"; and Snow and Machalek, "Sociology of Conversion." For a more general account, see Orbuch, "People's Accounts Count."

41. This closely corresponds with Brian Robert Calfano's emphasis on the two variables shaping clergy political action: personal ideology and contextual factors. Calfano argues that clergy are more prone to compromise on their own preferences in response to parishioner concerns about salient issues, and more likely to advance their personal agendas on matters to which laypeople give less attention. See his "Decision Theory." For a similar conclusion in a study of Roman Catholic priests, see Calfano, Oldmixon, and Gray, "Strategically Prophetic Priests."

42. This is not to suggest that the diocese was free of tension prior to the call to choose sides. The legal maneuverings in which Calvary Church engaged to clarify that church property belonged to the Episcopal Church, not the Diocese of Pittsburgh, drew the ire of Bishop Duncan and his supporters. The clashes between the rector of Calvary, Harold Lewis, and Bishop Duncan at diocesan conventions were the stuff of local legend. For Lewis's account of the situation before the schism, see his *Recent Unpleasantness*.

43. Juergensmeyer, "Thinking Globally About Religion," in *Global Religions*, 4.

CHAPTER 5

1. For the statement issued by the Primates' Meeting, see http://www.anglicancommunion.org/media/206038/Primates_Meeting_2016_Statement.pdf. For the ACC's statement in response to the communiqué, see Episcopal News Service, "ACC 'Neither Endorsed nor Affirmed.'"

2. See Simmel, *Conflict and the Web*. Our reading of Simmel has been influenced by Lewis Coser's *Functions of Social Conflict*. See also Hirschman, "Social Conflicts as Pillars."

3. See, for example, Hengel and Barrett, *Conflicts and Challenges*; Bryant, "Sect-Church Dynamic."

4. Bryan S. Turner argues that one of the basic requirements for any religious organization is to find a means of dealing with internal difference and disagreement. See his *Religion and Modern Society*.

5. See especially Weber, "'Churches' and 'Sects' in North America"; and Troeltsch, *Social Teaching of the Christian Churches*.

6. See Karagiannis, "Secularism in Context."

7. See Martin, "Denomination."

8. Swatos, "Beyond Denominationalism?"

9. Sect-like Anglicanism is by no means the exclusive province of conservative Evangelicals; paradoxically, it is also characteristic of some traditionalist Anglo-Catholics as well (see Pickering,

Anglo-Catholicism). Following Simmel, we would expect to find that Anglicans in environments where they are a minority subject to harassment and persecution also experience pressures that tend toward sectarian social forms.

10. Havel, "Power of the Powerless"; Wedeen, "Acting 'As If.'"

11. Sachs, *Transformation of Anglicanism*, 164–207.

12. Thompson, *Bureaucracy and Church Reform* (at home); Jacob, *Making of the Anglican Church*, 194–235 (abroad).

13. Strong, *Episcopalianism in Nineteenth-Century Scotland*, 11–21.

14. Turner, "Marginal Politics, Cultural Identities."

15. Neville, "Church of Ireland"; Morgan, "Church in Wales."

16. Prichard, *History of the Episcopal Church*, 101–38.

17. Jacob, *Making of the Anglican Church*, 151–93.

18. Prichard, "Lambeth Conferences," 92.

19. The document that grants an office, issued by the monarch.

20. Jacob, *Making of the Anglican Church,* 150.

21. Ibid.

22. The Mothers' Union is an international organization of Anglican women, founded in England in 1876. It has been particularly influential in Africa, where, in many dioceses, the bishop's wife becomes ex-officio president of the diocesan chapter. See Colin Buchanan, "Mother's Union," in *Historical Dictionary of Anglicanism*, 422; Moyse, *History of the Mothers' Union*.

23. A children's game played with a piece of string looped back and forth between the fingers of both hands.

24. See Martin, "Denomination."

25. Samuel Crowther (1809–1891) was the first African to be made a bishop in the Anglican Communion, as a missionary bishop to the Niger Delta in 1864. See Ward, *History of Global Anglicanism*, 124–25.

26. See Ashley, "Diversity and Episcopal Governance."

27. This is not to discount the very frequent presence of charismatic leaders in sects. Such leaders' authority, however, stems not from an office but from personal authority bestowed directly by God without mediation. See Max Weber, "The Sociology of Charismatic Authority," in *From Max Weber*, 245–63.

28. On the long history of these misunderstandings, see Locke, *Church in Anglican Theology*, 45–128.

29. For the more general point about how culture becomes institutionalized, see Berger and Luckmann, *Social Construction of Reality*.

30. Sennett, *Together*, 23. A small qualification is perhaps worth noting. While not unknown to the people of Scotland (in the north there is a stronger tendency toward the plain-speaking tradition), it is not uncommon to hear Scots complain that they wish the English would say what they mean.

31. For contemporary debate over the established status of the Church of England, see Chapman, Maltby, and Whyte, *Established Church*.

32. Keenan, "Separating Church and God"; see also Keenan, "Conditional Love?"

33. See Brown and Woodhead, *Church That Was*.

34. OutRage! activist Peter Tatchell publicly displayed the names of ten allegedly gay bishops at General Synod in 1994. This was considered an invasion of privacy, and their names were not published in the UK, but they were published in the Australian Press. Several months later, Dr. David Hope, bishop of London and the third-most senior bishop in the Church of England, soon to become archbishop of York, came out because he believed that he was about to be outed. The scene has since threatened to replay itself. See Gallagher, "Tatchell Threatens to 'Out' Bishops."

35. Peter Wheatley, suffragan bishop of Edmonton in the Diocese of Lincoln,

had the misfortune of similar publicity in 2003. See Gledhill, "Evangelicals to Meet Williams."

36. Lines and Jensen, "GAFCON Statement."

37. See One Body One Faith, "Bishop of Grantham."

38. For more on power, establish-ment, and the appointment of bishops, see McKinnon, "Religion and Social Class," 15.

39. See, for example, Smith, "Oligarchies in America." The passage from Tocqueville's classic study is to be found in book 1, section 1, chapter 7 of *Democracy in America*.

40. Primates of the Anglican Communion, "Walking Together."

41. They are "services of dedication and thanksgiving," which are the same services that are used following the civil marriage of a heterosexual couple, includ-ing that of the Prince of Wales and Camilla, Duchess of Cornwall, in 2005. See Seed, "Church Services After a Civil Partnership."

42. Wynne-Jones, "Male Priests Marry."

43. The nature and status of establish-ment continue to be debated within the Church of England; see Chapman, Maltby, and Whyte, *Established Church*.

CHAPTER 6

1. For the statement, see Anglican Communion, "News from Primates 2016."

2. For church media coverage of the meeting, see Folkins and Forget, "Order of Bishops."

3. National Indigenous Bishop Mark MacDonald, Bishop Lydia Mamakwa, of the Indigenous Spiritual Ministry of Mishamikoweesh, and Bishop Adam Halkett of Missinippi released a joint statement following the 2016 Canadian General Synod, explaining how First Nations Anglicans were reacting to the vote in support of same-sex marriage. Among the issues they listed was that the study guides and other material published by the national church had yet to be translated into indigenous languages. See MacDonald, Mamakwa, and Halkett, "Statement." For discussion of the historical roots of tensions between the Canadian Church and its indigenous members, see Woods, *Cultural Sociology of Anglican Mission*.

4. For a position defending the need for orderly procedures in the Communion, see Cameron, "Ardour and Order." For a defense of the value of persuasion through relationship, see Driver, "Beyond Lambeth 2008." It is noteworthy that Cameron's essay was written in the wake of an optimistic reception of the *Windsor Report* of 2004, whereas Driver's article appeared when the *Windsor Report*'s proposed covenant was in obvious jeopardy and after the *indaba* dialogue process had been introduced at Lambeth 2008. For a discussion of the *Windsor Report*, the Anglican covenant, and the *indaba* process, see below.

5. For an account of canon law in the Anglican tradition, see Doe, "Canon Law."

6. Doe, "Canon Law and Communion." The groundwork for Doe's argument was first established in his book *Canon Law in the Anglican Communion*.

7. For additional discussion of chal-lenges inherent in the notion that canon law might serve as a unifying instrument for the global church, see Hill, "Ecclesiological and Canonical Observations"; Atkin, "Language and Anglican Canon Law." Atkin highlights in particular the uneasy relation-ship between particular linguistic concepts originating in ecclesial canon law and some secular legal concepts, particularly in Anglican provinces in which the church is not established.

8. Doe, "Canon Law and Communion," 246.

9. Ibid., 260.

10. An illustration of the difficulty of achieving collective agreement among the different provinces is found in the debate that followed the call for all member prov-inces to formally approve the creation of the Anglican Consultative Council (ACC).

Debate soon arose over which bodies had the authority to bestow such approval, and recognition emerged that the answer to this question would be very different among the many distinct provinces. In Canada, for example, after much deliberation, the issue was sent to each diocese of the national church, although even there debate often ensued over whether the local diocesan synod had the authority to vote on establishing a body like the ACC. See Howe and Craston, *Anglicanism and the Universal Church*, 85–91. Our thanks to Alan Hayes for drawing our attention to this example.

11. Sachs, *Transformation of Anglicanism*, 201–5; Jacob, *Making of the Anglican Church*, 158–84.

12. Liebman, Sutton, and Wuthnow, "Exploring the Social Sources"; Sutton and Chaves, "Explaining Schism."

13. The significance and role of diocesan synods is of particular concern to a number of theologians. See Chapman, "Does the Church of England Have a Theology"; Kaye, *Introduction to World Anglicanism*, 210–31; Podmore, *Aspects of Anglican Identity*, 103–33.

14. For discussion of the covenant, see Goddard, "Anglican Communion Covenant"; Chapman, *Anglican Covenant*; Adams, "Unfit for Purpose"; Avis, "Anglican Covenant"; Clatworthy, "Instead of the Anglican Covenant"; Meyers, "Baptismal Covenant"; Zink, "Patiently Living with Difference."

15. Lambeth Commission, *Windsor Report* 48, §§117–18, and 68, articles 16 and 18.

16. For responses to various drafts submitted by member churches of the Communion, see the Anglican Communion's website: http://www .anglicancommunion.org/search.aspx ?q=covenant&f=document_library (accessed 4 May 2016).

17. These documents are available at Anglican Communion, "Anglican Covenant."

18. This version was amended at the fourteenth meeting of the ACC in Jamaica in May 2009. These revisions focused on the fourth and final section, where issues of mediating disputes were discussed. A new provision (4.2.3) was added to specify that a dispute should be referred to the standing committee only as a last resort, after a process of mediation had already been attempted.

19. Some Anglo-Catholics have suggested that the description of the church in sections 1–3 is overly Protestant, since the Eucharist and sacramental theology receive scant attention. See Clatworthy, "Case Against the Anglican Covenant."

20. For a generally sympathetic collection of essays, see Guyer, *Pro Communione*.

21. Wright, "Rowan's Reflections."

22. Goddard, "Commitment in Word and Deed."

23. Williams, "Why the Covenant Matters."

24. Atta-Baffoe, "Anglican Covenant," 148.

25. Avis, "Anglican Covenant," 294–95.

26. Doe, "Anglican Covenant," 160.

27. GAFCON, "Oxford Statement."

28. Wabukala, "Global Communion."

29. Powell, "Synod Opposes Anglican Covenant." For a list of supporters and critics of the proposed covenant, see Modern Church, "Supporters and Opponents."

30. Chapman, "What Is Going on in Anglicanism?," in *Anglican Covenant*, 28.

31. Adams, "Unfit for Purpose."

32. For some of the results in different provinces, see Anglican Communion, "What the Churches Have Done."

33. Ormsby, "English Church Votes Down Pact."

34. Avis, "Anglican Covenant," 293.

35. Quoted in Malnick, "Traditionalist Anglican Leaders to Meet."

36. It is noteworthy that such an adaptation of the *indaba* model is by no means unique, as it has been adopted as a process in some other contexts. See, for

example, Newenham-Kahindi, "Transfer of Ubuntu and Indaba."

37. Anglican Communion, "Lambeth Conference Resolutions."

38. Lee, "Indaba as Obedience," 150.

39. Wolf, "That They May All Be One," 142.

40. See Groves and Draper, *Creating Space*.

41. Hylden, "What Lambeth Wrought."

42. Noll, "Orthodox Anglican Divide."

43. Wabukala, "Global Communion."

44. Bridger and Goddard, "Learning From Indaba," 45.

45. For the documents generated by the process, see Anglican Church of Canada, "Consultation of Anglican Bishops."

46. See Seventh Consultation of Anglican Bishops, "Testimony of Unity in Diversity."

47. The principles behind the process are outlined in the Church of England's guide for participants, *Grace and Dialogue*.

48. Davies and Williams, "Synod Prepares for 'Relational Road.'"

49. Farley, "Divisions Deepen in Church." For the press release issued by the group, see Anglican Church of Canada, "Consultation of Anglican Bishops."

50. Paul, "Synod's Shared Conversations."

51. One might suggest that Paul's statement here is in some tension with what he has written elsewhere: "it is not possible to argue that the only thing which matters is the truth. . . . Jesus' example of restoration and the rebuilding of relations, and Paul's profound concern that the body of Christ be 'one,' will not allow us off the relational hook so easily." Paul, "Reconciliation in the New Testament," 40.

52. For personal reactions to the process from a variety of participants, see Davies, "Synod Members Thanked." Anglican Mainstream's conservative network published a series of additional criticisms of the process; see Anglican Mainstream, "Regional Shared Conversations Conclude."

53. For such criticism of the concept of tolerance from the discipline of theology, see Milbank, "End of Dialogue"; Hauerwas, "Creation, Contingency, and Truthful Nonviolence." On further engagement with the ideal of tolerance, see Asad, *Formations of the Secular*; Khameh, "Political Toleration, Exclusionary Reasoning"; Galeotti, "Range of Toleration."

54. An established text along these lines is Bevans, *Models of Contextual Theology*.

55. Sykes, *Integrity of Anglicanism*, 44.

56. See, for example, Smith, *Muslims, Christians, and the Challenge*, 86–96. For further discussion of these issues in interfaith literature, see Brown, *Communication Perspective on Interfaith Dialogue*; Pratt, "Theology After Dialogue." For analysis of similar concerns in more general literature, see Stains, "Reflection for Connection"; Siebt and Garsdal, *How Is Global Dialogue Possible*; Heath et al., "Processes of Dialogue"; Nagle, "Politics of Agonistic Recognition."

57. Quoted in Anglican Church of Canada, *"This Holy Estate."*

58. Sunarko, "Interfaith Dialogue and Cooperation," 51. On this point, see also Brittain, "Partnership Not Dialogue."

59. Mombo, "Response to 'A Testimony.'"

60. *Religion and Ethics Newsweekly*, "Lambeth Conference Wrap Up."

61. Thompsett, "Passion for Intercessory Prayer" ("strengthened"); Carroll, "Restoring the Bonds of Affection" ("restored"); Cameron, "Ardour and Order" ("survival").

62. See Lewis, "By Schisms Rent Asunder?"

63. For additional laments over the state of Anglican theological education, see Percy, "Sacred Sagacity"; Williams, "Conflicting Paradigms"; Williams, "Theological Education." For a more general survey, see Spencer, "Theological

Education." For attention to issues in the African context, see Galgalo and Mombo, "Theological Education in Africa"; Trisk and Pato, "Theological Education and Anglican Identity."

64. Braddock, *Book of Common Prayer*; Sampson, "Scripture, Tradition, and *Ressourcement*." For a study of how these issues have historically affected debates over prayer book revision, see Maiden, "English Evangelicals." For a philosophical defense of the significance of liturgy, see Pickstock, *After Writing*.

65. Radner and Turner, *Fate of Communion*, 123, 127.

66. For theological discussion of the formative role of practice, see Dykstra and Bass, "Theological Understanding." This notion is often attributed to the work of Pierre Bourdieu. However, the conception of *habitus* employed in such discussions is much closer to the concept found in one of the sources from which Bourdieu drew, the work of the early twentieth-century anthropologist Marcel Mauss. See Bourdieu, *Outline of a Theory*; and Mauss, "Techniques du corps."

67. See, for example, Gitari, *Anglican Liturgical Inculturation*; Holeton, *Liturgical Inculturation*; Dowling, "Text, Shape, and Communion"; Eare, *Beyond Common Worship*.

68. Percy, "Engagement, Diversity, and Distinctiveness," 20–21.

69. Percy, *Anglicanism*, 138 (emphasis added).

70. Avis, *Vocation of Anglicanism*, 95–96.

71. In this regard, one might note an emerging literature on the significance of civility for contemporary democracies. See Rucht, "Civil Society and Civility"; Rouner, *Civility*; Žižek, "Big Other"; Kingwell, *Unruly Voices*; Goldfarb, *Civility and Subversion*.

72. See Scapp and Seitz, *Etiquette*; Wouters, *Sex and Manners*; Davidson, *Hypocrisy and the Politics*; Lowell, *Anthropology of Cultural Performance*.

73. Percy, "Engagement, Diversity, and Distinctiveness," 22.

74. For attention to this issue within the culture of the New Testament, see Olivares, *(Im)polite Jesus*.

75. Jacob, *Making of the Anglican Church*, 292–93.

76. The classic argument, from which almost all subsequent discussion of the history of manners draws, is Norbert Elias's *Civilizing Process*. In that book, Elias argues that we cannot understand the growth of manners apart from the processes of state formation, which are together part of the civilizing process. But Elias does not think that religion has much to do with the civilizing process; for a critical reconstruction that shows the role of religion in this historical process, see McKinnon, "Religion and the Civilizing Process."

77. Such cultural tensions can also be observed in theological discussions of the situation in the Communion. Colin Podmore, for example, has published a series of articles aimed at identifying the distinctive structures and ecclesiology of the American church, which explain why American Episcopalians behave as they do. He emphasizes in particular that TEC has a more democratic ethos than many other Anglican churches. This is evidenced in a variety of ways, including the fact that laity have historically held more power in their congregations than laity do elsewhere in the Communion; that bishops cannot overrule the decisions of their diocesan conventions; that there are no archbishops or metropolitans in TEC; and that baptism is generally understood to be a commissioning for ministry. See Podmore, "Tale of Two Churches"; "Baptismal Revolution"; and "Two Streams Mingling."

CHAPTER 7

1. Kaye, *Introduction to World Anglicanism*, 208. Kaye bases this perspective on an analysis of the *Virginia Report*, produced by the Inter-Anglican Theological and Doctrinal

Commission in 1997 and presented to the 1998 Lambeth Conference. The text of that report can be found in Dyer et al., *Official Report of the Lambeth Conference*, and Anglican Consultative Council, *Virginia Report*. Reception of the report has been mixed, and its status as an authoritative document remains in dispute. Carlos Calvani, for example, has accused it of being "superficial" and of collapsing the invisible "mystical" church into the institutional life of the Communion; see his "Myth of Anglican Communion," 143. Timothy Bradshaw, by contrast, has criticized the report for implying that the Communion should have a centralized bureaucracy run by academic experts. See his "Unity, Diversity, and the Virginia Report."

2. This basic issue is often described in ecclesiological debates as the tension between catholicity (a universal normative relationship) and locality (the needs and concerns of a particular context). It also emerges in debates over the distinction between "core doctrine" (which must be adhered to) and matters *adiaphora* (things of secondary importance, about which disagreement is acceptable). See Percy, *Anglicanism*, 153–70; Brittain, "Confession Obsession?"

3. Benhabib, *Claims of Culture*; Morlino, *Changes for Democracy*.

4. Wiarda, *Globalization*; Ninsin, *Globalized Africa*; Smith, *Latin American Democratic Transformations*.

5. See, for example, Ferrara, *Democratic Horizon*.

6. For more on the role of conflict in organizations, see DeSanctis and Fulk, *Shaping Organizational Form*. For a further defense of the value of agonistic confrontation from the field of political philosophy, see Connolly, *Identity/Difference*. For a theological discussion of the role of conflict in the Anglican tradition, see Avis, *Authority, Leadership, and Conflict*, 119–32. For alternative perspectives, see Ephraim Radner's account of serious division in the church as a sin against the Holy Spirit, in *End of the*

Church. John Webster, by contrast, argues that when an ecclesial community is in conflict, it is not in fact a "church"; see his "Theology and the Peace."

7. For further analysis of this dimension of globalization, see Obadia, "Globalization and the Sociology of Religion"; Beck, "Cosmopolitan Society and Its Enemies"; Featherstone, Lash, and Robertson, *Global Modernities*.

8. Lambeth Commission, *Windsor Report*, 60, §157.

9. Brown and Woodhead, *Church That Was*, chapters 2–3; Jones, *Sexual Politics*, chapter 6.

10. The struggle to live with differences in the church has long been a dominant theme in Anglican publications. See, for example, Saywell, *Evangelical and Catholick unity*; Haselmayer, *Lambeth and Unity*; Paton, *Anglicans and Unity*; Beckwith, *Prayer Book Revision*; Whisenant, *Fragile Unity*.

11. Phillip Cantrell explores the impact of the 1994 genocide on the internal dynamics of the Anglican Church of Rwanda (PEAR); he illuminates, for example, the fact that many clergy do not speak French in a predominantly francophone church, and shows how PEAR's policies align closely with those of the ruling government. See Cantrell, "Anglican Church of Rwanda"; "Rwanda's Anglican Church."

12. Emma Wild-Wood's ethnographies provide rich insight into the impact of civil war and foreign missionaries on the identity of Anglican congregations in that province. See her *Migration and Christian Identity*, 203–18; "Attending to Translocal Identities"; "'Free from Shackles'"; and "Boundary Crossing and Boundary Marking."

13. Mkunga Humphrey Percival Mtingele's ethnographic work in Tanzania exposes the extent to which tribalism affects church appointments in the province, which in turn influence the nature of the province's relationship with external partners. He also sheds light on rivalries between

Anglo-Catholics and Evangelicals in the province. See his *Leadership and Conflict*.

14. For a brief history of the churches in this region, see Ward, *History of Global Anglicanism*, 274–95; Pickard, "'Home Away from Home.'"

15. Hilliard, "Diocese, Tribes, and Factions," 57.

16. For discussion of controversies surrounding previous prayer book revisions in Australia, see Fletcher, "Re-Shaping Australian Anglicanism."

17. Tong, "Anglican Church of Australia," 394.

18. See Porter, *Sydney Anglicans*; Porter, *New Puritans*; McGillion, *Chosen Ones*; Jensen, *Sydney Anglicans: An Apology*; Thompson, "Serious Flaws."

19. One factor that helps explain the relatively scant attention is the fact that the Australian government has not passed laws allowing same-sex marriage, thus relieving church leaders of the pressure take a public position on the issue. On 15 November 2017, however, the results of a national mail-in poll on same-sex marriage indicated that 61.6 percent of Australians were in favor of legalizing such unions. This development suggests that the church in Australia will soon be compelled to address the issue directly.

20. Kaye, *Conflict and the Practice*, 26–40; Sachs, *Homosexuality and the Crisis*, 114–38.

21. Whisenant, *Fragile Unity*.

22. Avis, *Anglicanism and the Christian Church*, 349–50; Norris, "Episcopacy," 334, 340.

23. Kaye, *Introduction to World Anglicanism*, 147–52.

24. For a discussion of the novelty of this practice, see Turner, "Bonds of Discord."

25. Avis, *Identity of Anglicanism*, 167.

26. Ironically, it is precisely this concept of a flying bishop that has fueled further tensions and political maneuverings within the Communion. This way of revising and adapting the notion of episcopal oversight is what encouraged Anglicans in the United States to withdraw from the Episcopal Church and place themselves under the oversight of the archbishop of the Southern Cone. The same tactic has been employed by the provinces of Nigeria, Kenya, Rwanda, and Congo, which have sent "missionary bishops" into the jurisdiction of other provinces, chiefly the United States but subsequently also the Church of England.

27. Sachs, *Transformation of Anglicanism*, 2.

28. Ward, *History of Global Anglicanism*, 296–318; Pui-Lan, "Legacy of Cultural Hegemony"; Grau, *Rethinking Mission in the Postcolony*, 206–47.

29. Goddard, *Rowan Williams: His Legacy*, 135–73; Kaye, *Conflict and the Practice*, 108–37.

30. For a similar point, see Vanderbeck et al., "Meanings of Communion." For further analysis of the relationship between local identity and loyalties to wider national and transnational communities, see Pultar, *Imagined Identities*; Elliott, *Identity Troubles*. For the impact of these dynamics on the churches, see Kalu, *Interpreting Contemporary Christianity*; Bean, *Politics of Evangelical Identity*.

31. See Croxton, "Peace of Westphalia of 1648."

32. Fraser, "Transnationalizing the Public Sphere," 19. For a discussion of the impact of this shift on religious communities, see Beyer, *Religion in the Context of Globalization*.

33. One ought not to exaggerate the novelty of this situation; missionary societies have long straddled the geographical boundaries of different global regions, and Evangelicals and Anglo-Catholics have historically sought contact with fellow members of their parties in other nations. Nevertheless, the scope, intensity, and frequency of such interactions have grown significantly in recent years. Thus the new post-Westphalian networks have mobilized within the Communion to push

for significant change in ways never before possible.

34. The *Windsor Report* singles this out as a significant problem. See Lambeth Commission, *Windsor Report*, 19, §29.2.

35. See, for example, Kaye, *Conflict and the Practice*, 26–40; Percy, *Anglicanism*, 153–70.

36. Lambeth Commission, *Windsor Report*, 35, §76.

37. The challenge of making a shift toward a post-Westphalian model is all the more challenging for the Church of England, given its establishment and self-identity as the church of the English nation.

38. Akinola, "Akinola's Speech at Gafcon."

39. References to the "plain sense" of scripture are not uncommon in contemporary theology, but the meaning and implications of this notion are much debated, and there is no consensus on the matter—far from it. See, for example, Williams, "Literal Sense of Scripture"; Webster, "Clarity of Holy Scripture"; Tanner, "Theology and the Plain Sense"; Seitz, "Canon, Covenant, and Rule."

40. For Anglican discussions of such issues, see Webster, *Holy Scripture*; Null, "Thomas Cranmer and the Anglican Way"; Ndungane, "Scripture: What Is at Issue"; Booty, *Hooker and the Holy Scriptures*; Greer, *Anglican Approaches to Scripture*.

41. Bielo, *Social Life of Scriptures*, 2. For a related analysis of Biblicism, see Smith, *Bible Made Impossible*.

42. For a similar argument, see Rosman, "We Are Anglicans."

43. Calvani, "Myth of Anglican Communion," 142.

44. Jesse Zink, while avoiding the idealism that concerns us here, endorses a view that often encourages this line of argument. Zink suggests that his visits with an Anglican congregation in Nigeria call into question the "posturing" of the Anglican primates. "I often wonder what would happen," he writes, "if our thinking about the future of the Anglican Communion [was] more genuinely informed by voices from all levels of the church, such as those congregants in the small village in Nigeria I met. . . . It is these relationships that are foundational to and flourishing in the Anglican Communion." See Zink, "On Beyond Primates."

45. The phrase Archbishop Williams used in the version of the address released to the press was "a wounded Body." Williams, "Archbishop Opens the Lambeth Conference."

46. Yates, "Gospel Unity," 40.

47. For an analysis of the concept of the church as "holy," and how this concept functioned in the dispute within the two dioceses in Pittsburgh (ACNA and TEC), see Brittain, *Plague on Both Their Houses*, 199–216.

48. Rose, *Mourning Becomes the Law*, 15. See also Rose, *Broken Middle*.

49. Avis, *Vocation of Anglicanism*, 24.

50. Williams, "Archbishop's First Presidential Address."

51. Bruce N. Kaye offers an analysis of Williams's speech in *Conflict and the Practice*, 161–72.

52. Avis, *Vocation of Anglicanism*, 25.

53. For a critique of the view that Anglican churches should base their interrelationships on the model of Eastern Orthodoxy, see ibid., 26–27.

54. See, for example, the detailed discussion by the Evangelical Stephen Noll, "Communion Governance." For an "admittedly schematic" and nuanced defense of the conciliar ideal, see Radner, *Brutal Unity*, 264. For a detailed analysis of this theological tradition, see Valliere, *Conciliarism*.

55. Ayers, *Nicaea and Its Legacy*; Edwards, *Catholicity and Heresy*; MacMullen, *Voting About God*.

56. Radner, "Anglicanism and the Search," 256, 257.

57. Nicholas Healy refers to this approach as a "blueprint ecclesiology." Such accounts "describe the church in terms of its final perfection rather than its concrete and

sinful existence." Healy, *Church, World, and the Christian Life*, 9.

58. Ibid., 25–51.

CONCLUSION

1. Welby, "Letter to the Primates."

2. See Congar, "What Is Welby Saying"; Virtue, "GAFCON Primates Will Not Be Attending."

3. This is not our view, as discussed in chapter 6.

4. For a discussion in political theory that echoes this concern, see Seyla Benhabib's critique of Alessandro Ferrara's defense of the idea of a "multivariate polity" in her essay "Multivariate Polity or Democratic Fragmentation."

5. Percy, "Engagement, Diversity, and Distinctiveness," 21.

Adams, Marilyn. "Unfit for Purpose—or Why a Pan-Anglican Covenant at This Time Is a Very Bad Idea!" *Modern Believing* 49, no. 4 (2008): 23–45.

Agence France-Presse. "Uganda Tells West It Can 'Keep Its Aid' After Anti-Gay Law Criticism." *Telegraph* (UK), 27 February 2014.

Akinola, Peter. "Archbishop Peter Akinola's Speech at Gafcon." *Guardian*, 23 June 2008.

Allen, John L., Jr. "Lay Ecclesial Ministry and the Feminization of the Church." *All Things Catholic* (blog), *National Catholic Reporter*, 29 June 2007. http://ncronline .org/blogs/all-things-catholic /lay-ecclesial-ministry-and-femi nization-church.

Ammerman, Nancy Tatom. "American Evangelicals in American Culture: Continuity and Change." In *Evangelicals and Democracy in America*, edited by Steven Brint and Jean Reith Schroedel, 2 vols., 1:44–73. New York: Russell Sage Foundation, 2009.

———. *Baptist Battles: Social Change and Religious Conflict in the Southern Baptist Convention*. New Brunswick: Rutgers University Press, 1990.

Anderson, John. "Conservative Christianity, the Global South, and the Battle over Sexual Orientation." *Third World Quarterly* 32, no. 9 (2011): 1589–1605.

Anglican Church of Canada. "The Consultation of Anglican Bishops in Dialogue." http://www.angli can.ca/gr/bishopsconsultation/.

———. *"This Holy Estate": The Report of the Commission on the Marriage Canon of the Anglican Church of Canada*. N.p.: Anglican Church of Canada, 2015. http://www .anglican.ca/wp-content /uploads/Marriage_Canon _REPORT_15Sept22.pdf.

Anglican Communion. "An Anglican Covenant." N.d. http://www .anglicancommunion.org/iden tity/doctrine/covenant.aspx.

———. "The Anglican Covenant: What the Churches Have Done So Far." http://www.anglicancommunion .org/media/39753/provincial -reception-of-the-anglican-cove nant-for-acc-rev.pdf.

———. "Lambeth Conference Resolutions." http://www.lam bethconference.org/lc2008/news /news.cfm/2008/4/23/Archbishop -of-Canterbury-Better-Bishops -for-the-sake-of-a-better-Church.

Anglican Communion—Primates 2016. "News from Primates 2016." 14 January 2016. http://www.pri

mates2016.org/articles/2016
/01/14/statement-primates-2016/.

Anglican Consultative Council. *The Virginia Report: The Report of the Inter-Anglican Theological and Doctrinal Commission.* London: Anglican Consultative Council, 1997. http://www.anglicancommunion .org/media/150889/report-1.pdf.

Anglican Mainstream. "Regional Shared Conversations Conclude." 11 March 2016. http://anglican mainstream.org/regional-shared -conversations-conclude/.

Asad, Talal. *Formations of the Secular.* Baltimore: Johns Hopkins University Press, 2003.

Ashley, Christopher. "Diversity and Episcopal Governance in Recent Anglican Constitutions." In *The Open Body: Essays in Anglican Ecclesiology*, edited by Zachary Guiliano and Charles M. Stang, 45–78. New York: Peter Lang, 2012.

Ashworth, Pat. "Software Suggests Minns Rewrote Akinola Letter." *Church Times,* 23 August 2007. https:// www.churchtimes.co.uk/articles /2007/24-august/news/uk/soft ware-suggests-minns-rewrote -akinola-s-letter.

Atherstone, Andrew. "Identities and Parties." In *The Oxford Handbook of Anglican Studies*, edited by Mark D. Chapman, Sathianathan Clarke, and Martyn Percy, 77–91. Oxford: Oxford University Press, 2015.

———. "The Keele Congress of 1967: A Paradigm Shift in Anglican Evangelical Attitudes." *Journal of Anglican Studies* 9, no. 2 (2011): 175–97.

Atkin, Bill. "Language and Anglican Canon Law—Dabbling Briefly into Another Legal World." *Victoria University of Wellington Law Review* 42, no. 2 (2011): 387–98.

Atta-Baffoe, Victor. "The Anglican Covenant: An African Perspective." In *The Anglican Covenant: Unity and Diversity in the Anglican Communion*, edited by Mark D. Chapman, 143–56. London: T&T Clark, 2008.

Avis, Paul D. L. "The Anglican Covenant." *Ecclesiology* 7, no. 3 (2011): 293–96.

———. *Anglicanism and the Christian Church: Theological Resources in Historical Perspective.* London: T&T Clark, 2002.

———. *Authority, Leadership, and Conflict in the Church.* London: Mowbray, 1992.

———. *Church, State, and Establishment.* London: SPCK, 2001.

———. *The Identity of Anglicanism: Essentials of Anglican Ecclesiology.* London: T&T Clark, 2007.

———. *The Vocation of Anglicanism.* London: Bloomsbury T&T Clark, 2016.

Awondo, Patrick, Peter Geschiere, and Graeme Reid. "Homophobic Africa? Toward a More Nuanced View." *African Studies Review* 55, no. 3 (2012): 145–68.

Ayers, Lewis. *Nicaea and Its Legacy: An Approach to Fourth-Century Trinitarian Theology.* Oxford: Oxford University Press, 2006.

Bane, Mary Jo. "The Catholic Puzzle: Parishes and Civic Life." In *Taking Faith Seriously*, edited by Mary Jo Bane, Brent Coffin, and Richard Higgins, 63–93. Cambridge: Harvard University Press, 2005.

Bates, Stephen. *A Church at War: Anglicans and Homosexuality.* London: Hodder and Stoughton, 2005.

Battles, Kathleen, and Wendy Hilton-Morrow. "Gay Characters in Conventional Spaces: *Will & Grace* and the Situation Comedy Genre." *Critical Studies in Media*

Communication 19, no. 1 (2002): 87–105.

BBC News. "UK Confrontation at Lambeth Conference." 5 August 1998. http://news.bbc.co.uk/1/hi /uk/145420.stm.

Bean, Lydia. *The Politics of Evangelical Identity: Local Churches and Partisan Divides in the United States and Canada*. Princeton: Princeton University Press, 2014.

Beardsley, Christina. "It's a (Church of England) Lock Out." http:// changingattitude.org.uk /archives/8788.

Beck, Ulrich. "The Cosmopolitan Society and Its Enemies." *Theory, Culture, and Society* 19, nos. 1–2 (2002): 17–44.

Becker, Penney Edgell. *Congregations in Conflict: Cultural Methods of Local Religious Life*. Cambridge: Cambridge University Press, 1999.

Beckford, James A. "Accounting for Conversion." *British Journal of Sociology* 29, no. 2 (1978): 249–62.

Beckwith, R. T. *Prayer Book Revision and Anglican Unity*. London: Church Book Room Press, 1967.

Benford, Robert D., and David A. Snow. "Framing Processes and Social Movements: An Overview and Assessment." *Annual Review of Sociology* 26 (2000): 611–39.

Benhabib, Seyla. *The Claims of Culture: Equality and Diversity in the Global Era*. Princeton: Princeton University Press, 2015.

———. "The Multivariate Polity or Democratic Fragmentation: On Alessandro Ferrara's *The Democratic Horizon*." *Philosophy and Social Criticism* 42, no. 7 (2016): 649–56.

Berger, Peter L., and Thomas Luckmann. *The Social Construction of Reality: A Treatise in the Sociology of Knowledge*. New York: Anchor Books, 1967.

Bevans, Stephen B. *Models of Contextual Theology*. Maryknoll, N.Y.: Orbis Books, 2002.

Beyer, Peter. *Religion and Globalization*. London: Sage Publications, 1994.

———. *Religion in the Context of Globalization*. London: Routledge, 2013.

Bielo, James S., ed. *The Social Life of Scriptures: Cross-Cultural Perspectives on Biblicism*. New Brunswick: Rutgers University Press, 2006.

Bleys, Rudi. *The Geography of Perversion: Male-to-Male Sexual Behavior Outside the West and the Ethnographic Imagination, 1750–1918*. London: Cassell, 1996.

Bohan, Janis S. *Psychology and Sexual Orientation: Coming to Terms*. New York: Routledge, 1996.

Bongaarts, John. "Human Population Growth and the Demographic Transition." *Philosophical Transactions of the Royal Society of London B: Biological Sciences* 364, no. 1532 (2009): 2985–90.

Bonner, Jeremy. *Called Out of Darkness into Marvelous Light: A History of the Episcopal Diocese of Pittsburgh, 1750–2006*. Eugene: Wipf and Stock, 2009.

———. "The Pittsburgh Paradigm: The Rise of Confessional Anglicanism in Southwestern Pennsylvania, 1950–2000." *Anglican and Episcopal History* 77, no. 3 (2008): 257–86.

Booty, John E. *Richard Hooker and the Holy Scriptures*. Alexandria, Va.: Scholarly Engagement with Anglican Doctrine, 1995.

Bourdieu, Pierre. *Outline of a Theory of Practice*. Translated by R. Nice. Cambridge: Cambridge University Press, 1977.

Bowers, Paul. "African Theology: Its History, Dynamics, Scope, and Future." *Africa Journal of*

Evangelical Theology 21, no. 2
(2002): 109–25.

Boyd, Lydia. "The Problem with
Freedom: Homosexuality and
Human Rights in Uganda."
Anthropological Quarterly 86, no. 3
(2013): 697–724.

Braddock, Andrew. *The Role of the Book of
Common Prayer in the Formation
of Modern Anglican Church
Identity: A Study of English
Parochial Worship, 1750–1850.*
Lewiston: Edwin Mellen Press,
2010.

Bradshaw, Timothy. "Unity, Diversity, and
the Virginia Report." In *Grace
and Truth in the Secular Age*,
edited by Timothy Bradshaw,
180–93. Grand Rapids: Eerdmans,
1998.

Bridger, Francis, and Andrew Goddard.
"Learning from Indaba:
Some Lessons for Post-Pilling
Conversations." *Anvil* 30, no. 1
(2014): 41–56.

Brittain, Christopher Craig. *Adorno and
Theology*. London: T&T Clark,
2010.

———. "Confession Obsession? Core
Doctrine and the Anxieties of
Anglican Theology." *Anglican
Theological Review* 90, no. 4
(2008): 777–99.

———. "Partnership Not Dialogue: Lent
and Ramadan Under the Same
Roof." *Ecclesial Practices* 3, no. 2
(2016): 190–209.

———. *A Plague on Both Their Houses:
Liberal vs. Conservative
Christians and the Divorce of the
Episcopal Church USA*. London:
Bloomsbury T&T Clark, 2015.

Brittain, Christopher Craig, and Andrew
McKinnon. "Homosexuality
and the Construction of
'Anglican Orthodoxy': The
Symbolic Politics of the Anglican
Communion." *Sociology of
Religion* 72, no. 3 (2011): 351–73.

Broersma, Marcel, and Todd Graham.
"Social Media as Beat." *Journalism
Practice* 6, no. 3 (2012): 403–19.

Brown, Andrew. "African Christians Will
Be Killed If C of E Accepts Gay
Marriage, Says Justin Welby."
Guardian, 4 April 2014.

Brown, Andrew, and Linda Woodhead. *That
Was the Church That Was: How the
Church of England Lost the English
People*. London: Bloomsbury,
2016.

Brown, Daniel S., Jr., ed. *A Communication
Perspective on Interfaith Dialogue:
Living Within the Abrahamic
Traditions*. Lanham, Md.:
Lexington Books, 2013.

Bruce, Steve. "Authority and Fission: The
Protestants' Divisions." *British
Journal of Sociology* 36, no. 4
(1985): 592–603.

Bryant, Joseph M. "The Sect-Church
Dynamic and Christian
Expansion in the Roman
Empire." *British Journal of
Sociology* 44, no. 2 (1993): 303–39.

Buchanan, Colin. *Historical Dictionary
of Anglicanism*. Lanham, Md.:
Scarecrow Press, 2006.

Byrne, Tracey, and Jeremy Pemberton.
"Open Letter to the House
of Bishops of the Church of
England." One Body One Faith.
http://www.lgcm.org.uk/news
/ol-hob/.

Cadge, Wendy, Heather Day, and
Christopher Wildeman.
"Bridging the Denomination-
Congregation Divide: Evangelical
Lutheran Church in America
Congregations Respond to
Homosexuality." *Review of
Religious Research* 48, no. 3
(2007): 245–59.

Calfano, Brian Robert. "A Decision Theory
of Clergy Political Behaviour."
Social Science Journal 47 (2010):
836–44.

Calfano, Brian Robert, Elizabeth A. Oldmixon, and Mark Gray. "Strategically Prophetic Priests: An Analysis of Competing Principal Influence on Clergy Political Action." *Review of Religious Research* 56, no. 1 (2014): 1–21.

Calvani, Carlos. "The Myth of Anglican Communion." *Journal of Anglican Studies* 3, no. 2 (2005): 139–54.

Cameron, Gregory K. "Ardour and Order: Can the Bonds of Affection Survive in the Anglican Communion?" *Ecclesiastical Law Review* 9, no. 3 (2007): 288–93.

———. "A Tortoise in a Hurry: The Ordering of the Anglican Communion." *International Journal for the Study of the Christian Church* 8, no. 2 (2008): 69–80.

Campbell, Heidi A. "Religious Authority and the Blogosphere." *Journal of Computer-Mediated Communication* 15, no. 2 (2010): 251–76.

Campbell, Heidi A., and Stephen Garner. *Networked Theology: Negotiating Faith in Digital Culture.* Grand Rapids: Baker Academic, 2016.

Cantrell, Phillip. "The Anglican Church of Rwanda: Domestic Agendas and International Linkages." *Journal of Modern African Studies* 45, no. 3 (2007): 333–54.

———. "Rwanda's Anglican Church and Post-Genocide Reconciliation." *Peace Review* 21, no. 3 (2009): 321–29.

Carroll, R. William. "Restoring the Bonds of Affection." *Anglican Theological Review* 87, no. 4 (2005): 619–28.

Castells, Manuel. *The Rise of the Network Society: The Information Age; Economy, Society, and Culture.* New York: John Wiley and Sons, 2011.

Chapman, Mark D., ed. *The Anglican Covenant: Unity and Diversity in the Anglican Communion.* London: Continuum, 2008.

———. *Anglicanism: A Very Short Introduction.* Oxford: Oxford University Press, 2006.

———. "Does the Church of England Have a Theology of General Synod?" *Journal of Anglican Studies* 11, no. 1 (2013): 15–31.

Chapman, Mark, Judith Maltby, and William Whyte, eds. *The Established Church: Past, Present, and Future.* London: T&T Clark, 2011.

Chaves, Mark. *American Religion: Contemporary Trends.* Princeton: Princeton University Press, 2011.

———. *Ordaining Women: Culture and Conflict in Religious Organizations.* Cambridge: Harvard University Press, 1999.

Christian Today. "Africa Anglicans Criticise Church of England over New Direction on Homosexuals." 9 September 2005. https://www .christiantoday.com/article/africa .anglicans.criticise.church .of.england.over.new.direction .on.homosexuals/3913.htm.

Church of England. "Grace and Dialogue: Shared Conversations on Difficult Issues." https://www.churchofeng land.org/media/2529621/grace _and_dialogue.pdf.

———. "Statistics for Mission 2014." London: Archbishops' Council, 2016. https://www.churchofeng land.org/media/2432327/2014stati sticsformission.pdf.

Churchmen's Union for the Advancement of Liberal Religious Thought. "Objects." *Church Gazette,* 19 November 1898. https://modern church.org.uk/173-modern -church/our-history?start=5.

Clatworthy, Jonathan. "The Case Against the Anglican Covenant." *Search:*

A Church of Ireland Journal (2011). http://searchjournal.ireland.angli can.org/AnglicanCovenant.php.

———. "Instead of the Anglican Covenant." *Modern Believing* 53, no. 2 (2012): 152–58.

Colenso, John W. *St. Paul's Epistle to the Romans: Newly Translated and Explained from a Missionary Point of View.* New York: D. Appleton, 1863.

Congar, George. "Fraud Complaint Filed in Tanzania Archbishop's Election." *Anglican Ink,* 25 February 2013. https://fcasa.wordpress.com /2013/03/01/.

———. "What Is Welby Saying in His Letter to the Primates?" *Anglican Ink,* 21 January 2017. http://www .anglican.ink/article/what-welby -saying-his-letter-primates.

Connolly, William E. *Identity/Difference: Democratic Negotiations of Political Paradox.* Minneapolis: University of Minnesota Press, 2002.

Coser, Lewis A. *The Functions of Social Conflict.* New York: Simon and Schuster, 1956.

Coward, Colin. "The Primates' Meeting—A Busted Flush?" *Unadulterated Love* (blog), 9 January 2016. http://www.unadulteratedlove .net/blog/2016/1/9/the-primates -meeting-a-busted-flush.

Crockett, Alasdair, and David Voas. "A Divergence of Views: Attitude Change and the Religious Crisis over Homosexuality." *Sociological Research Online* 8, no. 4 (2003). http://www.socresonline.org .uk/8/4/crockett.html.

Croxton, Derek. "The Peace of Westphalia of 1648 and the Origins of Sovereignty." *International History Review* 21, no. 3 (1999): 569–91.

Currier, Ashley. "Political Homophobia in Postcolonial Namibia." *Gender and Society* 24, no. 1 (2010): 110–29.

Davidson, Jenny. *Hypocrisy and the Politics of Politeness: Manners and Morals from Locke to Austen.* Cambridge: Cambridge University Press, 2004.

Davies, Godfrey, and Paul H. Hardacre. "The Restoration of the Scottish Episcopacy, 1660–1661." *Journal of British Studies* 1, no. 2 (1962): 32–51.

Davies, Madeleine. "Synod Members Thanked for Staying on to Talk About Differences." *Church Times,* 15 July 2016. https://www .churchtimes.co.uk/articles /2016/15-july/news/uk/synod -members-thanked-for-staying -on-to-talk-about-differences.

Davies, Madeleine, and Hattie Williams. "Synod Prepares for 'Relational Road.'" *Church Times,* 24 June 2016. https://www.churchtimes .co.uk/articles/2016/24-june/news /uk/synod-prepares-for-relational -road.

Davis, Nancy, and Robert V. Robinson. "Are the Rumors of War Exaggerated? Religious Orthodoxy and Moral Progressivism in America." *American Journal of Sociology* 102, no. 3 (1996): 756–87.

DeSanctis, Geraldine, and Janet Fulk. *Shaping Organization Form: Communication, Connection, and Community.* Thousand Oaks, Calif.: Sage Publications, 1999.

Dhingra, Neil. "The Primates and the 'Reality' of the Anglican Communion." *Living Church,* 13 January 2016. http://livingchurch .org/covenant/2016/01/13/the -primates-and-the-reality-of-the -anglican-communion/.

DiMaggio, Paul J., and Walter W. Powell, eds. *The New Institutionalism in Organizational Analysis.* Chicago: University of Chicago Press, 1991.

Doe, Norman. "The Anglican Covenant Proposed by the Lambeth Commission." *Ecclesiastical Law Journal* 8, no. 37 (2005): 147–161.

———. "Canon Law." In *The Oxford Handbook of Anglican Studies*, edited by Mark D. Chapman, Sathianathan Clarke, and Martyn Percy, 527–44. Oxford: Oxford University Press, 2015.

———. "Canon Law and Communion." *Ecclesiastical Law Journal* 6, no. 30 (2002): 241–63.

———. *Canon Law in the Anglican Communion: A Worldwide Perspective*. Oxford: Clarendon Press, 1998.

Donald, Peter. *An Uncounselled King: Charles I and the Scottish Troubles, 1637–1641*. Cambridge: Cambridge University Press, 2004.

Donovan, James M. "Homosexual, Gay, and Lesbian: Defining the Words and Sampling the Population." *Journal of Homosexuality* 24, nos. 1–2 (1993): 27–47.

Dowling, Ronald L. "Text, Shape, and Communion: What Unites Us When Nothing's the Same Anymore?" *Anglican Theological Review* 95, no. 3 (2013): 435–46.

Drake, Gavin. "New Zealand Postpones Decision on Same-Sex Blessings." *Anglican Communion News Service*, 12 May 2016. http://www.anglicannews.org/news/2016/05/new-zealand-postpones-decision-on-same-sex-blessings.aspx.

Driver, Jeffrey. "Beyond Lambeth 2008 and ACC14: Tuning a Polity of Persuasion to the Twenty-First Century." *Journal of Anglican Studies* 7, no. 2 (2009): 195–211.

Dugan, Marie. "A Nested Theory of Conflict." *Leadership Journal* 1, no. 1 (1996): 9–20.

Duncan, Robert. "Anglicanism Come of Age." *Trinity Journal for Theology and Ministry* 2, no. 2 (2008): 47–66.

———. "Bishop Duncan Addresses GAFCON." Episcopal Café, 20 June 2008. http://www.episcopalcafe.com/bishop_duncan_addresses_gafcon/.

Dyer, J. M., E. Gbonigi, M. Rumalshah, R. Etchells, R. Symon, and E. G. Clark, eds. *The Official Report of the Lambeth Conference, 1998*. Harrisburg, Pa.: Morehouse, 1999.

Dykstra, Craig, and Dorothy C. Bass. "A Theological Understanding of Christian Practices." In *Practicing Theology: Beliefs and Practices in Christian Life*, edited by Miroslav Volf and Dorothy C. Bass, 13–32. Grand Rapids: Eerdmans, 2002.

Earey, Mark. *Beyond Common Worship: Anglican Identity and Liturgical Diversity*. London: SCM Press, 2013.

Edwards, Mark J. *Catholicity and Heresy in the Early Church*. Aldershot: Ashgate, 2009.

Elias, Norbert. *The Civilizing Process: Sociogenetic and Psychogenetic Investigations*. Oxford: Blackwell, 2000.

Eliason, Michele J. "An Exploration of Terminology Related to Sexuality and Gender: Arguments for Standardizing the Language." *Social Work in Public Health* 29 (2014): 162–75.

Elliott, Anthony. *Identity Troubles: An Introduction*. New York: Routledge, 2016.

Englund, Harri, ed. *Christianity and Public Culture in Africa*. Athens: Ohio University Press, 2011.

Episcopal Café. "Who Speaks for Africa?" 23 August 2007. http://www.episcopalcafe.com/lead/anglican_communion/who_speaks_for_africa.html.

Episcopal News Service. "ACC 'Neither Endorsed nor Affirmed' Primates' Action, Six Outgoing Members Say." 6 May 2016. http://episco paldigitalnetwork.com/ens /2016/05/06/acc-neither -endorsed-nor-affirmed-primates -action-six-outgoing-members -say/.

Epprecht, Marc. *Heterosexual Africa? The History of an Idea from the Age of Exploration to the Age of AIDS*. Athens: Ohio University Press, 2008.

———. *Sexuality and Social Justice in Africa: Rethinking Homophobia and Forging Resistance*. London: Zed Books and the Royal African Society, 2013.

———. "The 'Unsaying' of Indigenous Homosexualities in Zimbabwe: Mapping a Blindspot in an African Masculinity." *Journal of Southern African Studies* 24, no. 4 (1998): 631–51.

Essien, Kwame, and Saheed Aderinto. "'Cutting the Head of the Roaring Monster': Homosexuality and Repression in Africa." *African Study Monographs* 30, no. 3 (2009): 121–35.

Farley, Harry. "Divisions Deepen in Church of England as Conservatives Express 'Lack of Confidence' in Gay Marriage Talks." *Christian Today*, 20 July 2016. http://www .christiantoday.com/article/divi sions.deepen.in.churh.of.england .as.conservatives.express.lack .of.confidence.in.gay.marriage .talks/91048.htm.

Faulds, Ian. "The Anglican Communion: Crisis and Opportunity." *Ecclesiastical Law Journal* 9, no. 2 (2007): 222–24.

Featherstone, Mike, Scott Lash, and Roland Robertson, eds. *Global Modernities*. London: Sage Publications, 1995.

Ferrara, Alessandro. *The Democratic Horizon: Hyperpluralism and the Renewal of Political Liberalism*. Cambridge: Cambridge University Press, 2014.

Fletcher, Brian H. "Re-Shaping Australian Anglicanism, 1962–1978: From Book of Common Prayer to an Australian Prayer Book." *Journal of the Royal Australian Historical Society* 85, no. 2 (1999): 120–38.

Fletcher, Wendy L. *Beyond the Walled Garden—Women and the Priesthood in Anglicanism: Canada and England, 1920–1978*. Dundas, Ont.: Artemis, 1995.

Folkins, Tali, and André Forget. "Order of Bishops Unlikely to Support Gay Marriage." *Anglican Journal* 142, no. 4 (2016): 1, 13. http://cdn .agilitycms.com/anglican-journal /NewspaperArchives/PDFs/aj -apr2016-web.pdf.

Fraser, Nancy. "Transnationalizing the Public Sphere: On the Legitimacy and Efficacy of Public Opinion in a Post-Westphalian World." In *Transnationalizing the Public Sphere*, edited by Kate Nash, 8–42. Cambridge: Polity Press, 2014.

GAFCON (Global Anglican Future Conference). "The Complete Jerusalem Statement." 22 June 2008. https://www.gafcon .org/resources/the-complete -jerusalem-statement.

———. "Nairobi Communique and Commitment." 26 October 2013. http://gafcon.org/news/nairobi -communique-and-commitment.

———. "Oxford Statement." http://gafcon .org/news/oxford_statement _from_the_gafcon_fca_primates _council.

Galeotti, Anna Elisabetta. "The Range of Toleration: From Toleration as Recognition Back to Disrespectful

Tolerance." *Philosophy and Social Criticism* 42, no. 2 (2016): 93–110.

Galgalo, Joseph D., and Esther Mombo. "Theological Education in Africa in the Post-1998 Lambeth Conference." *Journal of Anglican Studies* 6, no. 1 (2008): 31–40.

Gallagher, Paul. "Peter Tatchell Threatens to 'Out' Bishops He Believes Are Gay After Hospital Chaplain Jeremy Pemberton Has His License to Preach Revoked." *Independent* (UK), 25 July 2014.

Garner, Clare. "How I Felt the Wrath of a Bishop . . . Fury as the Church Votes for Gay Ban." *Independent* (UK), 5 August 1998.

Gifford, Paul. *Christianity, Development, and Modernity in Africa.* London: Hurst, 2015.

———. "Trajectories in African Christianity." *International Journal for the Study of the Christian Church* 8, no. 4 (2008): 275–89.

Gilliat-Ray, Sophie. "The Fate of the Anglican Clergy and the Class of '97: Some Implications of the Changing Sociological Profile of Ordinands." *Journal of Contemporary Religion* 16 (2001): 209–25.

Gitari, David, ed. *Anglican Liturgical Inculturation in Africa: The Kanamai Statement.* Nottingham: Grove Books, 1994.

———. "The Claims of Jesus in the African Context." *International Review of Mission* 71 (1982): 12–19.

Gledhill, Ruth. "Evangelicals to Meet Williams over Gay Bishop." *Times* (London), 23 June 2003.

Goddard, Andrew. "The Anglican Communion Covenant." In *The Wiley-Blackwell Companion to the Anglican Communion*, edited by Ian S. Markham, J. Barney Hawkins IV, Justyn Terry, and Leslie Nuñez Steffensen, 119–33.

Chichester: Wiley-Blackwell, 2013.

———. "Commitment in Word and Deed." *Living Church,* 29 April 2011. http://www.livingchurch .org/section-4-commitment -word-and-deed.

———. *Rowan Williams: His Legacy.* Oxford: Lion, 2013.

Goldfarb, Jeffrey C. *Civility and Subversion.* Cambridge: Cambridge University Press, 1998.

Goodhew, David, ed. *Growth and Decline in the Anglican Communion: 1980 to the Present.* London: Routledge, 2017.

Goodstein, Laurie. "Openly Gay Man Is Made a Bishop." *New York Times,* 3 November 2003.

Goodstein, Laurie, and Neela Banerjee. "Money Looms in Episcopalian Rift with Anglicans." *New York Times,* 20 March 2007.

Gore, Charles, ed. *Lux Mundi: A Series of Studies in the Religion of the Incarnation.* London: John Murray, 1890.

Grafton, Charles Chapman. *The Lineage from Apostolic Times of the American Catholic Church: Commonly Called the Episcopal Church.* Milwaukee: Young Churchman, 1911.

Grau, Marion. *Rethinking Mission in the Postcolony: Salvation, Society, and Subversion.* London: T&T Clark, 2010.

Greenberg, David F. *The Construction of Homosexuality.* Chicago: University of Chicago Press, 1990.

Greer, Rowan A. *Anglican Approaches to Scripture: From the Reformation to the Present.* New York: Crossroad, 2006.

Groves, Phil, and Jonathan Draper, eds. *Creating Space.* 2nd ed. London: Anglican Communion Office, 2012.

Groves, Phil, John Holder, and Paula Gooder. "The Witness of Scripture." In *The Anglican Communion and Homosexuality: A Resource to Enable Listening and Dialogue,* edited by Phil Groves, 81–154. London: SPCK, 2008.

Guelzo, Allen C. *For the Union of Evangelical Christendom: The Irony of the Reformed Episcopalians.* University Park: Pennsylvania State University Press, 1994.

Guyer, Benjamin M., ed. *Pro Communione: Theological Essays on the Anglican Covenant.* Eugene: Pickwick, 2012.

Hamill, Sean D. "Pittsburgh Episcopal Diocese Votes for Split." *New York Times,* 4 October 2008.

Handcock, Mark S., and Krista J. Gile. "On the Concept of Snowball Sampling." *Sociological Methodology* 41, no. 1 (2011): 367–71.

Handley, Paul. "ACNA Primate Was Given Ballot Paper to Vote on Episcopal Church." *Church Times,* 22 January 2016. https://www .churchtimes.co.uk/articles /2016/22-january/news/uk/acna -primate-was-given-ballot-paper -to-vote-on-episcopal-church-1.

Hardinge, Leslie. *The Church in Celtic Britain.* London: SPCK, 1972.

Harvey, David. *The Condition of Postmodernity.* Oxford: Blackwell, 1989.

Haselmayer, Louis August. *Lambeth and Unity.* New York: Morehouse-Gorham, 1948.

Hauerwas, Stanley M. "Creation, Contingency, and Truthful Nonviolence: A Milbankian Reflection." In *Wilderness Wanderings: Probing Twentieth-Century Theology and Philosophy,* 188–98. Boulder: Westview Press, 1997.

Havel, Vaclav. "The Power of the Powerless." In *Living in Truth: Twenty-Two Essays Published on the Occasion of the Award of the Erasmus Prize to Vaclav Havel,* edited by Jan Vladislav, 36–122. London: Faber and Faber, 1986.

Hassett, Miranda K. *Anglican Communion in Crisis: How Episcopal Dissidents and Their African Allies Are Reshaping Anglicanism.* Princeton: Princeton University Press, 2007.

Healy, Nicholas M. *Church, World, and the Christian Life: Practical-Prophetic Ecclesiology.* Cambridge: Cambridge University Press, 2000.

Heath, Robert L., W. Barnett Pearce, John Shotter, James R. Taylor, Astrid Kersten, Ted Zor, Juliet Roper, Judy Motion, and Stanley Deetz. "The Processes of Dialogue: Participation and Legitimation." *Management Communication Quarterly* 19, no. 3 (2006): 341–75.

Hegel, G. W. F. *The Phenomenology of Spirit: Selections.* University Park: Pennsylvania State University Press, 1994.

Held, David. "Regulating Globalization? The Reinvention of Politics." *International Sociology* 15, no. 2 (2000): 394–408.

Hengel, Martin, and C. K. Barrett. *Conflicts and Challenges in Early Christianity.* Edited by Donald A. Hagner. Harrisburg, Pa.: Trinity Press International, 1999.

Hill, Christopher. "Ecclesiological and Canonical Observations on the Principles of Canon Law Common to the Churches of the Anglican Communion." *Ecclesiastical Law Society* 14, no. 3 (2012): 400–407.

Hilliard, David. "Diocese, Tribes, and Factions: Disunity and Unity in Australian Anglicanism." In *Agendas for Australian*

Anglicanism: Essays in Honour of Bruce Kaye, edited by Tom Frame and Geoffrey Treloar, 57–84. Adelaide: ATF Press, 2006.

———. "UnEnglish and Unmanly: Anglo-Catholicism and Homosexuality." *Victorian Studies* 25 (1982): 181–210.

Hirschman, Albert O. "Social Conflicts as Pillars of Democratic Market Society." *Political Theory* 22, no. 2 (1994): 203–18.

Hoad, Neville. *African Intimacies: Race, Homosexuality, and Globalization.* Minneapolis: University of Minnesota Press, 2006.

Hoffer, Eric. *True Believer: Thoughts on the Nature of Mass Movements.* San Francisco: Harper Collins, 1951.

Holeton, David R., ed. *Liturgical Inculturation in the Anglican Communion: Including the York Statement "Down to Earth Worship."* Nottingham: Grove Books, 1990.

Hooton, W. S., and J. Stafford Wright. *The First Twenty-Five Years of the Bible Churchmen's Missionary Society: (1922–47).* London: Bible Churchmen's Missionary Society, 1947.

House of Bishops (Church of England). *Issues in Human Sexuality.* London: Church House Publishing, 1991.

Howe, John, and Colin Craston. *Anglicanism and the Universal Church: Highways and Hedges, 1958–1990.* Toronto: Anglican Book Centre, 1990.

Hunter, James Davison. *Culture Wars: The Struggle to Define America.* New York: Basic Books, 1991.

Hunter, James Davison, and Alan Wolfe. *Is There a Culture War? A Dialogue on Values and American Public Life.* Washington, D.C.: Pew Research Center, 2006.

Hylden, Jordan. "What Lambeth Wrought." *First Things,* October 2008, 15–17.

Jacob, William M. *The Making of the Anglican Church Worldwide.* London: SPCK, 1997.

Jacobsen, Douglas. *The World's Christians: Who They Are, Where They Are, and How They Got There.* Oxford: Wiley-Blackwell, 2011.

Jasper, R. C. D. *The Development of the Anglican Liturgy, 1662–1980.* London: SPCK, 1989.

Jenkins, Philip. *The New Faces of Christianity: Believing the Bible in the Global South.* Oxford: Oxford University Press, 2006.

———. *The Next Christendom: The Coming of Global Christianity.* Oxford: Oxford University Press, 2007.

Jensen, Michael P. *Sydney Anglicans: An Apology.* Eugene: Wipf and Stock, 2012.

Jerven, Morten. *Poor Numbers: How We Are Misled by African Development Statistics and What to Do About It.* Ithaca: Cornell University Press, 2013.

Johnson, Todd M., and Kenneth R. Ross, eds. *Atlas of Global Christianity.* Edinburgh: University of Edinburgh Press, 2009.

Johnston, Ian. "Church of England Leaders Defy Liberals and Condemn Same-Sex Marriage." *Independent* (UK), 14 January 2016.

Jones, Ian. *Women and Priesthood in the Church of England: Ten Years On.* London: Church House Publishing, 2004.

Jones, Timothy Willem. *Sexual Politics in the Church of England, 1857–1957.* Oxford: Oxford University Press, 2012.

———. "The Stained Glass Closet: Celibacy and Homosexuality in the Church of England to 1955." *Journal of the History of Sexuality* 20, no. 1 (2011): 132–52.

Juergensmeyer, Mark, ed. *Global Religions: An Introduction*. Oxford: Oxford University Press, 2003.

Kalu, Ogbu U., ed. *Interpreting Contemporary Christianity: Global Processes and Local Identities*. Grand Rapids: Eerdmans, 2008.

Karagiannis, Evangelos. "Secularism in Context: The Relations Between the Greek State and the Church of Greece in Crisis." *European Journal of Sociology* 50, no. 1 (2009): 133–67.

Kaye, Bruce. *Conflict and the Practice of Christian Faith: The Anglican Experiment*. Eugene: Cascade, 2009.

———. *An Introduction to World Anglicanism*. Cambridge: Cambridge University Press, 2008.

Keenan, Michael. "Conditional Love? Assimilation and the Construction of 'Acceptable Homosexuality' in Anglicanism." In *Contemporary Issues in the Worldwide Anglican Communion: Powers and Pieties*, edited by Abby Day, 95–112. Farnham, Surrey: Ashgate, 2016.

———. "Separating Church and God: An Exploration of Gay Clergymen's Negotiations with Institutional Church." In *The Ashgate Research Companion on Sexuality and Religion*, edited by Stephen Hunt and Andrew K. T. Yip, 173–88. Farnham, Surrey: Ashgate, 2012.

Kemp, Nathaniel, and Stephen Macedo. "The Christian Right, Public Reason, and American Democracy." In *Evangelicals and Democracy in America*, edited by Steven Brint and Jean Reith Schroedel, 2 vols., 2:209–46. New York: Russell Sage Foundation, 2009.

Khameh, Armin. "Political Toleration, Exclusionary Reasoning, and the Extraordinary Politics." *Philosophy and Social Criticism* 42, no. 11 (2016): 1–21.

Kingwell, Mark. *Unruly Voices: Essays on Democracy, Civility, and the Human Imagination*. Toronto: Biblioasis, 2012.

Kitschelt, Herbert. "Political Opportunity Structures and Political Protest: Anti-Nuclear Movements in Four Democracies." *British Journal of Political Science* 16 (1986): 57–85.

Klinken, A. S. van. "Homosexuality, Politics, and Pentecostal Nationalism in Zambia." *Studies in World Christianity* 20, no. 3 (2014): 259–81.

Kniss, Fred L. *Disquiet in the Land: Cultural Conflict in American Mennonite Communities*. New Brunswick: Rutgers University Press, 1997.

Kollmuss, Anja, and Julian Agyeman. "Mind the Gap: Why Do People Act Environmentally and What Are the Barriers to Pro-Environmental Behavior?" *Environmental Education Research* 8, no. 3 (2002): 239–60.

Lambeth Commission on Communion. *The Windsor Report*. London: Anglican Communion Office, 2004. http://www.anglican communion.org/media/68225 /windsor2004full.pdf.

Lambeth Conference. "Resolutions of the Lambeth Conference of 1920," Resolution 34. http://www .lambethconference.org /resolutions/1920/1920–34.cfm.

Larmondin, Leanne. "New Westminster Synod and Bishop Approve Same-Sex Blessings." Anglican Church of Canada, 15 June 2002. http:// www.anglican.ca/news/new -westminster-synod-and-bishop -approve-same-sex-blessings /3001541/.

Lasorsa, Dominic, Seth C. Lewis, and Avery E. Holton. "Normalizing

Twitter: Journalism Practice in an Emerging Communication Space." *Journalism Studies* 13, no. 1 (2012): 19–36.

Lederach, John Paul. *Building Peace: Sustainable Reconciliation in Divided Societies.* Washington, D.C.: United States Institute of Peace Press, 1997.

Lee, Peter John. "Indaba as Obedience: A Post Lambeth 2008 Assessment; 'If Someone Offends You, Talk to Him.'" *Journal of Anglican Studies* 7, no. 2 (2009): 147–61.

Levin, Steve. "Letter Shows Rift Among Episcopal Conservatives." *Pittsburgh Post-Gazette,* 30 January 2008.

Lewis, Harold T. "By Schisms Rent Asunder? American Anglicanism on the Eve of the Millennium." In *A New Conversation: Essays on the Future of the Episcopal Church*, edited by Robert Boak Slocum, 9–12. New York: Church Publishing, 1999.

———. *The Recent Unpleasantness: Calvary Church's Role in the Preservation of the Episcopal Church in the Diocese of Pittsburgh.* Eugene: Wipf and Stock, 2015.

Liebman, Robert C., John R. Sutton, and Robert Wuthnow. "Exploring the Social Sources of Denominationalism: Schisms in American Protestant Denominations, 1890–1980." *American Sociological Review* 53, no. 3 (1988): 343–52.

Lindsay, D. Michael. "Politics as the Construction of Relations: Religious Identity and Political Expression." In *Evangelicals and Democracy in America*, edited by Steven Brint and Jean Reith Schroedel, 2 vols., 2:305–30. New York: Russell Sage Foundation, 2009.

Lines, Andy, and Peter Jensen. "GAFCON Statement on the Appointment of the Bishop of Grantham." 3 September 2016. http://gafcon .org/2016/09/gafcon-statement -on-the-appointment-of-the -bishop-of-grantham/.

Locke, Kenneth A. *The Church in Anglican Theology: An Historical, Theological, and Ecumenical Exploration.* Farnham, Surrey: Ashgate, 2009.

Lowell, Lewis J. *The Anthropology of Cultural Performance.* Basingstoke: Palgrave, 2013.

MacCulloch, Diarmaid. "Putting the English Reformation on the Map: The Prothero Lecture." *Transactions of the Royal Historical Society* 15 (2005): 75–95.

MacDonald, Alan R. "James VI and I, the Church of Scotland, and British Ecclesiastical Convergence." *Historical Journal* 48, no. 4 (2005): 885–903.

MacDonald, Mark, Lydia Mamakwa, and Adam Halkett. "Statement." http://cdn.agilitycms.com /anglican-journal/Images /Articles/2016-articles/09sep 2016/A%20Statement%20by%20 the%20Bishops%20Mark%20 MacDonald.pdf.

Machen, J. Gresham. *Christianity and Liberalism.* Grand Rapids: Eerdmans, 2009.

MacMullen, Ramsay. *Voting About God in Early Church Councils.* New Haven: Yale University Press, 2006.

Maiden, John G. "English Evangelicals, Protestant National Identity, and Anglican Prayer Book Revision, 1927–1928." *Journal of Religious History* 34, no. 4 (2010): 430–45.

Maiden, John, and Peter Webster. "Parliament, the Church of England, and the Last Gasp of Political Protestantism, 1963–4."

Parliamentary History 32, no. 2
(2013): 361–77.

Malnick, Edward. "Traditionalist Anglican
Leaders to Meet over Homosexual
Bishops 'Crisis.'" *Telegraph* (UK),
15 April 2012.

Mana, Ka. *Christians and Churches of Africa:
Salvation in Christ and Building a
New African Society.* Maryknoll,
N.Y.: Orbis Books, 2004.

Markham, Ian S., J. Barney Hawkins IV,
Justyn Terry, and Leslie Nuñez
Steffensen, eds. *The Wiley-
Blackwell Companion to the
Anglican Communion.* Chichester:
Wiley-Blackwell, 2013.

Martey, Emmanuel. *African Theology:
Inculturation and Liberation.*
Maryknoll, N.Y.: Orbis Books,
1994.

Martin, David A. "The Denomination."
British Journal of Sociology 12
(1962): 1–14.

Masuzawa, Tomoko. *The Invention of World
Religions, or How European
Universalism Was Preserved in the
Language of Pluralism.* Chicago:
University of Chicago Press, 2005.

Mauss, Marcel. "Les techniques du corps."
Journal de Psychologie 32, nos. 3–4
(1936): 365–86.

Mbogo, Stephen. "Election of Homosexual
Bishop 'Could Fuel Anti-
Christian Persecution.'" CNS
News, 7 July 2008. http://
cnsnews.com/news/article
/election-homosexual-bishop
-could-fuel-anti-christian-perse
cution.

McAdoo, H. R. *Anglicans and Tradition
and the Ordination of Women.*
Norwich, UK: Canterbury Press,
1997.

McCarthy, John D., and Mayer N. Zald.
"Resource Mobilization and
Social Movements: A Partial
Theory." *American Journal of
Sociology* 82 (1977): 1212–41.

McGillion, Chris. *The Chosen Ones: The
Politics of Salvation in the Anglican
Church.* Crows Nest, New South
Wales: Allen and Unwin, 2005.

McGowan, Michael. "Sydney Anglican
Diocese Donates $1M to No
Campaign for Same-Sex Marriage
Vote." *Guardian,* 10 October
2017.

McKinnon, Andrew. "Elective Affinities of
the Protestant Ethic: Weber and
the Chemistry of Capitalism."
Sociological Theory 28, no. 1
(2010): 108–26.

———. "Metaphors in and for the
Sociology of Religion: Towards a
Theory After Nietzsche." *Journal
of Contemporary Religion* 2, no. 2
(2012): 203–16.

———. "Religion and the Civilizing
Process: The Pax Dei Movement
and the Christianization of
Violence in the Process of
Feudalization." In *Sociological
Theory and the Question of
Religion,* edited by Andrew
McKinnon and Marta
Trzebiatowska, 105–26. Aldershot:
Ashgate, 2015.

———. "Religion and Social Class:
Theory and Method After
Bourdieu." *Sociological Research
Online* 22, no. 1 (2017): 1–13.

———. "Sociological Definitions,
Language Games, and the
'Essence' of Religion." *Method
and Theory in the Study of Religion*
14, no. 1 (2002): 61–83.

McKinnon, Andrew, Marta Trzebiatowska,
and Christopher Craig Brittain.
"Bourdieu, Capital, and Conflict
in a Religious Field: The Case
of the 'Homosexuality' Conflict
in the Anglican Communion."
Journal of Contemporary Religion
26, no. 3 (2011): 355–70.

McLuhan, Marshall. *Understanding Media:
The Extensions of Man.* New York:
McGraw-Hill, 1965.

McQuillan, Kevin. "When Does Religion Influence Fertility?" *Population and Development Review* 30, no. 1 (2004): 25–56.

Mercer, Joyce Ann. "Conflicting Identities: An Ethnographic Account of Conflict and Schism in an Episcopal Parish." *Ecclesial Practices* 3, no. 2 (2016): 210–30.

Merino, Stephen M. "Contact with Gays and Lesbians and Same-Sex Marriage Support: The Moderating Role of Social Context." *Social Science Research* 42, no. 4 (2013): 1156–66.

Meyer, Birgit. "Christianity in Africa: From African Independent to Pentecostal-Charismatic Churches." *Annual Review of Anthropology* 33 (2004): 447–74.

Meyers, Ruth A. "The Baptismal Covenant and the Proposed Anglican Covenant." *Journal of Anglican Studies* 10, no. 1 (2012): 31–41.

Milbank, John. "The End of Dialogue." In *Christian Uniqueness Reconsidered: The Myth of a Pluralistic Theology of Religions*, edited by Gavin D'Costa, 174–91. Maryknoll, N.Y.: Orbis Books, 1990.

Millard, Jonathan. "Making the Case: Explaining the Rationale for Resolution 1." http://www.stand firminfaith.com/media /JonathanMillard_Making TheCase.pdf.

Mitchell, Donn. "Lambeth's Forgotten Teaching: The Universal Declaration of Human Rights." *Anglican Theological Review* 90, no. 1 (2008): 65–83.

Modern Church. "Supporters and Opponents of the Anglican Covenant." N.d. https://modern church.org.uk/anglican-covenant /introduction/for-and-against.

Mombo, Esther. "Response to 'A Testimony of Our Journey Toward Reconciliation' (Fifth Consultation)." http://www .anglican.ca/wp-content/uploads /2014/05/EstherMombo _DialogueResponse.pdf.

Morgan, Barry. "The Church in Wales." In *The Wiley-Blackwell Companion to the Anglican Communion*, edited by Ian S. Markham, J. Barney Hawkins IV, Justyn Terry, and Leslie Nuñez Steffensen, 452–63. Chichester: Wiley-Blackwell, 2013.

Morlino, Leonardo. *Changes for Democracy: Actors, Structures, Processes*. Oxford: Oxford University Press, 2011.

Morris, Nigel. "Commonwealth Nations to Have Aid Cut for Gay Rights Abuses." *Independent* (UK), 31 October 2011.

Moyse, Cordelia. *A History of the Mothers' Union: Women, Anglicanism, and Globalisation, 1876–2008*. Woodbridge, UK: Boydell and Brewer, 2009.

Mtingele, Mkunga Humphrey Percival. *Leadership and Conflict in African Churches: An Anglican Experience*. New York: Peter Lang, 2016.

Muñoz, Daniel. "North to South: A Reappraisal of Anglican Communion Membership Figures." *Journal of Anglican Studies* 14, no. 1 (2016): 71–95.

Murphy, Caryle. "Most U.S. Christian Groups Grow More Accepting of Homosexuality." Pew Research Center, 18 December 2015. http:// www.pewresearch.org/fact -tank/2015/12/18/most-u-s-chris tian-groups-grow-more-accept ing-of-homosexuality/.

Murray, Jocelyn. *Proclaim the Good News: A Short History of the Church Missionary Society*. London: Hodder and Stoughton, 1985.

Murray, Stephen O. "The Will Not to Know." In *Islamic Homosexualities: Culture, History,* and Literature, edited by Stephen O. Murray and Will Roscoe, 14–54. New York: NYU Press, 1997.

Nagle, John. "From the Politics of Agonistic Recognition to Agonistic Peace Building." *Peace and Change* 39, no. 4 (2014): 468–94.

Nardi, Bonnie A., and Steve Whittaker. "The Place of Face-to-Face Communication in Distributed Work." In *Distributed Work*, edited by Pamela Hinds and Sarah Kiesler, 83–110. Cambridge: MIT Press, 2002.

Naughton, Jim. "Following the Money." *Washington Window*, April 2006, 1–8.

Ndungane, Njongonkulu Abp. "Scripture: What Is at Issue in Anglicanism Today?" *Anglican Theological Review* 83, no. 1 (2001): 11–23.

Neill, Stephen. *Anglicanism*. Oxford: Mowbray, 1977.

Neville, Robyn M. "The Church of Ireland." In *The Wiley-Blackwell Companion to the Anglican Communion*, edited by Ian S. Markham, J. Barney Hawkins IV, Justyn Terry, and Leslie Nuñez Steffensen, 426–40. Chichester: Wiley-Blackwell, 2013.

Newenham-Kahindi, Aloysius. "The Transfer of Ubuntu and Indaba Business Models Abroad: A Case of South African Multinational Banks and Telecommunication Services in Tanzania." *International Journal of Cross Cultural Management* 9, no. 1 (2009): 87–108.

Niebuhr, Gustav. "Episcopal Priest Absolved in Gay Ordination." *New York Times*, 16 May 1996.

Nieman, James R. "Congregational Studies." In *The Wiley-Blackwell Companion to Practical Theology*, edited by Bonnie J. Miller-McLemore,

133–42. Oxford: Wiley-Blackwell, 2011.

Ninsin, Kwame A., ed. *Globalized Africa: Political, Social, and Economic Impact*. Accra: Napasvil, 2012.

Noll, Stephen. "Communion Governance: The Role and Future of the Historic Episcopate and the Anglican Communion Covenant." Virtue Online, 2 August 2010. http://www.virtue online.org/communion-gover nance-stephen-noll.

———. "Lambeth Diary 1998: Week Three (Diary from the Third Week of the Lambeth Conference of Anglican Bishops, August 2–9, 1998)." http://www.stephenswit ness.org/2007/12/lambeth-diary -1998-week-two.html.

———. "The Orthodox Anglican Divide." 17 September 2010. http://gafcon .org/resources/the_orthodox -anglican_divide/.

Norris, Richard A., Jr. "Episcopacy." In *The Study of Anglicanism*, rev. ed., edited by Stephen Sykes, John Booty, and Jonathan Knight, 333–48. London: SPCK, 1998.

Null, Ashley. "Thomas Cranmer and the Anglican Way of Reading Scripture." *Anglican and Episcopal History* 75, no. 4 (2006): 488–526.

Obadare, Ebenezer. "Sex, Citizenship, and the State in Nigeria: Islam, Christianity, and Emergent Struggles over Intimacy." *Review of African Political Economy* 42, no. 143 (2015): 62–76.

Obadia, Lionel. "Globalization and the Sociology of Religion." In *The New Blackwell Companion to the Sociology of Religion*, edited by Bryan S. Turner, 477–97. Oxford: Blackwell, 2010.

O'Connor, Daniel. *Three Centuries of Mission: The United Society for the Propagation of the Gospel,*

1701–2000. London: Continuum, 2000.

Ogungbile, David O., and Akintunde E. Akinade, eds. *Creativity and Change in Nigerian Christianity*. Lagos: Malthouse Press, 2010.

Olivares, Carlos. *The (Im)polite Jesus: An Analysis of Jesus' Verbal Rudeness in Matthew's Gospel*. New York: Peter Lang, 2016.

One Body One Faith. "The Bishop of Grantham." http://lgcm.org.uk /news/the-bishop-of-grantham/.

Orbuch, Terri L. "People's Accounts Count: The Sociology of Accounts." *Annual Review of Sociology* 23 (1997): 455–78.

Ormsby, Avril. "English Church Votes Down Pact to Unite Anglicans." *Reuters,* 24 March 2012. http:// uk.reuters.com/article/2012 /03/24/uk-britain-religion-cove nant-idUKBRE82N0EJ20120324.

Orombi, Henry Luke. "What Is Anglicanism?" *First Things,* August 2007. https://www .firstthings.com/article/2007 /08/001-what-is-anglicanism.

Parkin, Frank. *Max Weber*. London: Tavistock, 1982.

Parsons, Talcott. *The Structure of Social Action*. New York: Free Press, 1949.

"A Pastoral Statement to Lesbian and Gay Anglicans from Some Member Bishops of the Lambeth Conference." 5 August 1998. http://www.whosoever.org/v3i2 /lambeth2.html.

Paton, David M. *Anglicans and Unity*. London: A. R. Mowbray, 1962.

Paul, Ian. "Reconciliation in the New Testament." In *Good Disagreement? Grace and Truth in a Divided Church,* edited by Andrew Atherstone and Andrew Goddard, 23–42. Oxford: Lion, 2015.

———. "Synod's Shared Conversations." Psephizo, 13 July 2015. http:// www.psephizo.com/sexuality-2 /synods-shared-conversations/.

Percy, Martyn. *Anglicanism*. Farnham, Surrey: Ashgate, 2013.

———. "Engagement, Diversity, and Distinctiveness." In *A Point of Balance: The Weight and Measure of Anglicanism*, edited by Martyn Percy and Robert Boak Slocum, 13–28. New York: Morehouse, 2012.

———. "Sacred Sagacity: Formation and Training for Ministry in a Church of England Seminary." *Anglican Theological Review* 90, no. 2 (2008): 285–96.

Pickard, Stephen. "'Home Away from Home': Displacement, Identity, and Anglican Ecclesiology in Australasia." In *The Oxford Handbook of Anglican Studies*, edited by Mark D. Chapman, Sathianathan Clarke, and Martyn Percy, 205–17. Oxford: Oxford University Press, 2015.

Pickering, W. S. F. *Anglo-Catholicism: A Study in Religious Ambiguity*. Cambridge: James Clarke, 2008.

Pickstock, Catherine. *After Writing: On the Liturgical Consummation of Philosophy*. Oxford: Blackwell, 1998.

Podmore, Colin. *Aspects of Anglican Identity*. London: Church House, 2005.

———. "The Baptismal Revolution in the American Episcopal Church: Baptismal Ecclesiology and the Baptismal Covenant." *Ecclesiology* 6 (2010): 8–38.

———. "A Tale of Two Churches: The Ecclesiologies of the Episcopal Church and the Church of England Compared." *International Journal for the Study of the Christian Church* 8, no. 2 (2008): 124–54.

———. "Two Streams Mingling: The American Episcopal Church in the Anglican Communion." *Journal of Anglican Studies* 9, no. 1 (2011): 12–37.

Porter, Muriel. *The New Puritans: The Rise of Fundamentalism in the Anglican Church*. Melbourne: Melbourne University Press, 2006.

———. *Sydney Anglicans and the Threat to World Anglicanism: The Sydney Experiment*. Aldershot: Ashgate, 2011.

Powell, Russell. "Synod Opposes Anglican Covenant." *Sydney Anglicans*, 13 October 2011. http://sydney anglicans.net/news/synod _opposes_anglican_covenant/.

Pratt, Douglas. "Theology After Dialogue: Christian-Muslim Engagement Today and Tomorrow." *Islam and Christian-Muslim Relations* 26, no. 1 (2015): 89–101.

Prichard, Robert W. *A History of the Episcopal Church: Complete Through the Seventy-Eighth General Convention*. New York: Church Publishing, 2014.

———. "The Lambeth Conferences." In *The Wiley-Blackwell Companion to the Anglican Communion,* edited by Ian S. Markham, J. Barney Hawkins IV, Justyn Terry, and Leslie Nuñez Steffensen, 91–104. Chichester: Wiley-Blackwell, 2013.

Primates of the Anglican Communion. "Walking Together in the Service of God in the World." 15 January 2016. http://www.primates2016 .org/articles/2016/01/15 /communique-primates/.

Pui-Lan, Kwok. "The Legacy of Cultural Hegemony in the Anglican Church." In *Beyond Colonial Anglicanism: The Anglican Communion in the Twenty-First Century*, edited by Ian T. Douglas and Kwok Pui-Lan, 47–70. New York: Church Publishing, 2001.

Pultar, Gönül, ed. *Imagined Identities: Identity Formation in the Age of Globalization*. Syracuse: Syracuse University Press, 2014.

Putnam, Robert D., and David E. Campbell. *American Grace: How Religion Divides and Unites Us*. New York: Simon and Schuster, 2010.

Quimby, Karin. "*Will & Grace*: Negotiating (Gay) Marriage on Prime-Time Television." *Journal of Popular Culture* 38, no. 4 (2005): 713–31.

Radner, Ephraim. "Anglicanism and the Search for Christian Concord." In *Change and Transformation: Essays in Anglican History*, edited by Thomas P. Power, 246–66. Eugene: Pickwick, 2013.

———. *A Brutal Unity: The Spiritual Politics of the Christian Church*. Waco: Baylor University Press, 2012.

———. *The End of the Church: A Pneumatology of Christian Division in the West*. Grand Rapids: Eerdmans, 1998.

Radner, Ephraim, and Philip Turner. *The Fate of Communion: The Agony of Anglicanism and the Future of a Global Church*. Grand Rapids: Eerdmans, 2006.

Ranger, Terence O., ed. *Evangelical Christianity and Democracy in Africa*. Oxford: Oxford University Press, 2008.

Religion and Ethics Newsweekly. "Lambeth Conference Wrap Up." 8 August 2008. http://www.pbs.org/wnet /religionandethics/2008/08/08 /perspectives-lambeth-conference -wrap-up/14/.

Ritzer, George. *The McDonaldization of Society*. Newbury Park, Calif.: Pine Forge Press, 2010.

Robertson, Roland. *Globalization: Social Theory and Global Culture.* London: Sage Publications, 1992.

Rose, Gillian. *The Broken Middle: A Good Enough Justice.* Oxford: Blackwell, 1992.

———. *Mourning Becomes the Law: Philosophy and Representation.* Cambridge: Cambridge University Press, 1996.

Rosman, Rosamond C. "We Are Anglicans, They Are the Church of England." In *The Social Life of Scriptures: Cross-Cultural Perspectives on Biblicism*, edited by James S. Bielo, 100–113. New Brunswick: Rutgers University Press, 2009.

Roudometof, Victor. *Globalization and Orthodox Christianity: The Transformations of a Religious Tradition.* London: Routledge, 2014.

Rouner, Leroy, ed. *Civility.* Notre Dame: University of Notre Dame Press, 2000.

Rubenstein, Mary-Jane. "An Anglican Crisis of Comparison: Intersections of Race, Gender, and Religious Authority, with Particular Reference to the Church of Nigeria." *Journal of the American Academy of Religion* 72, no. 2 (2004): 341–65.

Rucht, Dieter. "Civil Society and Civility in Twentieth-Century Theorising." *European Review of History: Revue Européenne d'Histoire* 18, no. 3 (2011): 387–407.

Sachs, William L. *Homosexuality and the Crisis of Anglicanism.* Cambridge: Cambridge University Press, 2009.

———. *The Transformation of Anglicanism: From State Church to Global Communion.* Cambridge: Cambridge University Press, 2002.

Sadgrove, Joanna, Robert M. Vanderbeck, Johan Andersson, Gill Valentine, and Kevin Ward. "Morality Plays and Money Matters: Towards a Situated Understanding of the Politics of Homosexuality in Uganda." *Journal of Modern African Studies* 50, no. 1 (2012): 103–29.

Sadgrove, Joanna, Robert M. Vanderbeck, Kevin Ward, Gill Valentine, and Johan Andersson. "Constructing the Boundaries of Anglican Orthodoxy: An Analysis of the Global Anglican Future Conference (GAFCON)." *Religion* 40, no. 3 (2010): 193–206.

Salawu, Beshiru. "Ethno-Religious Conflicts in Nigeria: Causal Analysis and Proposals for New Management Strategies." *European Journal of Social Sciences* 13, no. 3 (2010): 345–53.

Sampson, Tyler. "Scripture, Tradition, and *Ressourcement*: Toward an Anglican Fundamental Liturgical Theology." *Anglican Theological Review* 96, no. 2 (2014): 305–22.

Sanneh, Lamin. *West African Christianity: The Religious Impact.* London: C. Hurst, 1983.

Saywell, William. *Evangelical and Catholick unity, maintained in the Church of England.* London: printed by T. H. for Robert Scott, 1682.

Scapp, Ron, and Brian Seitz, eds. *Etiquette: Reflections on Contemporary Comportment.* Albany: SUNY Press, 2007.

Schmitt, Carl. *The Concept of the Political.* Exp. ed. Chicago: University of Chicago Press, 2007.

Seed, Nigel. "Church Services After a Civil Partnership." Diocese of London, 2008. http://inclusive-church.org.uk/sites/default/files/files/Chancellor%20Nigel%20Seed%20Guidance.pdf.

Seitz, Christopher. "Canon, Covenant, and Rule of Faith—The Use of Scripture in Communion." *International Journal for the Study of the Christian Church* 8, no. 2 (2008): 81–92.

Sennett, Richard. *Together: The Rituals, Pleasures, and Politics of Cooperation.* London: Penguin, 2013.

Seventh Consultation of Anglican Bishops in Dialogue. "A Testimony of Unity in Diversity." 25–29 May 2016. http://www.anglican.ca/wp-content/uploads/Testimony-of-Unity-in-Diversity-2016.pdf.

Siebt, Johanna, and Jesper Garsdal, eds. *How Is Global Dialogue Possible?* Berlin: De Gruyter, 2014.

Silverman, Rachel E. "Comedy as Correction: Humor as Perspective by Incongruity on *Will & Grace* and *Queer as Folk.*" *Sexuality and Culture* 17, no. 2 (2013): 260–74.

Simmel, George. *Conflict and the Web of Group Affiliations.* Translated by Kurt Wolff. New York: Free Press, 1955.

Smith, Christian. *The Bible Made Impossible: Why Biblicism Is Not a Truly Evangelical Reading of Scripture.* Grand Rapids: Brazos Press, 2011.

Smith, Christian, with Michael Emerson, Sally Gallagher, Paul Kennedy, and David Sikkink. *American Evangelicalism: Embattled and Thriving.* Chicago: University of Chicago Press, 1998.

Smith, Gloria. "Response to the Ordination of Women as Priests in the Anglican (CPSA) Diocese of Pretoria, South Africa." *Journal of Theology for Southern Africa* 109 (2001): 83–93.

Smith, Jane Idleman. *Muslims, Christians, and the Challenge of Interfaith Dialogue.* Oxford: Oxford University Press, 2007.

Smith, Jonathan Z. "Religion, Religions, Religious." In *Critical Terms for Religious Studies,* edited by Mark C. Taylor, 269–84. Chicago: University of Chicago Press, 1998.

Smith, Rogers M. "Oligarchies in America: Reflections on Tocqueville's Fears." *Journal of Classical Sociology* 10, no. 3 (2010): 189–200.

Smith, William C., ed. *Latin American Democratic Transformations: Institutions, Actors, and Processes.* Chichester: Wiley-Blackwell, 2009.

Snow, David A. "Framing Processes, Ideology, and Discursive Fields." In *The Blackwell Companion to Social Movements*, edited by David A. Snow, Sarah Soule, and Hanspeter Kriesi, 380–411. Malden, Mass.: Blackwell, 2007.

Snow, David A., and Richard Machalek. "The Sociology of Conversion." *Annual Review of Sociology* 10 (1984): 167–90.

Solarz, Marcin Wojciech. "North-South, Commemorating the First Brandt Report: Searching for the Contemporary Spatial Picture of the Global Rift." *Third World Quarterly* 33, no. 3 (2012): 559–69.

Solheim, James. *Diversity or Disunity? Reflections on Lambeth 1998.* New York: Church Publishing, 1999.

———. "Sexuality Issues Test Bonds of Affection Among Bishops at Lambeth Conference." *Episcopal News Service,* 9 March 1998. http://archive.episcopalchurch.org/3577_70963_ENG_HTM.htm.

Sollis, David. "Bearing False Witness: The Media and the Gay Debate." *Theology and Sexuality* 12 (2000): 101–19.

Soothill, Jane E. *Gender, Social Change, and Spiritual Power: Charismatic*

Christianity in Ghana. Leiden: Brill, 2007.

Spencer, Leon P. "Theological Education in the Anglican Communion." In *The Wiley-Blackwell Companion to the Anglican Communion,* edited by Ian S. Markham, J. Barney Hawkins IV, Justyn Terry, and Leslie Nuñez Steffensen, 643–56. Chichester: Wiley-Blackwell, 2013.

Spickard, James V. "Religion in Global Culture: New Directions in an Increasingly Self-Conscious World." In *Globalization, Religion, and Culture,* edited by Peter Beyer and Lori Beaman, 235–50. Leiden: Brill, 2007.

Stains, Robert R., Jr. "Reflection for Connection: Deepening Dialogue Through Reflective Processes." *Conflict Resolution Quarterly* 30, no. 1 (2012): 33–51.

Starke, Frederick A., and Bruno Dyck. "Upheavals in Congregations: The Causes and Outcomes of Splits." *Review of Religious Research* 38, no. 2 (1996): 159–74.

Stevenson, Kenneth, ed. *A Fallible Church: Lambeth Essays.* London: Darton, Longman, and Todd, 2008.

Strong, Rowan. *Episcopalianism in Nineteenth-Century Scotland: Religious Responses to a Modernizing Society.* Oxford: Oxford University Press, 2002.

Sunarko, Adrianus. "Interfaith Dialogue and Cooperation Across Faiths: The Experience of Indonesia." *Theology Today* 73, no. 1 (2016): 46–59.

Sutton, John R., and Mark Chaves. "Explaining Schism in American Protestant Denominations, 1890–1990." *Journal for the Scientific Study of Religion* 43, no. 2 (2004): 171–90.

Swatos, William H., Jr. "Beyond Denominationalism? Community and Culture in American Religion." *Journal for the Scientific Study of Religion* 20, no. 3 (1981): 217–27.

Swidler, Ann. "Culture in Action: Symbols and Strategies." *American Sociological Review* 51, no. 2 (1986): 273–86.

Sykes, Stephen W. *The Integrity of Anglicanism.* New York: Seabury Press, 1978.

Tanner, Kathryn. "Theology and the Plain Sense." In *Scriptural Authority and Narrative Interpretation,* edited by Garrett Green, 59–78. Philadelphia: Fortress Press, 1987.

Tarsitano, Louis R., and Peter Toon. *Dear Primates.* Charlottetown, Prince Edward Island: St. Peter Publications, 2000.

Thinking Anglicans. "Will There Be Another Lambeth Conference?" 30 September 2014. http://www .thinkinganglicans.org.uk /archives/006744.html.

Thomas, Philip E. "Doctrine of the Church." In *The Study of Anglicanism,* edited by Stephen Sykes and John Booty, 222–23. London: SPCK, 1988.

Thomas, W. I., and D. S. Thomas. *The Child in America: Behavior Problems and Programs.* New York: Knopf, 1928.

Thompsett, Fredrica Harris. "A Passion for Intercessory Prayer." *Anglican Theological Review* 98, no. 2 (2016): 303–16.

Thompson, Kenneth. *Bureaucracy and Church Reform: The Organizational Response of the Church of England to Social Change, 1800–1965.* Oxford: Clarendon Press, 1970.

Thompson, Mark D. "The Global Anglican Future Conference (GAFCON)." In *The Wiley-Blackwell Companion to the Anglican Communion,* edited by Ian S. Markham, J.

Barney Hawkins IV, Justyn Terry, and Leslie Nuñez Steffensen, 739–49. Chichester: Wiley-Blackwell, 2013.

———. "Serious Flaws in Muriel Porter's Misguided Polemic." *ABC Religion and Ethics,* 31 August 2011. http://www.abc.net.au/religion/articles/2011/08/31/3306439.htm.

Tocqueville, Alexis de. *Democracy in America.* New York: Penguin, 2003.

Tong, Robert. "The Anglican Church of Australia." In *The Wiley-Blackwell Companion to the Anglican Communion,* edited by Ian S. Markham, J. Barney Hawkins IV, Justyn Terry, and Leslie Nuñez Steffensen, 387–406. Chichester: Wiley-Blackwell, 2013.

Trisk, Janet, and Luke Pato. "Theological Education and Anglican Identity in South Africa." *Journal of Anglican Studies* 6, no. 1 (2008): 59–67.

Troeltsch, Ernst. *The Social Teaching of the Christian Churches.* London: Allen and Unwin, 1956.

Tucker, Karen Westerfield. "Music Wars: A New Conflict?" *Liturgy* 24, no. 4 (2009): 3–9.

Turkle, Sherry. *Life on the Screen: Identity in the Age of the Internet.* New York: Simon and Schuster, 2011.

Turner, Bryan S. "Marginal Politics, Cultural Identities, and the Clergy in Scotland." *International Journal of Sociology and Social Policy* 1, no. 1 (1981): 89–113.

———. *Religion and Modern Society: Citizenship, Secularisation, and the State.* Cambridge: Cambridge University Press, 2011.

Turner, Philip. "The 'Communion' of Anglicans After Lambeth '98: A Comment on the Nature of Communion and the State of the Church." *Anglican Theological Review* 82, no. 1 (1999): 281–93.

Turner, Roger. "Bonds of Discord: Alternative Episcopal Oversight Examined in the Light of the Nonjurring Consecrations." *Ecclesiastical Law Journal* 3, no. 17 (1995): 398–409.

Tutu, Desmond. *No Future Without Reconciliation.* New York: Doubleday, 1999.

UK Census Office. *Religious Worship in England and Wales: Abridged from the Original Report.* Edited by Horace Mann. London: Routledge, 1851.

Ukiwo, Ukoha. "Politics, Ethno-Religious Conflicts, and Democratic Consolidation in Nigeria." *Journal of Modern African Studies* 41, no. 1 (2003): 115–38.

United Nations, Department of Economic and Social Affairs, Population Division. *World Population Prospects: The 2015 Revision,* vol. 1, *Comprehensive Tables* (ST/ESA/SER.A/379). https://esa.un.org/unpd/wpp/publications/Files/WPP2015_Volume-I_Comprehensive-Tables.pdf.

Valentine, David. "The Categories Themselves." *GLQ: A Journal of Lesbian and Gay Studies* 10, no. 2 (2004): 215–20.

Valliere, Paul. *Conciliarism: A History of Decision-Making in the Church.* Cambridge: Cambridge University Press, 2012.

Vanderbeck, Robert M., Gill Valentine, Kevin Ward, Joanna Sadgrove, and Johan Andersson. "The Meanings of Communion: Anglican Identities, the Sexuality Debates, and Christian Relationality." *Sociological Research Online* 15, no. 2 (2010). http://www.socresonline.org.uk/15/2/3.html.

Vasey-Saunders, Mark. *The Scandal of Evangelicals and Homosexuality: English Evangelical Texts, 1960–2010*. London: Routledge, 2015.

Village, Andrew. "Feeling In and Falling Out: An Individual Differences Approach to Sense of Belonging and Frequency of Disagreeing Among Anglican Congregations." *Archive for the Psychology of Religion* 29 (2007): 269–88.

Vincent, Louise, and Simon Howell. "'Unnatural,' 'Un-African,' and 'Ungodly': Homophobic Discourse in Democratic South Africa." *Sexualities* 17, no. 4 (2014): 472–83.

Virtue, David W. "GAFCON Primates Will Not Be Attending Meeting Called by Archbishop Welby." Virtue Online, 25 January 2017. http://www.virtueonline.org/gafcon-primates-will-not-be-attending-meeting-called-archbishop-welby.

Vonofakou, Christiana, Miles Hewstone, and Alberto Voci. "Contact with Out-Group Friends as a Predictor of Meta-Attitudinal Strength and Accessibility of Attitudes Toward Gay Men." *Journal of Personality and Social Psychology* 92, no. 5 (2007): 804–20.

Wabukala, Eliud. "A Global Communion for the Twenty-First Century." Keynote address at the GAFCON Leadership Conference, 24 April 2012. https://www.gafcon.org/news/a-global-communion-for-the-twenty-first-century.

Wallace, Ruth A. *They Call Her Pastor: A New Role for Catholic Women*. Albany: SUNY Press, 1992.

Wallerstein, Immanuel. *The Modern World-System I: Capitalist Agriculture and the Origins of the European World-Economy in the Sixteenth Century*. Berkeley: University of California Press, 2011.

Ward, Kevin. *A History of Global Anglicanism*. Cambridge: Cambridge University Press, 2006.

———. "The Role of the Anglican and Catholic Churches in Uganda in Public Discourse on Homosexuality and Ethics." *Journal of Eastern African Studies* 9, no. 1 (2015): 127–44.

Watson, J. R. "Ancient or Modern, Ancient and Modern: The Victorian Hymn and the Nineteenth Century." *Yearbook of English Studies* 36, no. 2 (2006): 1–16.

Weber, Max. "'Churches' and 'Sects' in North America: An Ecclesiastical Socio-Political Sketch." Translated by Colin Loader. *Sociological Theory* 3, no. 1 (1985): 7–13.

———. *From Max Weber: Essays in Sociology*. Translated and edited by Hans Gerth and C. Wright Mills. New York: Oxford University Press, 1946.

Webster, John. *Holy Scripture: A Dogmatic Approach*. Cambridge: Cambridge University Press, 2003.

———. "On the Clarity of Holy Scripture." In *Confessing God: Essays in Christian Dogmatics II*, 33–68. London: T&T Clark, 2005.

———. "Theology and the Peace of the Church." In *The Domain of the Word: Scripture and Theological Reason*, 150–70. London: T&T Clark, 2012.

Wedeen, Lisa. "Acting 'As If': Symbolic Politics and Social Control in Syria." *Comparative Studies in Society and History* 40, no. 3 (1998): 503–23.

Weeks, Jeffrey. *Sex, Politics, and Society: The Regulations of Sexuality Since 1800*. 3rd ed. Harlow, UK: Pearson, 2012.

Welby, Justin. "Archbishop's Message to GAFCON 2013: Seek Holiness

and Unity." 23 October 2013.
http://www.archbishopofcanter
bury.org/articles.php/5163
/archbishops-message-to-gafcon
-2013-seek-holiness-and-unity.

———. "Letter to the Primates from the
Archbishop of Canterbury."
Anglican Ink, 21 January 2017.
http://www.anglican.ink/article
/letter-primates-archbishop
-canterbury.

West, Gerald O. "Do Two Walk Together?
Walking with the Other Through
Contextual Bible Study." *Anglican
Theological Review* 93, no. 3 (2011):
431–49.

Wetherell, David. *Women Priests in
Australia? The Anglican Crisis.*
Melbourne: Spectrum, 1987.

Whisenant, James C. *A Fragile Unity:
Anti-Ritualism and the Division
of Anglican Evangelicalism in the
Nineteenth Century.* Carlisle, UK:
Paternoster Press, 2003.

White, Stephen Ross. *Authority and
Anglicanism.* London: SCM Press,
1996.

Wiarda, Howard J., ed. *Globalization:
Universal Trends, Regional
Implications.* Boston:
Northeastern University Press,
2007.

Wild-Wood, Emma. "Attending to
Translocal Identities: How
Congolese Anglicans Talk
About Their Church." *Journal of
Anglican Studies* 9, no. 1 (2011):
80–99.

———. "Boundary Crossing and Boundary
Marking: Radical Revival in
Congo and Uganda Since 1948."
In *Revival and Resurgence in
Christian History: Papers Read
at the 2006 Summer Meeting
and the 2007 Winter Meeting of
the Ecclesiastical History Society,*
edited by Kate Cooper and
James Gregory, 329–40. London:
Boydell Press, 2008.

———. "'Free from Shackles' or 'Dirtied'?
The Contested Pentecostalisation
of Anglican Congregations in
Democratic Republic of Congo."
Transformation 25, nos. 2–3
(2008): 103–15.

———. *Migration and Christian Identity in
Congo (DRC).* Leiden: Brill, 2008.

Wilkins, John. "Back from the Brink? The
Windsor Report on the Anglican
Communion." *Ecclesiology* 1, no. 3
(2005): 101–7.

Williams, John. "Conflicting Paradigms
in Theological Education for
Public Ministry in the Church of
England: Issues for Church and
Academy." *International Journal
of Public Theology* 7, no. 3 (2013):
275–96.

Williams, Rhys H. "Politicized Evangelism
and Secular Elites: Creating a
Moral Other." In *Evangelicals
and Democracy in America,* edited
by Steven Brint and Jean Reith
Schroedel, 2 vols., 2:143–78. New
York: Russell Sage Foundation,
2009.

Williams, Rowan. "The Archbishop Opens
the Lambeth Conference." 17 July
2008. http://rowanwilliams.arch
bishopofcanterbury.org/articles
.php/1354/the-archbishop-opens
-the-lambeth-conference.

———. "The Archbishop's First Presidential
Address." Lambeth Conference
of the Anglican Communion,
London, 20 July 2008. http://
rowanwilliams.archbishopof
canterbury.org/articles.php/1353
/archbishops-first-presidential
-address-at-lambeth-conference.

———. "Foreword." In *A Point of Balance:
The Weight and Measure of
Anglicanism,* edited by Martyn
Percy and Robert Boak Slocum,
ix–xii. New York: Morehouse,
2012.

———. "The Literal Sense of Scripture."
Modern Theology 7 (1993): 121–34.

———. "Theological Education in the Anglican Communion." *Journal of Anglican Studies* 3, no. 2 (2005): 237–40.

———. "Why the Covenant Matters." 5 March 2012. http://rowanwil liams.archbishopofcanterbury .org/articles.php/2380/archbishop -why-the-covenant-matters.

Willis, Justin. "The Nature of a Mission Community: The UMCA in Bonde." *Past and Present* 14 (1993): 127–54.

Wolf, Geralyn. "That They May All Be One: Anglican Communion in Prayer." *Journal of Anglican Studies* 7, no. 2 (2009): 139–46.

Woods, Eric Taylor. *A Cultural Sociology of Anglican Mission and the Indian Residential Schools in Canada: The Long Road to Apology.* London: Palgrave, 2016.

Wouters, Cas. *Sex and Manners: Female Emancipation in the West, 1890– 2000.* London: Sage Publications, 2004.

Wright, N. T. "Rowan's Reflections: Unpacking the Archbishop's Statement." Anglican Communion Institute, 30 June 2009. http://www.anglicancom munioninstitute.com/2009/07 /rowan%E2%80%99s-reflections -unpacking-the-archbishop%E2 %80%99s-statement/.

Wuthnow, Robert. *The Restructuring of American Religion: Society and Faith Since World War II.* Princeton: Princeton University Press, 1988.

Wynne-Jones, Jonathan. "Male Priests Marry in Anglican Church's First Gay 'Wedding.'" *Telegraph* (UK), 14 June, 2008.

Yates, John, III. "A Gospel Unity." In *A House Divided? Ways Forward for North American Anglicans*, edited by Isaac Arten and William Glass, 36–46. Eugene: Wipf and Stock, 2015.

Yinger, J. Milton. *Religion, Society, and the Individual: An Introduction to the Sociology of Religion.* New York: Macmillan, 1957.

Zahl, Paul F. M. *The Protestant Face of Anglicanism.* Grand Rapids: Eerdmans, 1998.

Zink, Jesse. "On Beyond Primates." *Medium*, 6 January 2016. https:// medium.com/@jessezink/on -beyond-primates-bf895fbb32c4 #.mm3eu5t2n.

———. "Patiently Living with Difference: Rowan Williams' Archiepiscopal Ecclesiology and the Proposed Anglican Covenant." *Ecclesiology* 9, no. 2 (2013): 223–41.

Žižek, Slavoj. "The Big Other Between Violence and Civility." In *The Universal Exception*, vii–xxxii. New York: Continuum, 2006.

Zoll, Rachel. "World's Episcopalians Watching Vote." *Fredericksburg (Va.) Free Lance-Star*, 3 August 2003. https://news.google.com /newspapers?nid=1298&dat=2003 0803&id=cjMzAAAAIBAJ&sjid =oQgGAAAAIBAJ&pg=6721,562 073&hl=en.